ONE MARINE'S WAR

ONE MARINE'S WAR

GERALD A. MEEHL

A COMBAT INTERPRETER'S
QUEST FOR HUMANITY IN THE PACIFIC

Naval Institute Press • Annapolis, Maryland

Naval Institute Press

291 Wood Road

Annapolis, MD 21402

Library of Congress Cataloging-in-Publication Data

Meehl, Gerald A.

One Marine's war : a combat interpreter's quest for mercy in the Pacific / by Gerald A. Meehl.

p. cm.

Includes bibliographical references and index.

ISBN 978-1-61251-092-7 (hbk. : alk. paper)—ISBN 978-1-61251-093-4 (ebook) 1. Sheek, Bob, 1922- 2. World War, 1939-1945—Pacific Area. 3. United States. Marine Corps—Officers—Biography. 4. United States. Navy. Japanese Language School—Alumni and alumnae. 5. Translators—United States--Biography. 6. Translating and interpreting—United States—History—20th century. 7. World War, 1939-1945—Naval operations, American. 8. World War, 1939-1945—Personal narratives. I. Title.

D767.9M395 2012

940.54'5973092--dc23

2011051957

To Bob Sheeks and his many contributions to this book—this is his story; and to Marla Meehl, whose unwavering support and partnership in this and all things is cherished greatly.

CONTENTS

PREFACE

Every so often I find myself telling stories from a now-distant conflict that took place in the 1940s; stories about events that enveloped my parents' generation, the world in general, and the tropical Pacific in particular; stories from exotic locales, tales of incredible happenings, told to me by those who were there. One veteran's stories I often relate are unusually compelling and typically evoke questions like, "Wow, that's amazing! How did you meet this guy?" Anticipating that query from prospective readers of this book, let me start right off by telling you how it happened.

It was in Sabah, north Borneo, in 1979, and one sultry hot day I was walking down a golden-sand beach. Like most tropical beaches, it was narrow, fewer than one hundred feet wide, and it arced off ahead in a gentle, gleaming curve. Feathery palm trees leaned casually over the sand in what could have passed for a classic South Pacific scene, but this was Southeast Asia. This particular beach at Tanjong Aru was near the little city of Kota Kinabalu (dubbed "KK" by the Malaysians) in a Malaysian part of the huge rain forest island of Borneo. Two Malaysian states had been carved off from Kalimantan, the Indonesian part of Borneo, on the island's north coast. One was Sabah, where KK was located, and the other was Sarawak to the southwest. The tiny, oil-rich sultanate of Brunei was wedged between Sarawak and Sabah and was oddly insular from the rest of Borneo, like a fabulously wealthy, eccentric relative.

It was late afternoon, and the crystalline water lapped quietly on the sand. A few little, green-tufted islands were scattered offshore out by the reef that protected Tanjong Aru from the larger ocean waves rolling in from the South China Sea. I'd spent two months looking out at a totally different version of that ocean, having been sent to Sarawak for an international meteorological field project to study the monsoons of Southeast Asia. Another American and I were leading a team of technicians from the Malaysian Meteorological Service to launch weather balloons at a place called Bintulu.

The town was perched between the rain forest, the South China Sea, and the sluggish Bintulu River that drained massive areas of dense rain forest in the interior of Borneo. The river's muddy, tepid water idled past the beaten-down little settlement and emptied into the ocean, making the waves from the South China Sea look unappetizingly like frothing, liquid milk chocolate. But here I was now at Tanjong Aru and it was totally different—clean, clear, paradise-like. I'd taken a weekend off to make the trip up the coast to what I had been told was the best beach in Borneo, and I wasn't disappointed.

Contemplating the idyllic scene, I looked out over the water in the direction of the offshore islands and saw an outboard motorboat in the distance. Though it was still a ways from shore, I could see that it was rocketing in toward the beach, its motor wound up to a high-pitched whine. The little boat was bouncing off the chop, white spray flashing in the low afternoon sun each time the bow slapped down. I tried to see if it was pulling a water skier, possibly justifying the manic speed. But there was no water skier, only four figures hunched low in the boat, hanging on for dear life as it raced toward the beach. As it got closer, it seemed impossible that it could stop before it hit the beach. Sure enough, to my startled surprise, it shot right out of the water and up onto the sand, outboard motor screaming crazily. It slid to a stop about thirty feet past the water's edge. Somebody on the boat quickly cut the motor, and three European men jumped out. Something was seriously wrong with the fourth, who lay motionless in the boat. The others grabbed him, hefted him out, and just as they did, they lost their grip and dropped him awkwardly onto the sand. Then two grabbed an arm each, the third picked up the feet, and they hustled the inert form toward a line of palm trees that screened a small parking lot behind the beach. One of the few cars parked there was a white Toyota. They opened the back door and heaved the unconscious man onto the seat. One jumped in after him, and the other quickly leapt behind the wheel. The car started with a loud rev, and the tires screeched as it accelerated out of the parking lot.

The remaining member of the group was left standing there as he watched his friends head off toward town. He turned slowly and walked back down to the boat, now stranded on the golden-sand beach. It had all happened quickly and within fifty feet of where I was standing. With considerable effort he started to drag the boat back into the water. I decided to walk over and help. "Can I give you a hand?"

He looked up at me and smiled. "Yeah, that would be great." He appeared to be in his mid-forties, and his graying hair was thinning a bit. He was slight and wiry and tan, obviously having spent much time in the sun. From his accent I knew he was American, which in itself was rare in Borneo in 1979.

I introduced myself, and he stuck out his hand and said, "Name's Bob Sheeks." His grip was strong, he nodded perfunctorily, and we started to move the boat back toward the water.

"Glad you came along," he said as the boat slid grudgingly over the sand.

He didn't offer further explanation, so I asked, "What was that all about, and what was wrong with that guy you stuffed into the car?"

Without looking up he said, "Oh, we were going to snorkel on the reef by that little island out there." His head motioned to one of the offshore islands. "We had just pulled the boat up on the beach and were wading out and putting our snorkeling gear on, when that guy stepped on a stonefish."

He didn't need to say more. I'd heard that stonefish were spectacularly dangerous, hideously ugly little creatures that lie motionless on the bottom in shallow water. The venomous spines on their back face upward, ready to impale any human feet unlucky enough to step on them. Stonefish venom was reputed to be as lethal as any in the natural world. To step on one meant there was a good chance you wouldn't survive.

"Yeah, I've heard about stonefish. He'll be lucky to make it." I immediately regretted saying this, but Bob didn't take any notice. We got the boat back into the water and he said, "When he stepped on it he gave out a yell and he knew right away what it was. We also knew he didn't have long to survive, so we got him into the boat and headed back here as fast as we could. His leg was already swelling and turning black and he'd lost consciousness by the time we ran up on the beach here, and that wasn't more than about five minutes after he first stepped on it. The other guys took him to the hospital, so I stayed here to take care of the boat." He paused and looked up. "Thanks for the help."

"Do you need to get to the hospital now?" I asked.

"No, they'll take care of him. I hope he makes it. He should be OK if they got to the hospital in time. I'll call in a while and visit later this evening. I don't know him very well—just met him this afternoon. I think he's an Englishman, a friend of a friend. He runs an export business here in KK." He paused, and then said, "Can you stick around and help put the boat away? We'll have to take it over there and winch it up into the shed behind the beach. Then I'll call over to the hospital to see how he's doing. There'd be a beer in it for you."

"Sure." We'd pushed the boat into the shallow water next to shore, and as we climbed in I asked, "So, you say there's good snorkeling out by those islands?"

"Yeah, it's fantastic. You know, we've got a couple hours of daylight left. Want to go out there for a quick snorkel? Then I'll phone when we get back here."

Of course this was ideal, but I felt bad about being a distraction. "Look, if you want to call the hospital now and skip the snorkeling, that's OK with me."

He looked sideways at me and with measured tones said, "He's on his own now. Not much anyone can do but get him to a hospital. With a stonefish you either live or you die." He sounded matter-of-fact, and there was no hint of emotion. I would come to find out that events in Bob's life had hardened him to such unpleasant realities.

So out we went in his boat to the scene of the stonefish incident. The island in the distance looked to be uninhabited and surrounded by a stunning white-sand beach. The interior was shrouded in palm trees, and it was smaller than a city block. Bob drove the boat at a leisurely pace. "So, where are you from?" He looked past me to keep the boat heading to the little island.

"I'm from Boulder, Colorado."

"Oh!" He perked up. "I learned Japanese in Boulder at the University of Colorado during the war. I got my Marine Corps commission there."

This seemed very odd. "You learned Japanese in Boulder and you were in the Marines?"

"Yes," he replied. "The Second Marine Division in the Pacific during the war."

World War II? How could that be? Here was this soft-spoken guy, definitely not the stereotypical, gung-ho Marine type, seemingly too young to have been in World War II. I tried to do the math quickly. If he was in his early twenties in 1943, he was probably born in the early 1920s. This was now 1979, and that put him in his late fifties. It was hard to believe—he looked and acted at least fifteen years younger.

Before I could ask any more questions, we arrived at the island. "We'll throw out this anchor so we don't have to wade out from the beach. Let's try to avoid any stonefish, if possible. We've run out of cars to go to the hospital, so if you step on one there's not much I can do for you."

With that, he quickly pulled on his fins, strapped on his face mask, and was in the water snorkeling while I was still fumbling around in the boat trying to get my fins on. I finally followed and was treated to a display of vivid purple and yellow-green coral in canted formations extending up from the shallow bottom to just beneath the surface of the crystal-clear water. The coral looked like surreal plants frozen into position and suspended motionless, with swirls of fluorescent blue and yellow fish swimming lazily in and around the branches that reached out into the blue-tinted void below.

The sun was getting lower, and I had the feeling I was keeping Bob from checking on the injured Englishman. Though I'd have preferred to stay out there until sunset, I reluctantly climbed back in the boat. Bob looked up from the coral and paddled over. "Great stuff, huh?" he said as he tossed his mask and fins in the boat and climbed in.

"Fantastic—thanks for bringing me out."

"Well, I owed you for helping me get the boat back in the water."

"No problem, and you don't know how great this is compared to what I've had to look at for the past two months in Sarawak."

As we headed back toward Tanjong Aru, he was curious about what I'd been doing in Borneo. I explained about the weather balloons, the monsoon field project, and the grim muddy South China Sea off Bintulu.

I pressed him about his World War II experiences. "So, you had to learn Japanese to be in the Marines?"

He smiled. "Well, that's what I did in the Marines. I was a Japanese language and intelligence officer. I translated captured Japanese documents and did a little interrogation of POWs." He actually did much more than that, as I was to find out later.

I knew nothing about how the Marine Corps worked and naively commented, "Well, at least that put you safely behind the front lines, right?"

Bob laughed. "You don't understand the Marine Corps. Every Marine is trained to be a combat rifleman in the front line. I went in on several landings with the rest of them."

"But that makes no sense," I objected. "You were a trained specialist and they risked you getting shot in the landings along with privates fresh out of boot camp?"

"It makes no difference to the Marine Corps," he said. "We were all in the same boat together, literally."

Before he could say more, we were idling up to the beach in front of a barren, one-story cinder block building that passed for the yacht club. We jumped out and winched the boat up to the shed. After we finished he said, "Look, I should call the hospital. You're welcome to come up to the roof of the yacht club and have that drink I promised you."

I thought it was an excellent suggestion. Bob went in to make the call, and I headed up to the second-floor terrace that featured a stunning panorama of Tanjong Aru beach, the offshore islands, and the glittering reflection of the low sun off the South China Sea. I ordered a Scotch and water and settled at a table by the railing. The words "yacht club" and this plain, cinder block building were incongruous to say the least. But it appeared to be the social center for European and American expats in KK, and the view was spectacular. Bob soon joined me and announced, "They got him to the hospital in time. Looks like he'll live after all."

I asked Bob what he was doing in Borneo, and he described a seaweed farming operation he'd organized on the east coast of Sabah in a little town called Semporna. He made frequent trips to KK for business. "If you're looking to see a bit more of Borneo, why don't you come over and visit our operation. If you like snorkeling, there are some of the best coral reefs in the world over there. We have a couple of other Americans working on the project and a bunkhouse with extra rooms—free lodging. We take boats out on the reef almost every day and you can tag along and snorkel when we make our rounds."

I thanked him for the invitation and then asked, "So, what do you do with the seaweed?"

"Well, it's an economic development project for the government of Sabah. The Bajau fishermen need a way to make cash to supplement their subsistence fishing. They sometimes use dynamite in the water to increase their catch. The explosions stun the fish and they can make big hauls, but it ruins the reefs. Since they're always out fishing anyway, we just have them plant a special type of seaweed in the reef shallows and then keep an eye on it. When it's ready, they harvest it and bring it in to our dock and we pay them. We dry it, bale it, and ship it to Maine. An outfit there, Marine Colloids Company, extracts carrageenan from the seaweed, and it's used as a colloiding agent in things like dairy products."

This, of course, sounded very interesting—not the seaweed, so much, but the prospect of more snorkeling in crystal-clear warm water before I headed back to face the brown waters of the South China Sea off Bintulu. I accompanied Bob the next morning on the one-hour flight over to the northeast coast to Tawau, followed by a nearly three-hour ride by car to his operations base in Semporna.

During the ride, I asked him how he got into the seaweed business.

"Well, my company does projects all over Asia," he said. "I'm usually based in Taiwan."

"Taiwan? How did you end up there?"

"Well, I was born and grew up in Shanghai, so I know some Chinese and I learned Japanese during the war. I've always had an interest in Asia. That's why I ended up in the Navy Japanese Language School. It's kind of a long story." And, indeed, from that first meeting in 1979 in Borneo, I've been compiling Bob's "long story" ever since. This book is the product of that effort.

Many veterans were profoundly changed by their experiences during World War II. Some came away with an abiding hatred for their wartime enemies. For Bob, the war in the Pacific had the opposite effect. It transformed his feelings about the Japanese from an initial intense hatred to subsequent profound empathy. This evolution was driven by seeing firsthand a bewildering range of human behavior, from ghastly atrocities so shocking that it is nearly impossible to imagine humans could do such things, to acts of decency so life affirming that it is difficult to picture individuals behaving so admirably.

The substantive events in this book are actual, not fictional—these things really happened. Bob puts it this way: "Real events can be incredible, more so than what one can imagine or make up." Truer words were never said.

Gerald Meehl
Boulder, Colorado
2012

ACKNOWLEDGMENTS

Thanks to Bob Sheeks for not only recounting the details of his experiences—from his formative years in Shanghai, to his training in the Navy Japanese Language School in Boulder, to his service as a Japanese language officer in island combat with the 2nd Marine Division in the Pacific—but also reading over and ensuring the accuracy of the written accounts. He made this book possible. To Bao-Mei Sheeks for her support and encouragement of this project; to Robert Sheeks, Bob's son, for his assistance and help with his father's World War II documents; to George Sheeks and his daughter, Diana Schneider, for making the Sheeks family photos available; to Dan Williams for providing vivid recollections of his childhood in Shanghai with Bob, and for recalling numerous details of his time in the Navy Japanese Language School in Boulder and subsequent adventures as a Japanese language officer in the 4th Marine Division in the Pacific; to Jan Williams for her patient attention paid to Bob and Dan as they told and retold stories about their experiences in China and the Pacific; to David Hays at the University of Colorado Archives for his vital role as the focal point for preserving the memories of the wartime graduates of the Navy Japanese Language School, and to Stephanie Hodges at the Archives for her help with some of the photos; to Walton Rawls for his publication suggestion and encouragement; to Adam Kane at Naval Institute Press for taking on this project and shepherding it through to completion; to Marla Johanning, Marlena Montagna, Claire Noble, and Susan Corrado, also at Naval Institute Press, for their professional and competent handling of the editorial aspects and for looking after the numerous details involved with the book's production; to Eileen Meehl, Mark and Jan Meehl, Janet and Pete Fox, and Paul Shankman for patiently listening to many Bob Sheeks stories over the years; and to Marla Meehl—her editorial advice, steadying encouragement, and sustaining resolve were invaluable in bringing this book to fruition.

PROLOGUE

A Remarkable Incident on Saipan,
Western Tropical Pacific, 1944

The battle for Saipan was a more complicated kind of Pacific island combat, different from the warfare that began on Guadalcanal two years before. The Japanese military forces were still fighting to the death as they had on other islands, but this time there were civilian enemy populations caught up in the struggle, including Japanese, Koreans, and local Chamorros, thus adding a difficult dimension for both the U.S. Marines and the Japanese military.[1] Saipan was a small island, and the civilians had no place to go. They often took shelter in the same caves as the Japanese soldiers, all crowded together, with few options.

On one particular day in the latter stages of the battle, Japanese snipers had pinned down a group of Marines. They were pressed to the ground, dungaree shirts mottled with sweat in the stifling heat, tropical sun beating down relentlessly, no breeze. It had been a couple of weeks since the Marines had battled their way ashore on Saipan,[2] another in a series of isolated dots of land where Americans were fighting and dying in the tropical Pacific, islands that almost invariably had never been heard of before in the United States. Though areas along the coast where the fighting was taking place had been blasted and burned by high explosives, like a shell-pocked, World War I no-mans'-land, Saipan was an otherwise exotic, green-dappled tropical paradise. Steep black volcanic cliffs in the northern part of the island stepped upward toward the nearly impenetrable interior. Golden coral reefs protected shallow azure lagoons and dazzling white-sand beaches. Decades later, in an ironic legacy of the Pacific war, those same beaches, now strewn with Marine and Japanese dead, would front exotic honeymoon resorts for descendants of the Japanese defenders. But in 1944 the soldiers of Imperial Japan were combatants, and the Marines were attempting to violently eliminate them from the island.

By this time, surviving remnants of the Japanese army had been driven into the narrow, steep, cliff- and cave-laced northern part, along with thousands of civilians. The Japanese were fighting to the death, grimly determined to kill as many Marines as possible before they themselves were killed. Their regimented culture, reinforced by intensive and, by American standards, abusive training, had drilled into them that surrender was unacceptable.[3] In a strange twist that was incomprehensible to the Marines, the Japanese soldiers were also trying to prevent civilians from surrendering. The Americans had seen Japanese refugees shot, the troops of the Empire of Japan preferring to kill them rather than stand by and watch them give up to the enemy. The civilians themselves had been told that the demonic Marines were brutal animals who would rape the women, and then torture and kill everyone.[4] It was no wonder that the Japanese were not inclined to come out. It was a tragic stalemate. Given that surrender was not an option for the Japanese, at least from the point of view of their cultural background and official military policy, it seemed to the Marines that there was little more they could do than kill them all. But this was easier said than done; the Japanese were mostly in concealed positions in caves, where they could bring the Marines under murderous fire, and it was not easy to get at them.

After the initial beach landing and northward sweep of American forces driving the Japanese before them, the battle had devolved into a series of small actions, with the Japanese holed up in caves that had to be taken out one at a time. All the while, American casualties were piling up. It seemed to the Marines that they were caught in a senseless, flaming Armageddon, with the Japanese determined to see everyone dead, friend and foe alike. Quite understandably, this did not sit well with the Marines. If you were losing and the situation was hopeless, why not surrender? To them it was stupid to keep fighting, and many of the Americans had developed a deep hatred of the Japanese because of it.[5]

Bob Sheeks, a Marine Corps Japanese language officer, had been called up to the front line. The boyish-looking lieutenant was crouched among the knot of fellow Marines under fire. They were dressed in characteristic Marine Corps combat uniforms—matching green dungaree long-sleeved shirts and pants, steel helmets covered with dappled tan- and light-green-camouflaged cloth—all clutching rifles. Bob could see other Marines scattered around, all lying flat or hunched close to the ground. They were pinned down by Japanese soldiers somewhere up in the vegetation-shrouded cliffs ahead. Bob was carrying an odd contraption: a small, electric megaphone with a portable amplifier attached to a truck battery.[6] As a trained Marine language officer, his job now was to attempt to talk the Japanese soldiers into surrendering. This was not because the Marines had developed a sense of compassion for their hated enemies, but American lives would be saved if Bob could somehow convince the Japanese to give up. He could see ahead, past where more Marines were lying low, and on up to where half a dozen lay in odd positions on the ground. He figured they were dead because the living always had at least some movement, and he could sense life in them, just as death brought an unnatural stillness.

Those Marines had been alive just half an hour ago. They had awakened in their tents at dawn, not knowing that by the middle of the morning their lives would be over. It was like a macabre lottery—if your number came up, that was it. Their sudden and violent deaths would set in motion an inevitable sequence of events, starting later in the day with graves registration personnel removing and cataloging dog tags. Their bodies would be transported to a temporary military cemetery on the island for burial, and then a telegram would go out to their families back in Des Moines or St. Louis or Seattle. Those telegrams would trigger profound grief that would stick with parents, siblings, and girlfriends for years, sometimes lifetimes. Nieces and nephews would hear stories of their uncle who was killed in the Pacific war, and they would wonder what he was really like. To all of them he would live on in fading black-and-white photos, always the strapping young Marine, hat at a cocky angle, a confident smile on his face.

But no one still alive on this particular day in this particular group of Marines was even close to thinking about any of that now. It was a simple fact that their buddies were dead, and they shelved that knowledge as far back in their minds as possible. Emotional numbness was a necessity in order to keep functioning, and Bob was no different from the rest of them. They never discussed this coping mechanism, but it had become automatic, as vital to their survival as their studied nonchalance in the face of violence and death. They simply had to put some things out of their consciousness, like the fact that any one of them could be dead or maimed in the next instant. For some, this cauterization of feeling would take years to overcome. Others would never get over it, their sleep and even their waking hours haunted by nightmares and flashbacks for the rest of their lives.[7] But now they were intently focused on how to get out of this situation alive.

Sweat dripped from Bob's face as he crouched next to the pinned-down Marines. He had been told to report to the regimental commander, Col. Bill Jones, an officer with an impressive military record.[8] He was a classic no-nonsense Marine and a highly effective combat leader. Bob asked one of the Marines near him where the colonel was; he motioned to another group of Marines to the left, and Bob crawled over to Jones. Though he was a lieutenant colonel and regimental commander, he was surprisingly young, looking to Bob to be in his late twenties. His company officers were in their mid-twenties; the platoons, about forty men each, were led by lieutenants who were typically in their early twenties; the ten-man-squad leaders, sergeants, were mostly in their late teens or early twenties; and the privates were nearly all in their late teens. It was difficult to comprehend that such young men, American and Japanese alike, almost exclusively shouldered the burden of combat and thereby determined the outcome of the Pacific war. Jones looked up from a map held by one of his company commanders and asked Bob if he was the language officer he had called for. Bob replied that he was and tried to sound confident in the presence of this tough combat commander.

Bob was only twenty-two years old, and he did not look like a typical Marine. Slight and wiry, Bob had grown a faint mustache in an attempt to look older. Plucked from the ranks of Harvard undergraduates after the Pearl Harbor attack, he had completed an intensive Navy Japanese language course at the University of Colorado. He had then gone through Marine combat training and had first experienced what it was like to be shot at during the hellish invasion of Tarawa Atoll the year before. On a tiny island with a total land area of no more than a few city blocks, about 1,000 Marines and more than 4,500 Japanese died in a battle that lasted fewer than four days.[9]

Colonel Jones was frustrated and impatient. The Japanese troops in the caves up ahead had them pinned down and were holding up the American advance. The Marines couldn't get close enough to kill them, and artillery couldn't touch them in the natural shelter of the caves. Every time the Marines tried to attack, some got shot, and when more Marines went up to try and bring their wounded comrades back, they also got shot. Six Marines were dead and they were no closer to eliminating Japanese resistance in the caves than when they started. Jones had his doubts about the role of interpreters in combat, but he had heard of Bob's success in being able to convince at least some Japanese to surrender. Besides, he was out of options.

Bob was far from confident. This was not a good situation for talking Japanese troops into coming out peacefully. They occupied a superior defensive position and had the Marines pinned down. Using amplified megaphones like the one he was carrying, Bob had previously achieved considerable success in getting Japanese civilians and a few troops to surrender from cave complexes in Saipan's contorted and twisted limestone cliffs. But well-armed Japanese soldiers were in the cave ahead. From their rock-sheltered position, their weapons controlled movement from the cliffs all the way down to the coast. They were determined to kill a lot of Marines, and to hold out to the end.

Bob's feelings toward the Japanese were, to say the least, complicated. At the most basic level, he knew that the more Japanese he could persuade to surrender, the more Marine lives would be saved. At least that's how he explained it to his fellow Marines. They, in turn, often looked upon his efforts as a nuisance and impediment to what they were trained for and sent there to do: namely, kill the Japanese enemy.

Bob spotted a couple of Koreans nearby who had been put to work dragging enemy corpses into a few long burial trenches that had been scooped out by bulldozers. He motioned them over to help, and they were thankful to get a break from their grisly work. A considerable number of Koreans had been shipped to Saipan by the Japanese administration before the war to work as tenant farmers and military labor.[10] The Koreans felt little affinity to the Japanese Empire, and many readily surrendered if given a chance. Bob could also use them as living proof to the Japanese holdouts that surrender was survival. The Koreans wore white headbands while on the burial detail so the Marines could distinguish them from the Japanese combatants. Thousands of enemy troops had already been killed, and in the hot, sultry, tropical climate, the sooner the bodies were buried, the better. No telegrams to relatives, no rows of white headstones to visit decades later. Just anonymous, quick burials in a random bit of land on an island far from their homes and families in Japan.

Decades later on Saipan, Japanese corpses in their unmarked graves turned up almost every time a new foundation was dug. Each time this happened, the Japanese government was notified, a team from Japan showed up to collect and cremate the remains, and the ashes were carefully saved, packaged, and sent to the Yasukuni Shrine in Tokyo where the Japanese war dead are honored.[11]

In his halting Japanese, Bob explained the situation to the Koreans. First he would use the amplified megaphone to try calling to the holdouts in the caves. His imperfect language skills would be an asset to establish his credibility as an American Marine calling for them to come out. Then the Koreans, with their better Japanese fluency and accent, would use the megaphone to repeat the message. As Bob prepared the instrument and fiddled with the connections to the truck battery, there was nearly dead silence except for the pop of distant gunfire and the boom of artillery elsewhere on the island. Occasionally there was the crack of rifle fire from up ahead in the cliffs, and bullets whizzed overhead, reminders that the Japanese in the cave were still there. The two Koreans crouched next to Bob, and after he had finished his initial pitch, speaking into the microphone slowly and calmly in his best Japanese, one of them took over as instructed. The message was repeated in the Korean's fluent Japanese: "Come out. There is water for you, and food, and medicines. You can come out honorably. Many hundreds of your comrades have already come out. There is a safe camp with much water and food."[12] Bob had told the Koreans to avoid using the Japanese word for "surrender." The phrase "come out" was preferable, leaving the enemy with an option that was culturally more palatable.

After several minutes of broadcast appeals, there was a muffled *whumph* from up ahead, one of the Marines yelled "Incoming!", and just as quickly there was a loud, flat *wham* as a mortar shell exploded just behind them. Dirt and gravel showered the Marines. Startled but undaunted, Bob grabbed the microphone and repeated his message, then handed it off again to the Koreans, who kept up the appeals. The mention of water was especially compelling. Most of the limestone caves in the cliffs on Saipan were dry, and it was nearly impossible for the Japanese to get out and find drinking water without being shot. Many of them were almost dying of thirst, somewhat counterintuitive on a tropical island, but a significant and unavoidable fact of life for many of the Japanese holdouts.[13]

Suddenly there was a flurry of rifle fire from the direction of the cliffs, and a Japanese soldier appeared, scampering downhill and dodging bullets fired by his comrades in the cave. The Japanese troops were trying to kill him. As he got closer, Bob motioned him over to where he was crouched with the Koreans and handed him a canteen. It was like the Japanese soldier had just come out of a waterless desert, and he eagerly gulped the cool water. Bob spoke to him in Japanese, telling him he had acted sensibly and honorably. Then he asked him how many more soldiers were in the cave and whether he thought they would also come out.

The soldier was a young boy, no more than seventeen years old. His eyes were wide open as he handed the canteen back to Bob, and he was clearly angry. He said that after hearing Bob's broadcast appeals he began talking to his fellow soldiers in the cave, trying to convince them that it was pointless to continue, and that they should come out, or at least allow the Marines to retrieve their dead. This was not what the rest of the Japanese soldiers wanted to hear, and they had cursed and punched him for even suggesting such a thing. That was when he started to get angry. He realized he would have to sneak out by himself. He waited a few minutes and then slipped out between two boulders near the front of the cave. The others spotted him leaving and started to shoot at him. As the bullets struck around him he became even more infuriated. He was able to use large rocks and ravines as shelter, and he made his way unscathed down to the American Marines. As Bob tried to settle him down, he asked how many more soldiers were in the cave. The boy thought there were about eight.

Sheeks kept talking to him calmly in Japanese, pointing out that every time the Marines advanced toward the cave they got killed. Others who went up to help them or to retrieve the bodies also got shot. The Japanese boy nodded quickly and said he had not done any shooting because he was an ammunition carrier. He was bristling with rage, not only for his comrades' futile insistence to fight to the death, but also because they had tried to kill him when he elected to come out. Then Bob quickly asked more questions: What weapons and ammunition did they have, how had they fortified the cave, and what about the route he had taken to get out?

Colonel Jones and his aides intently watched this scene unfold, frustrated that they could not understand a word that was being said. But they did not need to know Japanese to recognize that this soldier in the Japanese Imperial Army had somehow, in spite of all his training, realized it was pointless to continue fighting a hopeless battle, and had made the rational decision to come out, even as his fellow soldiers tried to kill him for doing so.

Bob paused, and then asked if the boy could show him how to get up to the cave without being shot. He figured the soldier could lead him and a couple of Marines to a sheltered position close enough to the cavern, and from there they could throw in an explosive charge. The boy agreed and Bob reported this to Colonel Jones, who welcomed this development with a certain amount of skepticism. Bob turned back to the boy and explained the plan. Still visibly angry, he shook his head and said he had changed his mind. He decided he would do it alone.

This was a decidedly unexpected development. Bob's Japanese was not perfect, so to make sure, he asked again whether the boy was indeed willing to take explosives up to the cave by himself and kill the Japanese soldiers there. The soldier stared back at him and nodded in agreement with an unmistakable look that Bob recognized. He often saw it in the faces of his fellow Marines. It was a mixture of anger, fear, and determination.

But this plan would be especially dangerous. It was unclear whether the boy would really risk his life to kill his fellow soldiers. Bob had never heard of a Japanese soldier, presumably just another cog in the Imperial Japanese machinery, doing such a thing. Sheeks turned to the colonel and told him the boy had agreed to carry explosives up to the cave single-handedly, and that he was sure he could get near the cave without being shot. But the Americans would have to trust him enough to give him the explosive satchel charges to do the job. Colonel Jones agreed to the plan, with the caveat that the Marines would cover the boy, so if he turned back to throw the satchel charges they would shoot him immediately.

Bob was trying to imagine what was about to happen: a Japanese soldier was going to kill his comrades willingly. This ran counter to everything Bob had witnessed personally or even heard of secondhand. Before he could contemplate it any further, a demolitions man appeared with two dark green knapsacks containing the satchel charges, and he quickly instructed the boy on how to use them. The young soldier listened intently, grabbed the charges, and, without hesitating, took off for the cave.

As Bob and the Marines watched anxiously, he disappeared among coral rock outcrops and the spiky clusters of pandanus leaves on their twisting trunks. Bob was thankful that none of the Marines had taken a shot him. Then the wait began. It would take a while for him to get close to the cave entrance. If the Japanese soldiers shot their former comrade, the Marines would not know it. Bob figured that if they had not heard the satchel charges detonate after about half an hour or so, they would assume the mission had failed and would have to try something else. Exactly what that would be, Bob didn't know.

A long, hot, sweating half hour came and went, and Bob was starting wonder if the boy had been killed. Then from the cliffs came a dull thud, and then another. Smudges of black smoke drifted above the rocks. Soon the boy reappeared, walking upright down the slope, no longer taking cover to dodge bullets. He approached Bob and calmly reported that everyone in the cave emplacement was dead. Bob relayed this information to Colonel Jones, who was astonished but visibly pleased. A squad of Marines was sent up to the cave to investigate and Bob went with them. The terrain got rougher as they got closer. They had to take care in making their way through the twisted and contorted limestone rock formations because their surfaces were the texture of cheese graters and sharp to the touch. Finally they saw the mouth of a large cave. Bob let his eyes adjust to the darkness of the opening, and then he could see what looked like about a half dozen bodies or parts of bodies tossed around, bloody ragged clothing, and legs and arms bent at strange angles by the blast. There were indeed no survivors. The squad returned and informed the colonel, who was relieved. His unit could now retrieve the bodies of the dead Marines and continue their advance.

Though Bob was quite familiar with the fanatic Japanese reputation of fighting to the death, he always believed some would give up. Yet this young Japanese soldier seemed to be operating on a different plane. On a purely rational level, Bob could comprehend that the boy had judged his comrades to be wrong and had used objective thought to see his way out. But rarely were humans in combat purely rational, and the decision to kill his former comrades, thereby actively helping the Marines do their job, was astounding.

The colonel ordered some Marines to go back up to the cave, pick up the Japanese weapons, and destroy the ammunition. Bob thanked the two Koreans who had helped with the broadcasts. Before they reluctantly returned to their burial detail, Bob loaded them down with rations and cigarettes he had quickly extorted from Colonel Jones' outfit. All that was left was for Sheeks to accompany the young Japanese soldier back to the prisoner of war camp. It all ended somewhat anticlimactically. But this one episode, inconsequential in the vast sweep of the Pacific war, would be remembered for a long time by everyone who had been there.

As they bounced along the dusty road to the rear area, Bob looked at the boy riding beside him in the truck. The Japanese soldier's actions were extraordinary, another remarkable piece in the complicated puzzle of human behavior. Was the Japanese boy driven by simple anger because his fellow soldiers had roughed him up and then tried to kill him? Was it revenge that motivated him? At face value, Bob figured the soldier could simply have been sick of the military and wanted out, but that didn't fully explain his unexpected conduct. Such experiences were changing Bob's attitude toward the Japanese from the mind-set he had formed when he was a boy growing up in Shanghai. There, he personally witnessed a dark side to human behavior that would affect the course of the rest of his life.

Robert Sheeks' Pacific Theater

ONE
An Unusual Childhood: Shanghai, 1932

Bob Sheeks' childhood in the Shanghai of the late 1920s and early 1930s had a storybook feel to it. For starters, a middle-aged Chinese peasant woman was his personal live-in nanny, or amah. His brother, George, two years older, had one as well. A number of other Chinese servants were integral parts of the household. His father, an American business executive for an international company with an office in Shanghai, could afford the servants as well as a spacious Western-style residence.

In 1932 Bob was ten years old, and Shanghai at that time was not a typical Chinese city. It was the center of a powerful and far-reaching international business empire, the most cosmopolitan city in China, and the Americans who worked there lived well. There was only one catch: in late January Shanghai was invaded by marines of the Japanese navy. They were soon joined by units of the Imperial Japanese Army. This event came to be known as the "Shanghai Incident." It was preceded by the Japanese seizure of Manchuria in 1931, and the establishment of a separate puppet nation called "Manchukuo." The consequence was a bitter Chinese resentment of Japanese influence. In Shanghai there were organized boycotts of Japanese products and large protest demonstrations, culminating in a presumed attack on several Japanese monks. Though widely publicized by the Japanese, the details of this attack were not totally clear. Nevertheless, the Japanese used this as a pretext for their invasion of Shanghai.[1]

The large expatriate community of Americans, British, and French, living in exclusive enclaves, were mostly sheltered from the conflicts between the Chinese and Japanese. Bob's father had moved his family into an apartment in downtown Shanghai in the International Concession area, which he thought was safer. Prior to their move, they had lived in the elite Western residential suburb of Shanghai called the French Concession, a quiet neighborhood with tree-lined avenues and large homes. It looked pretty much like a typical upper-middle-class neighborhood in any U.S. city, except it was in China. Well-maintained gardens surrounded homes occupied by expatriate Americans and Europeans who lived in relative luxury.[2] Most worked for the great multinational corporations in Shanghai. There was an American-style school that Bob and his brother attended.

The main concern of the Sheeks family in early 1932 was not the Japanese, however, but Bob's mother, who was dying of breast cancer. The poor lady had been converted by a Christian Scientist in Shanghai who interpreted the religious teachings literally and had convinced her not to go to a hospital or get medication. The cancer had spread, and now there was nothing that surgery or medicine could do.

Bob and his brother, George, had been told their mother's condition was not good, but just how serious things had become was evident some evenings after supper. They would peer through the open door of an upstairs bedroom to watch their father administer injections of morphine, arranged with the help of an American doctor. The shots provided relief from the pain so that she could tolerate her condition, hoping the merciful end would come soon.[3]

Bob's father came from a sturdy, North Dakota frontier farm background, and he believed boys should see the realities of life. He let them watch as he first put a white tablet and some water in a metal spoon. After heating the mixture over an alcohol flame, he drew the liquid into a glass syringe, gave the injection, and Mrs. Sheeks peacefully relaxed. To the boys it was a miracle, and they felt immense relief knowing the medication removed her pain. At the time, they didn't know exactly what the drug was, but to them it seemed like a magic elixir.

Their mother's grim health situation affected everyone in the Sheeks household, including the entire staff of servants—the two amahs, the cook, the cook's assistant, the "Number One Boy" who served the meals and supervised the servants, the chauffeur, and the house-cleaner "coolie." In the 1930s, such a large Chinese staff was fairly standard in major expatriate homes in Shanghai.

Bob's father's office in the heart of Shanghai was located in a multistory, redbrick building that looked like it had been transplanted directly from London. Such architecture was typical of the office buildings along and near the world famous Shanghai Bund, the grand riverfront avenue situated on a broad curve of the Huangpu River. Like evocative thoroughfares in other cities around the world—the Champs Élysées in Paris, the Unter den Linden in Berlin, or Broadway in New York—the Bund in Shanghai had its own unique look and atmosphere. There was incessant street traffic, and boats and barges of all sizes frenetically plowed up and down the Huangpu River. Imposing European-style buildings facing the Bund housed the offices of the multinational banks and corporations that drove Shanghai's economy. Also along the Bund was the British Consulate compound, the prestigious Cathay Hotel, and other landmarks. The atmosphere was one of exotic sophistication and excitement, energized by the large amounts of money being made.[4] It was a fascinating place to be in the 1930s, and the Sheeks family was hoping the Japanese conflict with the Chinese would be only a temporary annoyance.

But the intrigue of Shanghai continued to be dulled by the illness of Bob's mother. It was like a black shroud had been drawn over the household. Bob looked elsewhere for diversions and, when not attending school, occupied himself with activities that took his mind off the situation at home. When he was interested in something he threw himself into it whole hog, like his pigeon hobby. The Chinese were crazy about pigeons, especially racing pigeons, and Bob had become interested in raising homing pigeons. His father let him keep a dozen or more in loft cages on the roof of their apartment building. Bob's mother was convinced they were unsanitary, so his father made him promise he would keep them out of the apartment and confine them to the roof.

The challenge in Chinese pigeonry was to release the birds in the morning and get them to return in the evening, ideally bringing other pigeons back with them. The Chinese had many tricks to lure someone else's pigeons to join their flock, and they held contests to attract other owners' pigeons. One method was to put special scents on the pigeons. A favorite was "oil of clover" extract. Theoretically, after applying the scent and releasing the pigeons, nearby flocks owned by others would be attracted by the scent and follow your pigeons home, like perfumed streetwalkers luring drunken sailors on shore leave. Bob was an analytical boy interested in biology, and he was fascinated by the subtle intelligence of these seemingly unthinking, habit-driven birds. His interest in pigeons foreshadowed a broader interest in wildlife that would lead him to study biology at Harvard years later, before World War II overtook him and the rest of the world.

In that same biological vein, Bob also had a silkworm hobby. His amah had a rural upbringing, and when he asked about silkworms she brought home a sheet of paper with what looked like about two hundred little black dots on it. These were silkworm eggs, and she instructed Bob to pick leaves from a mulberry tree, cut them into small pieces, and spread them over the sheet of paper. Soon the eggs hatched and the tiny silkworms started eating the leaves. When they had grown to the size of small pencil leads, they needed more shredded mulberry leaves to keep them fed. Before too long, Bob's amah brought home some bamboo trays to contain the rapidly growing silkworms. By this time Bob had stripped virtually all the leaves from the mulberry tree in his neighborhood, so he had to look farther afield. It turned out there were several of the trees near his school in the French Concession. He would take a couple of pillowcases with him on his bike, fill them with mulberry leaves, pedal back to the apartment, and spread them over the bamboo trays. About six weeks into the great silkworm experiment, each of the voracious worms had grown to the size of half a ball-point pen and had molted. They were now ready to make cocoons. Bob's amah placed a few silkworms on the mosquito net over his bed, and Bob watched them rhythmically weave their cocoons, which, when completed, were harvested for the silk. To predict whether the color of the silk would be white or gold, Bob was instructed to turn the worms over and look at their legs—white legs meant white silk, gold legs, gold silk.

To retrieve the silk thread, Bob placed the finished cocoons in a pan of boiling water, thus killing the silkworms. After the outer coverings of the cocoons dissolved, a single, long silk strand that was wound around the cocoon would loosen. Bob would then use a chopstick to wind up the silk strands one after another, and then unwind them to make a ball of silk thread. After a couple of months he had two softball-sized blobs of silk thread, one white and one gold. They had no monetary value because silk was commercially produced in great quantities in Shanghai. It didn't matter to Bob. As far as he was concerned, the silk was just the tangible end product of a successfully conceived and meticulously executed biology experiment. Bob's father finally had enough when he realized the whole operation had run amok. Silkworm trays took up the greater part of two rooms, and there were cocoons on nearly every mosquito net in the apartment. Bob's amah got rid of the worms shortly thereafter.

Bob's father had encouraged the pigeon and silkworm hobbies, perhaps because of his upbringing as a farm boy from the prairies of North Dakota. As a young man he left the isolation of the high plains for more exciting locales. He found work with the Ford Motor Company, first in Seattle, and then in Hawaii. After World War I, he and his wife moved to Shanghai to make their fortune, and he was hired by an American industrial machine firm. He stuck with it and worked his way up to a position as a well-paid business executive with another large American corporation that produced and distributed automotive equipment. Both of his sons were born in Shanghai, and they had many friends within the close-knit expatriate community. The boys called each other "Bobbie" and "Georgie," and their mother often referred to Bob as the "Duke of China" and George as the "Prince of China." For the Americans in Shanghai, it was a kind of surreal suspended animation, a gilded existence far from the economic hardships that were gripping the United States during the Great Depression.

Surprisingly, the American families weren't all that worried about the combat taking place around Shanghai. They were reassured, probably over-optimistically in retrospect, by the presence of the U.S. 4th Marine Regiment. The 4th Marines were a beloved part of the Shanghai scene for the resident American community.[5] Given the political troubles, the

Marines were a steadying influence, like a firm hand on the tiller of a ship in a storm. The Marines were recognized not only as welcomed protection for the Americans' homes and businesses, but also as reliable and familiar symbols of the United States in Shanghai.

On American holidays like Memorial Day and the Fourth of July, the Marines suited up in their uniforms and snappily marched down one of the main avenues of Shanghai in impressive martial formation behind the Marine Regiment Band. Crowds lined the sidewalks, both Chinese and foreigners, and cheered and clapped like small-town citizens watching a homecoming parade. As they marched, the Marines typically sang the Marines' Hymn. A big treat for the Boy Scout troop at the Shanghai American School was to march along right behind the Marines.

On most Sundays the U.S. 4th Marine Regiment Band, conducted by the regimental chaplain, played a concert in the Grand Theater downtown after church services. Dan Williams, along with his parents who were missionaries in the Shanghai area, usually attended with the Sheeks family and the families of Bucky Freeman and Billy Allman, two other boys who were in school together with Bob and Dan. They usually sat together and enjoyed an uplifting offering of American music played expertly by the Marine band. It was made all the more poignant by the fact they were hearing it in the midst of Shanghai.

After the concert, the band and other members of the 4th Marines mingled with the audience. The young men were all self-assured, congenial, solid citizen types, and their casual confident manner was reassuring to the Americans in the theater. They wore their impressive dress blue uniforms with bright red trim and white caps. There was a sharp military competence to their presence, and it was all very exciting to the boys.

The boys gravitated to a group of Marines and one in particular known to them as "Mac." One of his duties was to work on the Marine newspaper, titled *Walla Walla*, which meant "yak yak."[6] Mac would occasionally take them over to the Marine NCO (Noncommissioned Officers') Club. The 4th Marines had many amenities, and the Marine NCO Club, also called the Privates' Club, was one of them. Like Mac, most of the Marines in Shanghai were single, but several of them had married local "white Russian" women, many of whom were beautiful blondes, some third generation. Their families had fled Russia after the revolution and had formed a community in Shanghai. Dan had vivid memories of the marriage ceremonies his father performed for Marines and white Russian women.

The Privates' Club had a carpeted outer room with a large mahogany bar at one end and plush, leather-covered chairs set around small tables. It had the look of an old-world gentlemen's club in London. In the living quarters, separate rooms were assigned to each private in the 4th Marines. Mac's room had a richly burnished dark-paneled door with a gleaming brass knob. A polished brass plate affixed to the door was emblazoned with the words "Private First Class John McElroy."[7] Inside was a huge, carpeted living room with furniture, lamps, a dining room table, and a bed in one corner.

Mac was assigned a personal valet and servant, a "batman" as it was known in the British army. He was a slight-built Chinese man of about forty, and he spent his time making sure Mac's clothes were pressed, his rifle was cleaned, and errands Mac needed were done. By any standard, this was a surprising level of luxury for a private in the Marine Corps. But this was Shanghai, and even the monthly pay for a PFC, thanks to a favorable exchange rate and prevailing low wages and prices, produced amazing buying power.

The boys were greatly impressed by Mac and the 4th Marines in Shanghai, and they all agreed excitedly on one thing: they would join the Marine Corps as soon as humanly possible. As it turned out, Bob and Dan would have this dreamy vision fulfilled in ways they could not have even vaguely anticipated. Indeed, they would become Marines, but certainly their future service would never include having their names emblazoned in gold letters on a door with a private room and a servant.

Even though the Sheeks family had moved downtown, Bob and his brother George continued to attend the Shanghai American School in the French Concession. It was a Christian missionary–owned and operated institution, and it provided high quality American-style education for the children of the Americans in Shanghai. American kids whose parents lived elsewhere in China could also attend. The Sheeks boys were usually driven to school by the family chauffeur, but if the weather was nice, they rode their bicycles.

There was another advantage to living downtown, and that was ready access to the Bund. Something interesting was happening there almost always, such as the frequent demonstrations by the Chinese urging boycotts of Japanese products. These demonstrations were intended to be serious, but they had a kind of lighthearted carnival atmosphere. This usually sparked a reaction when the International Settlement police, many of them turbaned Sikhs from British India, tried to break them up. It made for memorable entertainment for a ten-year-old boy.

Bob would take the elevator down to the street and walk the two blocks to the Bund. Along the riverfront were the usual crowds of Chinese, all hurrying to get somewhere, and Bob looked forward to the new sights he would encounter. On some days there were grisly things, like bodies floating in the river. His father told him that some were suicides or accidents, and others were the victims of murders and gang killings. Reportedly, according to his father, the Japanese had started rounding up resisting Chinese civilians, executing them, and dumping the corpses in the muddy water. Bob had come to accept a body simply as a package with no life left. Death was an accepted fact of life. As his father had frankly explained, "That's life and death in Shanghai."

On one of his excursions to the Bund, Bob turned from the riverbank walkway to cross back over the busy thoroughfare. A stream of traffic was going by, many bicycles and rickshaws, and among them were cars and trucks. In one truck Bob noticed a Chinese boy, about his own age, sitting on the back edge of the open bed. He was a peanut seller, holding a wide bamboo tray full of paper bags filled with peanuts. As the truck started to slow down for traffic at an intersection, the boy jumped down onto the street. But the truck had not stopped, and when the boy's feet hit the pavement, his forward momentum pitched him backward. His head smacked the pavement violently with a loud noise that sounded like a bowling ball being dropped onto a concrete slab. As Bob watched, the boy's skull cracked open and his brain popped out intact on the asphalt, bags of peanuts scattered around it. Bob felt sick to his stomach. Dead bodies in the river were bad enough, but watching something as gruesome as what he had just seen, right in front of him, was something else. Traffic had stopped and Bob turned quickly to hurry farther up the Bund. Several policemen ran by him in the other direction toward the scene of the accident. As he continued to hustle away quickly, he noticed traffic was again flowing normally. When he looked back, there was no sign of the police, the body, the truck, or the scattered bags of peanuts.

He went back to the family apartment, and his amah made him a snack for lunch. He could barely eat, and he had difficulty getting the image of the Chinese boy hitting the pavement out of his mind. That evening Bob didn't mention what he had seen on the Bund, and he tried hard to forget it. This was by now a familiar process for the young boy, a way of coping with sights and experiences that otherwise would be difficult to deal with consciously.

Occasionally Bob's father had errands to run in Shanghai, and he would invite Bob along for the ride. These trips began with Bob joining his father in the elevator down to the lobby of their apartment building, and then emerging on the street from under an ornate, awning-covered entrance. Their Chinese chauffeur, Mr. Ling, was waiting by the open door of a shiny, black Ford sedan with immense rounded fenders. He stood by as Bob and his father climbed into the backseat. Mr. Ling then closed the door behind them, got behind the wheel in the front seat, and expertly guided the vehicle through the frenzied streets of Shanghai. There were few other cars on the streets, but hordes of pedestrians swirled amidst darting fleets of bicycles and rickshaws. It was a driving nightmare, but Mr. Ling wove the big Ford through the congestion, clearing the way through the crowds by honking the horn constantly.

Sometimes the errands took them to the French Concession. It was like coming across a suburban oasis in the crowded chaos of Shanghai. The zone was governed like a colony of France and was garrisoned by two Annamese regiments of the French army, mainly composed of troops from Vietnam.[8] The adjoining International Settlement also was home to European and American expatriates, though the French Concession had been considered by the Sheeks family to be more upscale. The threat of combat between the Chinese and Japanese had caused security to be beefed up, and the French police and troops, as well as the U.S. 4th Marines, had erected checkpoints on the main streets leading into the French Concession. During one errand, Mr. Ling slowed the car as he approached one of the blockaded intersections. There were several French troops and two U.S. Marines in combat gear on patrol. Each carried a rifle. The French sported red berets and the Marines wore the World War I–style steel helmets with the wide brim. Bob could see several other French soldiers behind a machine-gun emplacement surrounded by sandbags. The car came to a halt and a French officer peered through the windows. After a moment, he straightened and motioned them forward.

They drove on and eventually turned onto a tree-shaded street lined with elegant French Victorian–style houses. Soon they were passing their former residence, a distinguished brick house that could have been located just as easily in one of the better neighborhoods of Boston or Baltimore. The move to the apartment downtown had advantages and disadvantages. Bob and his brother were farther away from school and their friends, but there was a lot more action downtown compared to the relative quiet of the French Concession. Bob had made friends with a few Chinese boys in his new neighborhood, and he'd been using the Chinese language he'd picked up to be able to communicate with them. But he still missed the house where he had spent the first nine years of his life.

Bob's father was proud of his sons. They were bright and excelled in school, and what they saw and experienced in Shanghai, even though some of it was raw and shocking, surely would help them mature. Yet, he was carrying the heavy burden of dealing with his sick wife. They had moved to Shanghai with high hopes of a happy, prosperous, exciting life together in one of the most fascinating cities in the world. Soon she would be gone. What would be best for the boys? They had their amahs' care, but that was no substitute for a mother.

Mr. Ling usually made a couple of stops for Bob's father's errands, but they were never away for long from the apartment downtown. Afterward, Bob returned to his schoolwork or his hobbies, and he often checked on his pigeons. He rode the elevator up to the top floor, climbed a flight of stairs, and emerged onto a flat area surrounded by sloping, corrugated, galvanized metal roofs. At one side, next to several vent pipes, were three cage lofts containing enthusiastic-looking pigeons, eager to be released for their daily flight. Bob opened the doors to each cage in turn. Cautiously, one by one, they edged out with a fluttering of wings, and then flapped off noisily into the sky over Shanghai.

One night near the end of January 1932, as they flew away, Bob could hear the dull thud of artillery in the distance, with occasional pops of rifle shots. Earlier that day his father had mentioned what they had all feared: actual combat could begin at any minute between the Chinese and Japanese, most likely in an area called Chapei on the outskirts of Shanghai. The sounds of gunfire, clearly audible over the constant background roar of the city traffic, indicated the battle had begun.[9]

As the long night wore on, the unsettling sounds of distant artillery explosions made sleep impossible. Bob and his father went up to the roof to check on the birds. All of them had returned safely. They were sitting contentedly inside their cages, waiting to be fed, and then for the doors to be closed. As Bob went through the motions of attending to the pigeons, he was more focused on what appeared to be a spectacular fireworks display taking place a couple of miles away around the North Train Station. The sounds of explosions echoed through the cool night air. There was an almost constant *pop, pop, pop*, and an occasional geyser of burning debris followed by a large *boom*. Tracers from gunfire, streams of glowing orange dots, arced in slow motion into the dark night sky, a pyrotechnic accompaniment to the sounds of machine guns and mortar explosions. A building burned furiously, its garish yellow flames shooting golden embers into the night sky. The low clouds overhead were lit with a dull, red glow. Bob and his father watched in silence for some time before they finally went inside.

The outbreak of hostilities had a disconcerting effect on the Sheeks family and the rest of the Americans living in Shanghai, even though they thought the conflict had little to do with them. They felt sorry for the Chinese, but rather than worrying about the larger geopolitical issues, they were mostly concerned with the safety of their families and the stability of the business community. As far as the Americans were concerned, there was an impenetrable wall of security around them provided by the armed French police and security troops, the Shanghai Volunteer Corps, and of course the U.S. Marines. The Japanese wouldn't dare confront the Americans or, for that matter, the French and British expatriates who also lived in Shanghai. A rumor had been circulating among the Americans that the U.S. Army was prepared to send a force from the Philippines to make a strong statement to the Japanese, the message being not to attack foreign interests in Shanghai. As it turned out, things were alright for the Americans in Shanghai, more or less, until after the attack on Pearl Harbor in December 1941. Nearly all of the 4th Marines narrowly escaped Shanghai as the Japanese closed in, and they made it safely to the Philippines. There they fought against the Imperial Japanese Army for the next six months. They were taken captive when Corregidor fell, after which they spent the next three and a half years in POW camps.[10] The American civilians who remained in China soon found themselves in internment camps.[11]

A few days later, Bob's father announced that a cease-fire had been declared, and he wanted to take a drive out to Chapei by the North Station to see what the "damned Japs" had been up to. Bob and George viewed this as fantastic news—a chance to pick up spent cartridge shells and pieces of shrapnel, trading fodder for all kinds of other collectibles with the boys at school.

Mr. Sheeks called down for Mr. Ling to bring the car around. As the family emerged from the front door of the apartment building, they were greeted by Ling's familiar smiling face and the gleaming Ford sedan. As usual, he had buffed the automobile's black finish to a high gloss while he had been waiting.

George and Bob loaded into the backseat, and their father spoke quietly to the chauffeur as he moved by him and got behind the wheel. He told Ling that he would drive since they were going out to Chapei to see what had been happening, and he gave Mr. Ling the afternoon off. Combat between the Japanese and Chinese had greatly upset all the Chinese in Shanghai, and the fact that the Chinese army seemed to be losing made it even worse. Mr. Sheeks wanted to spare Ling from having to see what was, most likely, a Chinese defeat.

Mr. Ling nodded dutifully and seemed visibly relieved. He had heard the fighting was not going well for the Chinese, and he didn't relish having to drive out to look at a battlefield. The whole situation was depressing for him. He lived nearby with his family, and his salary as a member of the Sheeks' household staff meant he was making a good living. But what if the Japanese attacked the Americans? The Sheeks family would almost certainly leave Shanghai, and then he'd be out of a job. And what would happen if the Japanese won? Like the Americans, he was concerned for his own family, but unlike the Americans, he couldn't leave Shanghai if things got bad.

Mr. Sheeks wove the car through the crowded streets and headed toward Chapei on the outskirts of Shanghai. Soon the traffic became sparse, and they began to see pieces of bricks and bits of roofing tile that had been blasted into the street by the mortar shells that had struck the surrounding buildings. He steered around the debris, hoping not to run over anything sharp that could puncture a tire. Ahead was what remained of the North Station. The blackened concrete shell was all that was left of the massive building. This is what they had seen burning from the roof of their apartment building.[12]

Several Chinese men and women were wandering around carrying big bamboo baskets and bags. These were the scrap collectors, the real pros. They would sell their finds for cash to salvage merchants, while the boys would keep or trade what they found for their own collections.

They also noticed something else in the streets near the ruins of the deserted train station—what seemed like crumpled piles of dirty clothing. These were corpses, casualties from the Chinese army. They did not see any Japanese bodies. Apparently the Japanese had taken the time to gather and remove their dead. The Chinese army was occupying positions near the station, but the area they were driving through seemed to be patrolled by Japanese marines, naval troops also called "bluejackets" by the expatriates living in the International Concession. Even though this was a combat zone, the lull made touring the battlefield relatively safe. As expatriates the Sheeks boys felt safe, oddly neutral in the midst of the strife between the Japanese and Chinese, and they looked out the car windows like curious tourists.

The Ford moved slowly past more buildings damaged by artillery fire. George had brought along his Brownie camera and frequently asked his father to stop so he could take pictures of the damaged buildings. A squad of Japanese soldiers crossed in front of the car. As they marched away down the street through the rubble, George snapped another photo.

Soon they were in the countryside, and the urban city area gave way to small farms. The verdant fields, scenes of recent combat, were eerily quiet. Here and there were old Chinese graves, mounds of earth, a few with concrete or stones carefully arranged around them. These grave mounds had been used by both sides as shelter from rifle and shell fire, and also as gun positions. A number of uniformed Chinese corpses were lying near some of the mounds.

Mr. Sheeks stopped the car and they got out to walk around. He was absorbed in trying to reconstruct the direction of the battle. The boys didn't pay much attention. They detoured around the corpses and focused on collecting brass cartridges. They ignored the few Japanese soldiers hanging around ominously in the distance, seemingly paying no attention to the American sightseers. Several other civilians were wandering through the battlefield also. The boys' father recognized a couple of his friends, and they joined the Sheeks party on their tour.

All around them the green patches of vegetable gardens were torn apart by blackened craters left by mortars and artillery. There were also muddy zigzag trenches still containing heaps of uniforms that were Chinese bodies. Mr. Sheeks warned them sternly not to touch an object he spotted on the ground that looked like a soup can with a wooden handle coming out of one end. It was actually a German-style hand grenade meant to be thrown by that handle. Bob and George understood the danger. George snapped a photo of the grenade, and then concentrated on picking up brass shell casings scattered nearby.

They didn't notice the group of Japanese officers approaching, and they heard them before they turned to see them. Excitedly speaking Japanese, they walked up to George, eagerly gesturing toward the little boy holding the camera. They then pointed to the Americans, and back toward themselves. Apparently they had seen George take a photo of the unexploded grenade. As the soldiers continued to laugh and gesticulate, it became clear they wanted George to take a group photo of the Japanese officers with the Americans. Bob's father smiled nervously at his friends, then at the boys. This was an awkward moment indeed. The brutality of the Japanese military toward the Chinese was an indisputable and widely publicized fact. Though the Americans were formally neutral in the present conflict, their sympathies generally were with the Chinese. Foreigners in Shanghai weren't big fans of the Japanese military, to say the least.

But this was not the moment to refuse the Japanese anything, so Bob's father motioned to his friends and Bob to obediently line up with the Japanese officers, as George, his little Brownie camera in hand, nervously stepped out in front of the group and snapped a photo. This made the Japanese even more cheerful, and they strolled off in quite a good mood. The Americans were left standing there shaking their heads. George's photo became a family curiosity for years to come, made especially incongruous in light of the horrors they were soon to witness.

But on that day the Japanese officers were soon forgotten by the boys, and by the end of the outing the Sheeks brothers had made a notable haul. They picked up about a dozen brass rifle cartridges and nearly ten jagged chunks of shrapnel. Their new finds would be eagerly displayed and perhaps traded for greater treasures at school.

For the students of the Shanghai American School, collections and collectibles of every type and description were all the rage, and they included bird eggs, stamps, stones, and toys. Since combat between the Chinese and Japanese had started, any tidbit associated with the fighting had become valued for growing collections of war artifacts. One day at the school sports field, Bob approached a group of four boys crouched over several objects on the ground. His brother, George, pointed to items for which Dan Williams had traded earlier that day. A studious-looking boy wearing wire-rimmed glasses, Dan was holding two jagged pieces of iron shrapnel.[13] Another boy, Houghton "Bucky" Freeman, was inspecting a large-caliber, shiny brass shell casing he was turning over and over in his hands. The other boys listened intently as Dan explained his transaction. He had been walking to school that morning and a couple of the older kids had been out to where there had been fighting. They had found the shrapnel pieces, the large shell casing Bucky was holding, and several smaller brass shell casings. Bill Allman, or "Billy" to the other boys, the son of a prominent attorney and court judge who presided over legal cases involving Americans, interrupted and added eagerly that Dan had traded a few other artifacts they had found for all of it. This was indeed great treasure. Dan added excitedly that after he shined up the big shell, he noticed Japanese lettering on the bottom. This added to the value. It was like a newly recognized date on a freshly polished old coin.

Dan paid attention to details. He'd become an expert on the various types and calibers of Japanese ammunition. He had a naturally inquisitive nature, though it sometimes had the potential of backfiring. On a subsequent outing to the site of the fighting, he found an unexploded shell and wanted to open it. He thought hard about the best way to do it and came up with a step-by-step procedure he reasoned should work. First he soaked it in water for a week, and then he took it to shop class at school, put it in a vise, and pried it open. Of course the shell could have exploded, but Dan was lucky. Instead of a debilitating detonation, he found a bounty of shrapnel pellets inside, each the size of a marble, and he gave them out to the other boys to great acclaim. It was this potentially fatal but detailed analytical nature that led Dan's friends in later years to remark on his incredible ability to remember even minute aspects of his experiences throughout his life.

It was this same curiosity that led Dan to uncover the Japanese characters on the shell casing. Bucky handed it carefully to Bob, and he examined it closely. Sure enough, he could see a series of kanji characters written along one side. He held the shell casing in his hands like a rare and delicate jewel.

The boys recognized some of the kanji because they were identical to those used in Chinese writing. Growing up around local household servants, they'd been able to pick up some of the language and had attained a bit of proficiency in spoken and written Chinese. But even though some of the written characters were familiar, Japanese was quite a different language. They couldn't have known it then, but ten short years later the Japanese meaning of the kanji characters would be drilled into each of the boys' heads at the Japanese Language School run by the U.S. Navy in Boulder, Colorado. In 1932, however, this was only another aspect of collecting and trading endlessly fascinating war souvenirs.

The lull that came with the cease-fire was only temporary, and soon combat resumed not far away. The teachers at the Shanghai American School had a difficult time getting the boys in the class interested in their schoolwork. They were too excited to concentrate, and it was a struggle to make them pay attention to anything being taught. The fighting intensified through the month of February.

The local English-language newspaper was delivered to the Sheeks' apartment daily, and the family was kept abreast of the developments in the combat taking place in Chapei. The fighting seemed to be spreading slowly into the countryside surrounding Shanghai. Stories of atrocities perpetrated by the Japanese military against the Chinese started to circulate. Chinese civilians were being rounded up and taken out of the city for interrogation, or worse. In one case, there was a report of a group of Chinese civilians who were herded together, bayoneted, and shot.[14] Almost every day since the Japanese invasion there were stories of this sort in the papers.

Initially, the Americans thought the Chinese would be intimidated by the Japanese invasion and give up right away, yet the fighting went on for more than a month. The Japanese had underestimated the Chinese will to fight. This was at least partly because the Japanese held the Chinese in such extraordinarily low regard, in spite of the fact that Japanese culture was largely derived from Chinese traditions. The Japanese felt superior, proud of their unique militaristic bushido and imperial system, and they viewed the Chinese with disdain.[15]

The arrogance of the Japanese military forces in Shanghai in 1932 was difficult for the Sheeks family to tolerate, particularly with their American sense of fair play. The widely publicized atrocities had numerous side effects. Before 1932, Bob's father would take his sons to eat at restaurants in "Japan Town," a section of Shanghai populated mostly by Japanese. One of Bob's favorite dishes was sukiyaki. During this period, Bob's father had a respect for the Japanese because they were competing with his U.S. automotive parts company and were worthy adversaries. Japan also was known for having the best steamship lines serving China. But the Shanghai Incident changed everything. As the fighting and the atrocities went on, some of the evocative restaurants of Japan Town were burned down by the vindictive Chinese. So ended the Sheeks' sukiyaki excursions.

Dan Williams' parents were good friends with a Japanese couple who were insistently apologetic for the militant direction of the Japanese government. They gave the Williams family attractively illustrated photo books of Japan to emphasize the beauty of their country. They tried to explain repeatedly the difference between the Japanese people and the misdeeds of their current militaristic government.[16]

Bob's father took note of newspaper reports that the Japanese were handily defeating the Chinese. This came as no surprise, since it was widely assumed that the Chinese army was outmatched. The boys at school could see Japanese planes easily shooting down the old Chinese planes in dogfights taking place over the city. So, why the atrocities? This is what Bob found hard to deal with. The Chinese, like the servants who were surrogate members of Bob's household, these kind, sensitive, thoughtful people, were apparently powerless against the fearsome invaders. To Bob, the Japanese seemed mindlessly inhuman.

At the same time, Bob's father was receiving alarming reports from some of his American business associates. He came home from the office one day to find his wife having one of her good days. She was sitting in the living room, and Bob and George were doing their homework on the dining room table. Their father sat down next to her and reported first on the deteriorating situation around Shanghai, and then that the Mitchell family had temporarily evacuated, having taken the steamer to Hong Kong that afternoon.[17] The Mitchells were British and old friends of the Sheeks family. They had lived in the northern Shanghai suburb of Hongkew. It had been an American business enclave along the Huangpu River, but most Americans and Europeans now chose to live in the more desirable areas in Shanghai's western suburbs. The Sheeks family had been to numerous parties at the Mitchells' beautiful rambling brick-and-timber home. Bob had vivid memories of broad, elaborate gardens tended by several gardeners. The Mitchells had decided to leave two of their Chinese household staff to tend to the place, and they had asked Bob's father to look in on them from time to time. A family evacuating as a result of the Japanese invasion was truly depressing news. Could the permanent departure of even more expatriates be far behind?

One weekend, their father asked the boys if they wanted to come along to check on the Mitchells' home. The brothers glanced at each other and shrugged. There was probably not much chance of finding any military artifacts, though there had been combat around the Hongkew area where the Mitchell house was located. They agreed to go along on the off chance there could be some remnants of the fighting laying around.

Chauffeur Ling and the Ford were waiting outside as usual. The drive didn't take long, and they were soon pulling up in front of the Mitchells' elegant residence. Manicured shrubs surrounded the house, and neatly maintained flower beds were in bloom in the front yard. But something was wrong. A broken lamp lay on the walkway leading to the large front porch, and the door to the house stood open.

They got out of the car, headed up the paved path to the house, stepped past the broken lamp, went up a couple of steps to the porch, and approached the open door. Their father walked through the doorway and called out to see if anyone was there. Bob and George peered around from behind. What greeted them was a scene of total chaos, as if a tornado had torn through the house. Furniture was overturned, cushions were ripped open, draperies were half off the windows, papers were strewn around, and broken glass littered the floor. Someone had completely looted the place. They silently picked their way through the mess of what had been a graciously furnished home.

Double French doors opened out to the back garden. The glass was broken out of the doors, and both were ajar. There was more debris on the brick patio, and beyond was a trail of trash that led to the lawn. Their father stepped over an end table that partially blocked the French doors and went out to the patio. Bob and George were close behind. Suddenly their father stopped and tried to turn the boys back, but it was too late. The brothers stood beside their father staring at the scene in the back yard. Someone had dug what looked like a barbeque pit in the center of the lawn. The blackened remains of a wood fire were left in the pit. Above the pit, trussed on two poles like grilled pigs, were the ghastly remains of what had been two human beings. It took only a moment for the sickening realization to sink in. The Chinese servants had been roasted to death.

The boys' father, true to his North Dakota pioneer grit, believed his boys should witness the realities of life and death, but this was too much. Quickly he grabbed them by the arms to turn back into the house. Right behind them stood Mr. Ling, his face turned into an ashen grimace. He was staring unmoving at the scene, blocking the way. He had been a personal friend of the gardener. He had heard of this type of thing happening before. The Japanese had searched the house for valuables. When they came up empty handed, they tortured and killed the servants, trying to get them to say where any money and jewelry were hidden.[18]

Quickly their father led the boys back through the ruined house and out the front door, stepping over the debris and broken lamp in the walkway. In the Ford on the way home, no one spoke another word until they got back to the apartment. The boys' father went inside and immediately called the Shanghai Municipal Police to report what they had seen.

The brothers sat in the living room, only absently listening to snatches of their father's phone conversation with the police. They agreed it was the worst thing they had ever seen. They could usually joke about the grisly sights they often saw in Shanghai, but this was too awful. Not only had the Mitchell's house, much like their former home in the French Concession, been trashed by the Japanese, but two household servants had been grilled to death over a barbecue pit. They had been gentle Chinese people, kind and considerate, just like the family's staff the boys had grown up with. It was too horrible to contemplate.

Bob's hatred for the Japanese was churning inside him. He wished he could join the 4th Marines right then and there, so he could fight and kill Japanese soldiers. What Bob saw in Shanghai that day would stay with him for many years to come.

It was only a short while later that the boys' mother died in that tragic spring of 1932. After that, it became a matter of when, not if, they would leave. Even though combat ended in early March, followed by a truce that grew out of a British-American proposal in May 1932, the threat of all-out war between the Japanese and Chinese never really went away.[19] By 1935 Bob's father had made up his mind. It was clear that the deteriorating relationship between China and Japan was not going to have a good outcome. Bob, George, and their father left Shanghai on an American President Line ship to America. Even though they were leaving Shanghai partly because of the increasing belligerence of the Japanese government, in a bizarre twist the ship's routing took them right through Yokohama, Japan.

At this point in their lives, the Sheeks boys had never been to the United States, but they had been to Japan before. Two years earlier, in 1930, when relations between Japan and the international community were more congenial, their mother had taken them on a cruise on an Australian ship called the SS *Tanda*. One of the stops was Japan. The cruise was a great adventure for the boys, at that time aged eight and ten. One of Bob's most vivid memories was an entertainment event for the kids on the ship. The crew got them all together and had them take off their shoes. The shoes were then tied together in mismatched pairs and thrown into a big pile. The children descended on the jumble of shoes and tried to find their own. The first kid to find his got a prize. Bob burrowed into the pile enthusiastically, applying his usual focus and determination, and was the first to find his shoes. As the big winner, he was awarded a silver-plated letter opener in the shape of a dagger with a cockatoo on the handle, and he kept it for many years.

When the cruise ship stopped in Japan on that first visit in 1930, Bob didn't think much about it because he was just a little kid. But there was one incident that made a lasting impression on him, an event that revealed a darker side of the Japanese. It was the end of the day and all the passengers had returned from their tours ashore. The ship was ready to leave, but there was a delay of several hours. It turned out that two of the Australian crew members had been arrested for rowdiness. For punishment, they weren't simply thrown in jail or fined. The Japanese police elected to punish them for their misdeeds by beating the soles of their feet with bamboo rods. The two ended up so sore and bruised they couldn't walk. Bob and some of the other passengers watched as they were carried on board by their crewmates. This seemed unusually cruel, and Bob felt sorry for them. The ship sailed and the incident, though odd, was forgotten. Bob remembered it later when he saw what the Japanese were capable of in Shanghai in 1932.

But it was now 1935 and the Sheeks family was leaving China by transiting Japan. The brutality of the Japanese military, witnessed firsthand in Shanghai, didn't stop Bob's father from typically bulldozing forward and seeing the sights, so they left the ship on a tour. They marveled at the manicured, orderly landscape, the smiling women in kimonos, and the massive bronze Buddha at Kamakura. Everything was well organized and the people were polite. But the ruthlessness of the Japanese military in China stuck in Bob's mind, and what he saw in Japan didn't change his low opinion of the Japanese.

The ship then steamed across the Pacific to Victoria, British Columbia, then to Seattle, and finally to San Francisco. It was there that the Sheeks boys finally set foot on U.S. soil for the first time. They had been raised as Americans but had never actually lived in the United States. It was an eye-opening experience for them, even though a few things, such as some of the food dishes, were familiar. It turned out that Bob had sampled his fair share of American cuisine in Shanghai. Their household cooks were trained to prepare American-style dishes, and there was an American restaurant in the International Concession called "Jimmy's Kitchen." It was a genuine slice of Americana, with gingham-checked tablecloths and a menu that included steak, apple pie, waffles, pancakes, and real maple syrup. And it wasn't only the food that was familiar. Bob had grown up with other Americans in the French Concession, and the Shanghai American School was almost like being in the United States because most of the kids were American. Yet it was quite a different story to suddenly be immersed in California. It was a kind of culture shock, but Bob found it invigorating and exciting. The Sheeks boys had read about America during their years in Shanghai, and they'd seen American movies, but to actually be in the United States was almost like they'd walked into one of those movies.

Bob's negative attitude toward the Japanese carried over to California, and if anything it became more intense. When he was in junior high school he created a little hate shrine on the dresser in his room, complete with photos of Emperor Hirohito and the Crown Prince that he'd clipped from a magazine. He posted them there so he could see them every morning and remind himself that he wanted to kill them one day. This could have been interpreted as a sign of typically immature teenage behavior, but at that point in his life, Bob truly believed the Japanese were, by nature, inherently evil.

A couple of years later their father moved them to Spokane, Washington, and Bob went to high school there. As he drew closer to seventeen years of age, the military eligibility threshold, he convinced his father to sign the papers so he could enlist early in the Marine Corps Reserve at age sixteen. This had been his goal ever since growing up admiring the 4th Marines in Shanghai, but now he had an additional motivation. He wanted to join the Marines to fight the Japanese and avenge the atrocities he had witnessed. However, there were a few glitches in his plan, chief of which was the United States wasn't yet at war with Japan. But simply having an affiliation with the Marines fulfilled a lifelong dream. His commitment would become much more serious all too soon.

TWO

Japanese Language Immersion: Berkeley, California, and Boulder, Colorado, 1942–43

Bob Sheeks' academic career really began when he took the Harvard National Exam while still in high school. He thought he'd failed the test and more or less forgot about it afterward. In 1940 he was still in the Marine Corps Reserve, and that summer he was in training at Bremerton Navy Yard in Puget Sound. President Roosevelt declared a limited emergency, and Bob heard Reservists were going to be called up for active duty. Then he got a letter from Harvard. It was typically understated, but to him it was spectacularly good news: words to the effect that if he were still interested in Harvard, they'd give him a full scholarship. Apparently he hadn't failed the qualification test as he'd thought, and of course he was interested in a scholarship to Harvard. The catch was that he had to arrange for a conditional release from Marine Corps duty. Since the war hadn't started yet, he could get a deferment to attend college, and that's how he ended up at Harvard. Right after he left for the East Coast, his fellow Reservists were sent off to American Samoa in the South Pacific, and then on to other duty stations. It turned out that by attending Harvard, Bob delayed his entry into the Pacific war by about two years.

There was a considerable cultural transition from high school in Spokane, Washington, to college in Cambridge, Massachusetts. Bob had to fill out a form for a housing request, and there was a space to specify the regional origin of the roommate he preferred. Because he had never been to the eastern United States before, he requested a roommate "from the east," and that ended up being Don Shively. But he hailed from quite a bit farther east than what Bob had in mind. Don's parents were American missionaries, and he had been born and grew up in Japan and spoke fluent Japanese. Meanwhile, Don had spent a brief time in the western United States as a teenager, so he filled out his housing form also requesting a roommate "from the east," thinking in terms of the eastern seaboard of the United States. He was matched with Bob who had never even been to the eastern United States, but had been born and raised in the Far East, namely China. When both Bob and Don said they preferred roommates "from the east," Harvard had taken the global view. That's how the two of them, both born and raised in Asia, ended up as freshman roommates in Weld Hall at Harvard for the 1940–41 academic year.

It would have been logical that Bob's roommate, Don, sparked Bob's interest in the Japanese language. But Bob was still carrying around a simmering hatred for the Japanese, ingrained from what he'd seen their military do to the Chinese in Shanghai. Though it was an uphill battle, Don set out to convince Bob that the Japanese weren't so bad. He provided a uniquely American perspective of growing up in a Japanese neighborhood, and he told humorous and positive stories of things he had experienced there. Bob wasn't sold. Don kept pointing out that the current problem with Japan was the military, not the Japanese people as a whole. Bob still wasn't convinced. But before long there were two factors that started Bob down a path that would directly influence his outlook: Japan's attack on Pearl Harbor, and a U.S. Navy commander named Hindmarsh.

With his freshman year completed and facing the start of the 1941–42 academic year, Bob and Don remained friends but went their separate ways for housing. Don moved into a campus residence, and Bob got a room in Adams House. It turned out he was assigned to the same suite where Franklin Roosevelt stayed during his tenure at Harvard.

During that fall of 1941, Bob spent a lot of time at the home of distinguished Harvard Law School professor Henry M. Hart Jr. and his wife, Mary. Their staid Victorian home was situated in a quiet, leafy neighborhood in Cambridge. Bob had met the Harts in Spokane that previous summer, and he had driven across the United States with them to return to Cambridge for the fall 1941 term. Henry Hart was in his forties, a senior member of the Harvard Law School, and an expert on Constitutional Law.

On the evening of December 7, 1941, the Harts went out to a formal dinner. Bob had been visiting them earlier in the afternoon, and they suggested he could stay at the house and study until they returned. The radio hadn't been on all day, so after they left Bob switched it on and settled down to read an assignment. He wasn't paying close attention, but then he heard something about Pearl Harbor being attacked by Japan earlier that morning. He dropped his book and leaned closer to the radio. A grim-voiced announcer reported that the attack had been from the air and had apparently inflicted casualties at the Navy base. Explosions had been heard in Honolulu, and there appeared to be injured civilians as well. It all seemed fairly confused, but there was little doubt as to the gravity of the situation.

Bob sat alone in the living room trying to make sense of what he was hearing. The Japanese had attacked Hawaii! The words were repeated again, but the news seemed unreal. Even before the Sheeks family left Shanghai, there had been speculation about the Japanese and what they were up to in the Pacific. Bob's father had always attempted to search out the facts, analyzing the chances of U.S. military help if the Japanese ever attacked Americans anywhere in the Pacific, specifically in Shanghai. Most of the talk was about how the U.S. Army in the Philippines would arrive quickly to lend a hand to the 4th Marines who were nominally protecting the American community. His father also used to mention the U.S. naval base at Pearl Harbor, and how extremely important it was for security in the entire Pacific.

The radio announcer continued repeating the news, but there didn't seem to be much more to add. Within an hour the Harts were back home. Bob motioned to the radio, where the announcer was again repeating information of the attack on Pearl Harbor. The Harts' somber expressions made it clear before they even said a word that they had already heard the news at dinner. They joined Bob in the living room in a kind of stunned silence. No one knew quite what to say. Finally they began discussing hesitantly what could happen next. Bob figured his deferment would be canceled, and he'd be called back into the Marine Reserves. Maybe Professor Hart would be drafted, though they agreed that because he was married and a bit older, he may be left to teach at Harvard. And what would be Japan's next move? Would they be eyeing a land invasion of Hawaii? What about the U.S. West Coast?

They stayed up late that night speculating on the implications of the news. Bob came to the conclusion that it was a fatal mistake for Japan to take on the U.S. military, and victory over the Japanese would take only a year or two. The longer they talked about it, the more convinced Bob became that he'd be called back into the Marines, and he would put in for duty at Shanghai. It would be his chance to vanquish the hated Japanese, and get a free ride back to China in the process.

The next morning Bob hurried across Harvard Yard, with its distinguished redbrick buildings. As he passed groups of students he could hear snippets of conversation, and everyone was talking about the Japanese attack on Pearl Harbor. Bob headed straight for one of the residence houses to search out Don Shively, the one person on campus he most wanted to see right then.

Given Bob's hatred of the Japanese and this current turn of events, all those hours spent during their freshman year debating whether the problem was Japanese society and culture as a whole, or just the military, now seemed irrelevant. As far as Bob was concerned, the events of December 7 demonstrated conclusively that the entire Japanese Empire, civilian and military, was at fault. Japan had now morphed into a threat for the world as a whole, and most likely for them personally.

Bob found Don deep in discussion with two other students. They were going over the current world political situation and the part Japan might now play. Bob joined them and after a quick recap to update each other on what they had heard, they decided to go see a mutual friend, Otis Cary. Otis was a close boyhood pal of Don's, and both had gone to school in Japan at the Canadian Academy in Kobe. Otis' parents were also missionaries, and he was now attending nearby Amherst College. They agreed that Otis would be more upset than either of them, since he was even more sensitive to Japanese culture and religion than Don. Bob's hatred of the Japanese military had always been disturbing to Otis.

When Bob and Dan arrived at Otis' dorm at Amherst, he was disconsolate indeed. He lamented repeatedly that his plan to go back to Japan after college to teach and do missionary work, as his father had done, was now in jeopardy. He took his religious commitment seriously. Like Don, Otis was fluent in Japanese, and missionary work there seemed like the natural thing for him to do. But a quick American victory might not be that certain, and his anticipated return to Japan could be delayed indefinitely.

Talk then turned to Japan and the Japanese, and the ensuing animated discussion went late into the night. One thing was clear: the United States was going to have to fight the Japanese. But then who knew what would happen?

There was something else that puzzled the students. It seemed odd that the Japanese attacked Pearl Harbor when the United States had so many facilities and troops in the Philippines. They thought Japan was overextended. The soldiers and sailors of the Empire would have to fight first in the Philippines against the huge U.S. military establishment there, and surely, the students thought, the Japanese could not defeat the reportedly powerful American-Filipino forces.

As classes continued at Harvard that week, news from the Pacific only got worse. The Philippines had been attacked. The British were in trouble in Hong Kong, Malaya, and Singapore. Suddenly, Japan's military machine seemed like an unstoppable juggernaut rolling over the Pacific.[1]

Returning to Spokane for the Christmas holidays and to study for finals, Bob rode along with a classmate, Bob Bates, whose home was in Ojai near Santa Barbara. It was a long three days and three nights in the car, but the best part was that it was free. Bob Bates' uncle wanted his giant new Buick sedan driven to Santa Barbara from Boston, so he supplied the car and paid for gas. From Santa Barbara, a bus ride brought Sheeks the rest of the way home. His brother, George, was on break from his classes at Gonzaga, and he joined Bob and their father for the holidays. Later known for its giant-killer basketball teams, Gonzaga's claim to fame in the early 1940s was a famous alumnus named Bing Crosby.

There was a sense of apprehension in the Sheeks household during that holiday season, with a lot of wondering and guessing as to how things would go for the boys in the next year. Everything was changing quickly in directions no one could predict. Though the boys were likely facing service in the military, with unknowable outcomes, their father didn't seem bothered by any of it.

After the holidays, Bob returned to Harvard in January 1942 to complete the fall term. This consisted of a couple of weeks of classes and the
dreaded final exams. Within a few days of his return, a letter showed up
in Bob's mailbox. The return address read, "Navy Department, Office of
the Chief of Naval Operations, Washington," and the letter was dated
January 16, 1942. *Here it is*, Bob thought. The Marine Corps was part
of the Navy, and he figured he was being called back into the service.
But to his surprise, the letter was a request to be interviewed later that
week. He was to report to a room at the Harvard-Yenching Institute, the
same building where he was taking a Chinese class. Though Bob was a
biology major, following up on his earlier inclinations along those lines
from Shanghai, he was taking a class in Chinese history and language as
an elective. Even with his demanding schedule of required classes for his
major, his interest in China remained strong and he relished learning
more about the country where he had been born and grown up.

Two days later at the appointed hour he appeared outside the room,
knocked, and heard a voice inside invite him in. Bob opened the door
and behind a desk sat a trim, distinguished naval officer in uniform. He
introduced himself as Commander Hindmarsh and motioned for Bob to
sit down in the one chair in front of his desk. Hindmarsh appeared to be
in his late thirties, with slightly graying close-cropped dark hair, round
wire-rimmed glasses, and a crisp manner. He told Bob he had received
his PhD at Harvard and also was a professor of international law there.
He related how he had joined the Naval Reserve, was an exchange professor at Tokyo Imperial University, and had learned Japanese.[2] After those
preliminaries, it was all business. He said that the Navy had ordered the
establishment of a Japanese language school at Berkeley, California. The
existing school at Pearl Harbor was being evacuated, and he was visiting Harvard to interview potential candidates.

Bob pointed out that he didn't speak Japanese, but he knew a bit of
Chinese. Hindmarsh informed him curtly that that was exactly why
he was being interviewed. Harvard records indicated he had been born
and raised in Shanghai and was presently taking a course related to Chinese history and culture. The Navy thus assumed he had an ongoing interest in Asia, must have picked up some Chinese language, and perhaps
had at least a passing familiarity with printed Chinese kanji characters.

He'd have a head start over someone trying to learn the similar Japanese kanji characters from scratch. Then came the bottom line: the training at Berkeley would qualify him for a commission in the Navy as a language and intelligence officer. It wasn't quite the Marine commission Bob had wanted, and he had the temerity to say so. Hindmarsh didn't have a problem with it, and he said he would recommend that Bob be admitted to the language school at Berkeley. If and when he successfully completed the course, he would receive a commission in the Marine Corps and serve in the Pacific.

That was exactly what Bob wanted to hear. He would be able to fulfill his lifelong dream of becoming a Marine Corps officer. The only seemingly minor catch was that he had to learn Japanese first. That little detail would turn out to be an exceedingly daunting task. Hindmarsh told him to go ahead and complete his courses at Harvard, since there was only a week left before finals, and then report to Berkeley for the start of the spring semester.

Bob headed to Don Shively's room to relay the news. Don also had received a letter from the Navy and had a meeting with Hindmarsh the next day. When they learned that Otis Cary had an interview scheduled later in the week at Amherst, they were astounded at how fast the Navy had worked. Within a few weeks of December 7, Hindmarsh had contacted several top academic institutions to recruit students with preexisting Japanese language skills, like Don and Otis. He had even gotten into the second tier of those, like Bob, who spoke no Japanese but had at least some Asia background that presumably qualified them for Navy language training in Japanese. It was a sign of how quickly the United States was ramping up for the epic effort to defeat the Japanese.[3]

In the next week Bob completed his third semester at Harvard, though he found it hard to concentrate on his studies. His thoughts were on naval training at Berkeley, the Japanese language school program, and his eventual commission in the Marine Corps. Though he only knew a little Chinese, there was no doubt in his mind he could learn Japanese.

A few weeks later Bob was in San Francisco being inducted into the Navy at Alameda Air Station. He was given the rank of Navy yeoman 2nd class and was told to report to the Naval Reserve Officers' Training Corps (ROTC) office at U.C. Berkeley. Bob made his way quickly to the nearby

Berkeley campus, and an officer in the ROTC office directed him to the Japanese language school in California Hall.

The campus basked in the February sun, sheltered by huge eucalyptus and pine trees. Bob entered California Hall and went into an office with a sign over the door that read, "U.S. Navy Japanese Language School." Inside, behind a fortress-like wooden desk, sat a formidable, distinguished-looking lady in her mid-forties, her gray hair wound in a swirl on top of her head. With a withering stare, she looked up at Bob through wire-framed glasses. He wasn't expecting such an imposing female presence.

She surveyed the tense young man in front of her and then made him feel much more at ease when she smiled and said she was Florence Walne, the administrative director of the Navy Japanese Language School. She stood and shook his hand with a firm, confident grip, then sat back down and shuffled through some folders on her desk. She noted casually, almost as an afterthought, that she and Bob had something in common—they both had attended Harvard, she had graduated with a degree in Japanese studies, and currently she was on the Japanese language faculty at Berkeley. Walne added that her parents were missionaries in Japan and she grew up there speaking the language.[4]

The door to her office opened and a stocky man in his mid-twenties entered the room and took a folder from her. He had dark hair combed straight back, a thin black mustache, and he looked vaguely Latino. She introduced him as Frank Huggins, a member of the first Navy Japanese language class at Berkeley.[5] He had an air of smug superiority about him, and he said something about the course being intense, as if it were some sort of threat.

Later, Bob learned the possible reason for Huggins' odd behavior. It was said he was nursing an unusually intense bitterness about the Japanese attack on December 7. It turned out his grandfather was Frank Brinkley, an American who had lived in Japan. Brinkley married the daughter of a samurai, and then founded the first English-language newspaper in Japan. Frank Huggins was one-quarter Japanese and had grown up in Japan.[6] He was fluent in the language and was slated to graduate early from the course. The school was under a lot of pressure to turn out interpreters as soon as possible.

After Frank brushed up his written skills and learned some military vocabulary, he would be sent directly to active duty in the Pacific, as would Don Shively, Bob's roommate during their freshman year at Harvard. Later on, Bob's boyhood chum Dan Williams would serve with Huggins, who was by then a senior Japanese language officer. They would land with the 4th Marine Division at Saipan, just down the beach from where Bob would come ashore with the 2d Marine Division.

Walne told Bob to go down the hall and look for some of the other new students who had been showing up that day. He passed an open door to an adjoining classroom, where he saw some familiar faces. There were his childhood pals from Shanghai, Bucky Freeman and Bill Allman, and his college friend from back east, Otis Cary. All had been recruited by Hindmarsh in an astonishing feat of rapid-fire organization and intelligence gathering.

That night they bedded down in a makeshift dorm near the campus, and the next morning felt like the first day of school when they were kids. The second wartime class of the expanding Japanese language school, forty-four students strong, squeezed into a classroom intended for far fewer.[7]

Florence Walne entered, accompanied by a distinguished-looking, middle-aged Japanese man. She welcomed them, apologized for the cramped conditions in the dorm and classroom, and introduced the chairman of the Japanese language department at Berkeley, Nakamura Susumu. She said from that point onward, he would be known to them as "Nakamura Sensei," meaning "Honored Teacher Nakamura."

Bob thought Nakamura looked like a Japanese Navy admiral. It hadn't occurred to him that some of their instructors would be ethnic Japanese. This struck him initially as a bit of a conundrum. Despite his negative feelings toward the Japanese military in Shanghai, what he felt as Nakamura stepped forward to the front of the classroom was mainly discomfort—not his own, but what he thought must be Nakamura's. He couldn't imagine what it must be like for Nakamura, with his cultural and academic ties to Japan, to be instructing students who would use what he would teach them to help defeat the Japanese.

Nakamura Sensei eyed the new students. He started speaking slowly and strongly. His English held little trace of a Japanese accent. There was formality in his manner that made it clear he meant business. He welcomed them to the Navy Japanese Language School and explained he was an American citizen, born in the United States, an American of Japanese descent, also called nisei. Most of their instructors would be nisei. He said that the students in the new class had been chosen carefully either for their existing Japanese language skill, or background in other Asian languages, or outstanding academic credentials, or a combination of all three. They had all come from top universities, and a number of them were Phi Beta Kappa. As Nakamura Sensei spoke, no one moved. His firm voice filled the room.

He warned them that what he was about to say would be the only full lecture in English they would hear for the next year. Over the next two weeks there may be some direction in English combined with Japanese, and then after that the instruction would be entirely in Japanese. This would force the students to either learn the language or fail the course. In that case, they may be reported to their draft boards. This little tidbit focused everyone's attention even more, and they all sat motionless in their seats, frozen by the prospect of flunking out and being drafted, the gilded promise of officer commissions going up in smoke in the face of unthinkable failure in the class.

Nakamura explained that the previous Japanese language schools' curricula in Tokyo and Hawaii were designed to be completed in three years, but the course on which they were about to embark would last a little over one year. To keep up, he warned, they would likely have to study fourteen hours a day, six days a week. Their teachers would work twelve hours a day teaching them Japanese. They would take a test once a week on the material learned during that week, with the tests being comprehensive and cumulative.

Then, more warnings: Slow learning would not be tolerated—they would learn fast, and thoroughly. Reading, writing, and speaking would be taught. Military texts would be studied only near the end. When they successfully finished the course, they would be able to read and write a minimum of 1,600 kanji characters; they would master a spoken vocabulary of 8,000 Japanese words; and they would be able to read a Japanese newspaper.[8]

Nakamura added that even though some of them had a background in Japanese, or learned Japanese in Japan, or grew up in China, or had at least a little familiarity with an Asian language, they would be taught as if they had no knowledge of Japanese. They would start from the beginning. Instructors would use the six-volume Naganuma Reader. He explained that Naganuma Sensei was the son of a samurai in Japan, had married the daughter of an American missionary, and had become the leader of the Japanese language school in Tokyo, where he taught Americans in the 1920s.[9] The course would follow his instruction method and use his materials. In a memorable understatement, Nakamura remarked that the students would "become familiar" with the Naganuma lessons.

On the desk at the front of the room was a stack of books, along with a pile of bound notebooks. Nakamura Sensei handed out the books, announcing that it was volume one of the Naganuma Reader, the point of departure for their journey in total Japanese language immersion. As he distributed the books he started describing the Japanese language, stating almost parenthetically, in another colossal understatement, that it was really quite simple.

Nakamura noted that Japanese is a totally different language from Chinese, although Japan adopted many Chinese words and concepts, mainly starting in the seventh and eighth centuries AD. This was because Japanese culture before that era was relatively primitive and had no writing system, and there had been limited contact between Japan and China prior to that time. Writing with Chinese ideographs was effectively introduced into Japan via Korea, mainly by Korean Buddhist and scholastic missionaries.[10]

He went on to describe how, at first, Japanese priests and scholars adopted Chinese as an elite language, much the same way Latin in Europe was used as the classical language of religion, high education, and culture. English is full of words borrowed from Latin, Greek, French, and other languages. Likewise, Japan adopted a large number of Chinese words and ideas into the basic Japanese language. Korea did the same. In Western Europe, however, the main languages are closely related, sharing Indo-European roots. The Japanese and Chinese languages have no such shared origins.

In Japanese, Nakamura explained, use of Chinese ideograph characters was widespread, but relatively few were used compared to their usage in Chinese writing. The Japanese call these ideographs of Chinese origin "kanji," which literally means "Chinese characters." In addition to the kanji, Japanese has two sets of written phonetic scripts for syllables. One is a set called katakana, which are small, angular letters written with one, two, or three strokes, like hand-printed English. Another, called hiragana, is exactly the same set of syllables, but written cursively, like handwriting in English. It is possible to write Japanese phonetically using one or the other of the phonetic kana. Except for the most elementary kindergarten texts, most published literature—newspapers, books, magazines—is written with some combination of kanji and kana. Then there is *sosho*, and Nakamura said this was entirely different. It is an artistic form of penmanship, and though it is somewhat stylized, it can be quite individualistic. It is a type of shorthand, or speed writing, and represents kanji and kana in a flowing style. It is mainly a fast way of writing kanji, not of writing katakana.

Nakamura went on to explain that there are five Japanese vowels. These five, plus combinations with ten consonants, constitute the basic fifty syllabic kana. In addition, there is another sound, which for some words is a final "n" at the end of a syllable. Thus, there are fifty-one basic kana. However, to extend the number of syllables, there is a system of putting small indicator symbols on the kana to change the consonant, thus increasing the total number of possible syllables. One indicator symbol looks like tiny quotation marks or a circle at the upper right side of the kana. He said this could change the sound from "ha" to "pa," from "ta" to "da," from "ka" to "ga," and so on.

With that, Nakamura wrote each of the katakana characters on the blackboard and pronounced each one. Bob and the rest of the students copied them into the notebooks they had been issued. Nakamura walked around the crowded classroom, watching the new students carefully write the unfamiliar characters. Occasionally he would stop and correct a student's mistakes. Bob's head was spinning with the level of complication. Nakamura seemed to recognize his students' confusion, and he moved around the room patiently, looking to help out. Because Nakamura was ethnic Japanese, Bob was initially wary. But he seemed like a reasonable person, impressive, thoughtful, and eloquent.

Later, the students were instructed to open book one of their Naganuma Reader to the first chapter and start translating sentences using their newly learned katakana characters. The assignment for the next day was to memorize all they had covered that day and read chapters one through four.

After an intense week there was a written test on Saturday morning, the first of what would become a weekly ritual, and it was difficult. But it was the cumulative nature of the course that the students found to be the most crushing challenge. Every Saturday test covered what had been taught the previous week, as well as everything presumably learned in previous weeks. The key to survival was memorization, memorization, and more memorization. It was like climbing an intellectual Mount Everest.

Bob did better on the written parts of the course because there was some correspondence with the Chinese characters and the Japanese kanji. Otis excelled in spoken Japanese, as was to be expected, though he had to work hard on the written lessons and learning new vocabulary; however, he did prove useful in teaching the students various Japanese slang words. Of course, all the students wanted to know how to swear in Japanese. Otis had to explain that cursing in Japanese was not the same as in English. The Japanese used subtle allegories in ways not entirely obvious that swearing was even involved. Bob and Otis compared notes on the relative characteristics of swearing in Japanese and Chinese. They decided that, as a language, there was much more graphic obscenity in Chinese than Japanese. They concluded that Japanese was a more polite language, so if you called someone a bad person, it was a real insult and considered obscene. But if you wanted to really curse at someone, Chinese had a breadth and depth of obscenities that was unmatched in Japanese. After learning these cultural nuances, the students could soon curse in a style that would impress a Japanese sailor on any waterfront in the world, though Otis, with his missionary background, rarely swore in any language.

Nakamura Sensei was the lead instructor, and the entire faculty of the Japanese language school was teaching and working with the students. Seven instructors on the faculty were American nisei; two more were Japanese nationals; and five were Caucasians who had learned Japanese while living in Japan.[11] Bob was genuinely impressed by the compassion and consideration of the nisei, and by their true interest in teaching Japanese to the Caucasian students. They seemed like some of the kindest, most forthright people he had ever met, a stark contrast to his impressions of the Japanese military he'd seen in action in Shanghai.

One day, some of the Japanese language students were walking back from lunch with Nakamura Sensei. It was a clear, blue-sky day, and as they passed Sather Gate and crossed campus, Nakamura decided to test the reaction of his students. In Japanese, he casually said, "It seems like it's about to rain today."[12] Then he looked around to gauge the reaction of the students. Bob and Otis looked at each other and immediately picked up on what Nakamura was doing. Otis said, in Japanese, "That's odd, no chance of rain today—impossible!" Then he and Bob both broke out laughing. Nakamura noted their reaction and was disappointed that none of the others caught on. They continued on to their classroom and resumed the rest of the day of instruction. Later, Bob and Otis had to explain to the rest of the students what it was all about.

They were only a few weeks into the class when news broke about a presidential order that stated all ethnic Japanese had to be moved away from the West Coast. It seemed to have something to do with the possibility of sabotage or spying. Because many of their teachers were ethnic Japanese, this presented a real complication. Soon, in reaction to Executive Order 9066, Florence Walne announced that the Navy Japanese Language School would have to move inland.[13]

Bob wondered how the United States could be doing something this ridiculous. Apparently, Japanese-American nisei were not quite U.S. citizens in the eyes of the government. They were somehow tainted, aliens in their own country, and had become the enemy in a way no one quite understood. Bob had quickly come to recognize that his nisei instructors, though of ethnic Japanese origin, were quite different from the brutal soldiers of the Imperial Japanese military in Shanghai. He now accepted that something had not gone haywire with an entire ethnic group, though his hatred for the Japanese military hadn't let up.

Sometime later, Bob and Otis stole a few precious moments of study time to walk a couple of blocks to one of the churches designated as an evacuation center. As they approached, they saw groups of ethnic Japanese filing down the street, carrying suitcases, dressed nicely as if going to church services. The nisei formed up and stood politely in line outside the church as uniformed U.S. Army soldiers tried to organize them into groups to board the buses parked along the street. Families were holding what looked like boarding passes. They all looked anxious, suddenly strangers in the town where they had grown up. There was almost total silence, as if they really were in church and not outside on the sidewalk.

To be forcibly removed from one's home and shipped somewhere else in one's own country was shocking in the extreme. Otis and Bob watched in silence. They wondered why no one was protesting or raging at this monstrous injustice. But the family groups stood in orderly lines, just as if they were catching a ride home, and deliberately boarded the buses.

Bob and Otis halfheartedly speculated that maybe it wouldn't be too bad, that it was just a short-term arrangement, that the Japanese-Americans were probably being moved to nice facilities somewhere. But in reality they acknowledged that they had no idea where the internees were being taken, or what kind of accommodation they would face, or for how long they would be interned. Plus, it just felt wrong to watch U.S. citizens being hauled off to camps. Soon, the last of the nisei were loaded and the buses drove off to an unknown destination. The street was again empty.

On their walk back to the boarding house to study, Bob and Otis agreed that the totalitarian military rulers of Japan had obviously crossed some line of human decency. But then, how could they reconcile this objectionable decision the U.S. leaders had made to forcibly remove elements of the U.S. population and put them in camps? Otis was unnerved by this latest turn of events and even more uncertain of his future, given the role he was about to play in the war. He was in a class where he was being taught skills that would contribute to defeating the Japanese. But since his lifelong dream was to return to Japan as a missionary, he feared that if the Japanese found out what he'd done in the war to help dishonor them in defeat, he could never go back. His previously well-thought-out life plan now seemed in total disarray.

There wasn't time to think too long about any of these incomprehensible big-picture questions. The inexorable pace of the class, and the relentless studying and memorizing, consumed most of the students' conscious moments. By mid-May they had finished the first book of the

Naganuma Reader. It had taken three months and they still had five more books to go. Then, on June 1, they got word to pack for their move inland to Boulder, Colorado. The last class at Berkeley was held on June 12, and the students were ordered to reassemble in Boulder on June 24.

Boulder, Colorado, June 1942

Otis and Bob packed their few belongings in Berkeley, caught a train to Cheyenne, Wyoming, and took the bus south to Boulder, Colorado. What greeted them was a small college town set at the foot of the Rocky Mountains. On its western edge, Boulder was backed by massive, steeply sloped pink sandstone slabs embedded in the ponderosa pine–dappled foothills that rose abruptly from the undulating plains of eastern Colorado. The locals appropriately called these stone behemoths "the Flatirons." Florence Walne had arrived earlier and had already set up the Japanese language school office on campus by the time they got there.[14] As the students straggled in from the West Coast, they were assigned to rooms in Fleming Hall, the men's dorm on the University of Colorado campus.

An early architect for the university had decreed that all buildings must be constructed of the same sandy pink stone as the Flatirons, with Italian-style red tiled roofs. The combination of the buildings and the setting made the JLS students feel like they'd wandered into a little slice of northern Italy set in the Rocky Mountains. Before they knew it, classes resumed and they tore into book two of the Naganuma Reader.

As his studies continued, Bob got to know some of the other members of his class. One was a tall, gangly student from Harvard named Dave Osborne. He was nearly 6'3", slim, and with the distinguished air of an academic quite beyond his years. Bob had first met Dave when they had taken a class together at the Harvard-Yenching Institute. Though clearly in the upper echelon of natural intelligence, even compared to the academic overachievers of the JLS class, what particularly distinguished Dave from the other students was his ability to read Braille, even though he had perfect eyesight. One late night in the dorm, Bob and Otis went to Dave's room to rouse him for a snack to cap off studying for the day. Bob knocked on the door, and a voice inside said to come in. They opened the door, and the room was totally dark. As their eyes adjusted, they could make out Dave sitting at his desk, his fingertips lightly touching the pages of an open book. He was reading Braille in the dark. This must have been a drawing card for Dave when he was being interviewed by Hindmarsh for the Japanese language school. After all, if a seeing person could learn Braille, Japanese kanji characters should come easy by comparison.

In his soft southern drawl, Dave had explained earlier that he had grown up in a poor Tennessee family. His parents couldn't afford newspapers or books, so he taught himself Braille to get a free subscription for the Braille edition of Readers Digest. It all made perfect sense to Dave, and his studies at Harvard seemed equally effortless. Now his relaxed confidence was propelling him smoothly through the intensity of the JLS coursework. The standing joke among the students was that on dates he could sense the intentions of a woman by caressing her arm and applying the sensory experience of his Braille training to good advantage.

One afternoon as Bob and Otis were studying in their dorm room on the CU campus, there was a knock on the open door. They looked up to see none other than Bob's brother, George Sheeks, and Dan Williams standing there, having somehow materialized in Boulder. Bob had last talked to his brother at home the previous Christmas, and he hadn't seen Dan for years, dating back to when they were kids in Shanghai. In the meantime, Dan had graduated from the University of Alabama and had been recruited by Hindmarsh, who had somehow found out about Williams' childhood in Shanghai and early Chinese-language skills. He still had a studious look about him, with gold wire-rimmed glasses framing inquisitive eyes. And they could see why George had a reputation as a ladies' man, with his dark good looks. George and Dan were there to start in the next Japanese language class just forming at CU, and they would be right behind Bob, Otis, Bucky, Bill, and the rest who were in the first Boulder class. The Shanghai kids had been reunited in Boulder to learn Japanese.

They all traded details of their interviews with Hindmarsh and subsequent trips to Boulder. Dan related how he replied to Hindmarsh's question of whether he knew any Japanese language. He said he knew some numbers, could say "hello" and "goodbye," and could recite the chant of a Japanese food vendor he had heard in the Hongkew district of Shanghai.

Hindmarsh asked about Chinese. Dan replied that he knew a few characters. To that, Hindmarsh replied, "OK, you're in." Like Bob, Dan requested and was promised a commission in the Marine Corps upon graduation.[15]

Bob then introduced his roommate, explaining that Otis, the son of missionaries, had enviable prior knowledge of Japanese from his childhood in Japan. George and Dan had heard rumors about the course requiring fourteen hours a day of studying. Otis and Bob ominously confirmed the intensity of the course and noted they were memorizing about eight pages of Japanese text every night.

There was a pause as that information sank in. Dan, himself the son of missionary parents in China, began to trade information with Otis. It turned out that Dan's father had not escaped China before the Japanese occupation and had been thrown into an internment camp. There were negotiations under way to have him returned as part of a deal to swap a group of Americans, caught in China when the Japanese invaded, with Japanese diplomats stranded in a similar way and interned in the United States.[16]

George and Dan moved into the men's dorm and soon fell in with the rest of the Japanese language students. Though the different class assignments and workloads kept them from socializing regularly, they all ate meals together in the faculty club on campus. Another activity that brought them together was when Dan bought a shortwave radio, a Zenith, the only one in the dorm. They occasionally gathered in Dan's room at night to listen to Radio Tokyo. Little by little, they could understand what was being said in Japanese.

Regular physical drills, called *undo* in Japanese, were added to the daily schedule. At first they were semivoluntary, though the faculty strongly suggested the students participate. Regular exercise was thought to be a way to diffuse the stress of the course.[17] There were also occasional outings to the mountains, and every week or so some of the nisei instructors would invite students to dinner. The most senior sensei, Ashikaga Enzo, of Japanese royal lineage and a member of a leading Buddhist family, welcomed Bob into his home for lessons in Japanese painting and calligraphy. Ashikaga was what the students referred to as the Japanese language school's in-house samurai. He was an expert in sword play and the art form of calligraphy, which was simply but elegantly performed with single strokes of brushed ink. Ashikaga had offered to teach this cultural art form to anyone in the class who was interested. Bob was the only one to take him up on it, all the while gaining an appreciation of Japanese art and culture, another unexpected surprise in his JLS experience. Almost imperceptibly, he was getting further and further away from his high school days of the Japanese hate shrine on his dresser.

One evening, Ari Inouye Sensei and his wife, Ida, invited Bob, Otis, and Dave Osborne to dinner. The three made their way through the residential neighborhood west of campus, then trudged up the Ninth Street hill. The sun had already set behind the immense rock slabs of the Flatirons, shading Boulder from the late afternoon sun. The long evening was lit mostly with the soft, indirect sunlight still shining out on the eastern plains. They approached the porch of a small bungalow, and Inouye greeted them with bottles of beer. Even though he was one of their teachers, he was only a few years older than the students he was instructing and they socialized almost as peers.

Ari was nisei, born in Oakland, California, his parents having moved from Japan to America in the early 1900s. Growing up in Alameda in the Bay Area, he was not allowed to swim in the public swimming pool. Another Japanese family in Alameda had a beachfront home and gave permission for Ari and the other nisei kids in the neighborhood to swim there. He was lucky to be admitted to UC Berkeley under the quota system for minorities, and he graduated in 1936 with a degree in political science. Ari had a Japanese professor at Berkeley who was familiar with his interest in international relations, and who encouraged him to spend some time in Japan. So in the late 1930s he lived in Japan for two years studying Japanese history, culture, and language. In that politically charged time, tensions were rising between Japan and the United States. Because he was both an American citizen and ethnic Japanese, Ari was routinely trailed by the police in Japan and was occasionally questioned. But he found Japan fascinating, particularly the intricate and ornate Japanese gardens that spurred his interest in landscapes. On his return to California, he enrolled again at Berkeley and completed a degree in landscape architecture in June 1941.

But the events of December 7, 1941, inexorably changed the course of his life, along with so many others. He was first put to work scrutinizing mail sent to Hawaii that was written in Japanese, though he never found any evidence of anti-government activities. Then he worked in the Office of War Information and was given the task of assessing how many of the Japanese fishing ships in the Aleutians could serve as troop transports. But he didn't stay long in that job. His excellent oral and written bilingual skills got him a position as an instructor in the newly formed U.S. Navy Japanese Language School at UC Berkeley.

His tenure there was cut short by the order to move all ethnic Japanese out of California, and he and Ida moved with the school to Boulder. In this way, he and the other nisei instructors and their families were able to avoid being sent to the internment camps. But Ari and Ida felt like they were without a country. On their trip to Colorado they were instructed to keep the blinds of their train car drawn, and about this time his parents were shipped to an internment camp in Utah. In spite of all this, Ari and the other nisei instructors were unfailingly patriotic and taught Japanese enthusiastically to the Caucasian students who would go on to help defeat the country of their parents' birth.[18]

Soon, dinner was ready and the students settled down in the dining room to a Japanese meal of sushi and tempura. Ida apologized for the simplicity of the servings, but the fact that she could put together anything resembling good Japanese food in Boulder was an astonishing feat. After dinner they moved out to the front porch and watched as the last fading light of the summer evening silhouetted the mountains. The conversation alternated between campus events, fellow students in the JLS, and war news.

A topic that didn't come up that evening was one Bob never heard openly discussed. As the JLS expanded with larger classes of new students, more instructors were also appearing. Some of the newly arrived nisei instructors had been recruited from the internment camps. Bob remembered watching the Japanese-Americans being loaded on buses in Berkeley, and he would have liked to have found out more about what went on in the camps. Later, he learned that several of the nisei who signed up to become instructors met with criticism from some of their friends in the camps.[19]

By late summer 1942, Bob's class was plunging ahead into Naganuma book three. After nearly eight months of intensive studying, they were only one-third of the way through the material. The students were struggling to keep up, furiously treading academic water to keep from sinking in a turbulent sea of Japanese kanji characters, grammar, and vocabulary. Voluntary lunchtime sessions were instituted where only Japanese was spoken in a more informal setting, in an attempt to get the students to become more familiar with the conversational aspects of the language.[20]

A popular pastime was to make entertaining guesses as to what could be jokes in Japanese. One popular reference was to Hindmarsh, the now legendary naval officer who had recruited them into the swirling vortex of the course. They referred to him as "Koshizawa," brazenly flouting grammatical correctness by running together the Japanese words for "behind" and "marsh."[21] But most of their time was spent on the more formal memorization and drills that continued routinely each day until midnight, building to the crescendo of the three-hour-long Saturday tests. They finished book three in the breathtakingly short time of just over three weeks. Without a pause, it was on to book four.

By the latter part of September, it was getting to be late in the course and they had yet to start learning military vocabulary. Most of the students, including Bob, didn't think their memorization exercises had much relevance to what they would need to know when they got out to the Pacific. A particularly egregious example cited by the students was "Momotaro," one of the stories they'd had to memorize in Japanese. It was an old fable reproduced in the Naganuma Reader about a boy who was magically bestowed upon an elderly childless couple. Somehow, a little boy child sprang from out of a peach that had come rolling down a mountain stream. He was called Momotaro, or "Peach Boy." Not only was the story somewhat bizarre, but also it seemed irrelevant to how they would soon be applying their Japanese language skills. Military terms would be taught at the end of the course, they were told, but in the meantime they were stuck with Momotaro.[22]

And then there were the movies. The faculty had located a few Japanese films, and they showed them in an auditorium on campus. The show times were publicized and any of the rank-and-file university students could attend, but mostly Japanese language school teachers and students showed up. The idea was to familiarize the JLS students with Japanese popular culture, while getting them to try and understand the plot in Japanese. But these movies did not even remotely resemble Hollywood hits of the time. The Japanese films were generally in the art genre, as opposed to the action and adventure movies more suited to the tastes of the young JLS students.

The style typically employed by the Japanese filmmakers was to reinforce a theme through the use of obvious symbolism and mind-numbing repetition. Perhaps the plot would call for a woman to cry, but she would not simply weep for a brief, comfortable interval. She would continue to cry and cry and cry some more, and it would not be enough for her tears to fall, but then rain had to fall, and it had to fall from this drop, to that leaf, and on and on as the woman cried and cried, all to the dreary accompaniment of dirge-like music.[23] But even after all of the complaining, most of the JLS students had to admit that the movies were still more entertaining than classwork.

Though there was little time for much of a social life, the JLS students did their best to squeeze in a few activities outside their relentless schedule. For Bob, this centered on a large Victorian brick house majestically anchoring one corner of the CU campus. The president of the university, Dr. Stearns, lived there. He had invited Bob's class to a reception at the house shortly after their course had started. At the reception, Bob met a couple of female students who boarded there, and he had asked one of them out on a few dates. These typically involved a movie at the Boulder Theater, an art deco masterpiece right across from the similarly styled County Courthouse in downtown Boulder, just down the hill north of campus. But because she lived in the house of the university president, there were not a whole lot of options for post-movie activities. Bob had vivid memories of saying goodnight to her on the porch of what he thought should have been renamed "House of Frustration." She had a twin sister living there, as well, and Bob and Otis managed to stage a couple of pleasant, albeit platonic, double dates with the sisters.

There were also "Barb dances," another option for meeting female students. These were held in the men's gym on campus and organized by "The Barbarians," or simply "The Barbs," a group of non-fraternity, civilian CU students who got together for social events. The Barbs were aware of the rigors of the Japanese language course, so their dances were often held on Saturday nights so the JLS students could attend and unwind after their weekly tests.[24]

Among the unique personalities of the JLS students, a notable stand-out was Sam Houston Brock. Brock was one of a group who hung around together, and as far as Bob could tell, they were united in their seemingly single-minded determination to be unnaturally serious. It turned out Brock was interested in the Chinese revolution and Chinese literature. He had a cover from *Time* magazine taped to the wall in his dorm room. It depicted an image of a revolutionary Chinese writer named Lu Hsun. Though not particularly typical wall decoration for a university student's dorm room, this seemed innocuous enough, but it ended up attracting the attention of the Navy. Even though the JLS students' exclusive active duty service at that point involved only the learning of Japanese, they were technically in the Navy. So there were routine inspections of their dorm rooms by naval officers, as if their campus dorm was some kind of military barracks. During one of these inspections, a rank-and-file Navy lieutenant noticed the picture and reminded Brock that he was not allowed to have anything hanging on the walls. But there was something else that bothered the Navy inspector. He admonished Brock, saying, "We hate him as much as you do, but you have to take it off the wall." The lieutenant thought it was a picture of Hirohito, and he made Brock take it down; it hadn't occurred to him that a student would tape a photo of a Chinese author to the dorm room wall.[25]

Bob was looking for more ways to diffuse the stress of the course, and he scouted around for some kind of additional physical exercise. Several of the nisei instructors were experts at judo, and they had started a class. Bob joined in. After the daily *undo* session on the lawn outside the men's dorm, the judo class would convene in the men's gym. During the second week, one of the instructors was demonstrating a judo move, using Bob as a subject, and it involved Bob being flipped over the instructor's hip. Midway through the maneuver, Bob turned awkwardly in the air and landed hard on his leg, twisting it underneath him. There was an audible snap that sounded like a drumstick being ripped from a roasted chicken, and everyone in the room groaned. With that gruesome sound, and the immediate shot of pain in his leg that followed, Bob knew his leg was broken. The instructor immediately apologized, and he organized several students in the class to make up a little convoy to carry Bob over to the student infirmary on campus. The doctor there took one look at his leg, stated it was indeed broken, determined that Bob was in the military, and shipped him off to Fitzsimons Army Hospital in Denver for treatment.

The nisei judo instructor, still feeling terrible, drove Bob to the hospital an hour away. The Army doctors there put his leg in a cast from toe to hip, and the instructor signed it apologetically before he left. Bob was then wheeled into a ward full of young men with various limbs in complicated-looking configurations of casts, cords, and pulleys. The patient in the bed next to him, a sailor with cables suspending his cast-encased leg like a freshly caught trophy fish, told him that the ward was filled with Pearl Harbor survivors. They were shipped as a group to Denver to free up hospital space in Hawaii to make room for waves of new casualties rolling in from combat in the Pacific.

Bob's judo injury suddenly seemed trivial compared to what the sailors in the ward had been through. He was intrigued, though. These guys were his peers, around his age, and were eyewitnesses to the Japanese attack of Pearl Harbor. Here was a chance, at last, to find out more about what happened on December 7. There had been few details in the papers or on the radio, other than it had been bad. The Japanese attack had been a frequent topic of discussion at the Japanese language school, but there was frustratingly little information to go on.

Most of the patients in the ward were willing to talk about their experiences. Typical stories usually started out with testimonials of how lucky they had been to be based in Hawaii before the war. It had been good duty, a paradise filled with beautiful beaches, girls, palm trees, and cold beer. By their accounts, most of them had been out raising hell in Honolulu that Saturday night of December 6. The battleship bands were having a big contest, and no matter where the sailors were that night,they all seemed to have had a good time, at least in retrospect. For the most part, they had to return before curfew to their ships in Pearl Harbor, where they slept off the partying of the night before. Early on Sunday morning, they were rousing out of the sack in various stages of post-party stupor, some to go to church services, others to breakfast. Then they told variations on the same theme of being dumfounded to see Japanese planes flying overhead, dropping bombs and torpedoes. One way or another, they all had near-death experiences that required them still to be hospitalized nine months after the attack.

Another near-universal sentiment in Bob's ward was that the sailors' friends did a lot more during the attack than they did, and some had been killed. Others had healed up and were back on duty, and that's how it should be. Bob felt embarrassed. Here were wounded combat veterans, and all he had done for the war effort so far was take classes in Japanese and have his leg broken by one of his nisei instructors.

The initial disasters of Pearl Harbor, Wake Island, Guam, and the Philippines had at least been answered in a preliminary way when the Marines landed on Guadalcanal the previous month. Now, in September 1942, it looked like they were holding their own.[26] But the reports on the radio said it was tough fighting, jungle fighting, and the Japanese were experts. There were accounts of Japanese fighting to the death. This didn't surprise Bob. From what he'd seen of the Japanese military in China, the Empire's soldiers were fanatics. Bob wondered if any of his buddies in his old Marine Corps Reserve unit from Portland were on Guadalcanal fighting the Japanese.

Many of Bob's ward mates autographed his cast. Meanwhile, he was struggling to keep up with his studies. When he got back to the dorm in Boulder, the Pearl Harbor stories he had heard in the hospital kept his fellow students entertained for many late nights. It was firsthand information and the only actual details they'd received about the extent of the disaster at Pearl Harbor. It made them even more determined to finish the course and get out in the Pacific to do something to help defeat the Japanese.

Thanksgiving was approaching, and they wound up book four with a flourish. They stampeded through book five, finishing it right before Christmas. At this point they were learning some military terms, but most were applicable to the Navy. Many ground combat applications were missing. Bob continued to worry about not being taught what he thought he would need to know in the Pacific. As it turned out, he was right.

Christmas came and went, and on a day in January 1943, Bob finished book six with Suzuki Sensei. He passed the final exam two days later.

That evening, he attended a dinner party for the graduating class at Florence Walne's house. The next day, January 15, the JLS graduates received their commissions in a graduation ceremony that was held in the cavernous Macky Auditorium on campus. Bob Sheeks was a newly minted second lieutenant in the U.S. Marine Corps, finally realizing a dream he'd had since boyhood. His childhood friends from Shanghai, Bill Allmann and Bucky Freeman, also graduated with him and were now U.S. Navy officers, along with Otis Cary, Dave Osborn, and the rest. His brother, George, and Dan Williams were in the class right behind his and would soon follow.

Most of the graduates in Bob's class, such as Bucky and Bill and Otis and Dave Osborn, took Navy commissions and were sent to various posts in the Pacific. Some went to the code-breaking operation at Pearl Harbor. Others went to Australia to serve with the Allied Translator and Interpreter Service, or ATIS, where they translated captured documents and did some interrogations. But before Bob could begin his language activities, because he was in the Marines, combat training was required. He got orders to report to Camp Elliot, near San Diego, California. This prompted another trip back to the West Coast. He was invited to ride along with a classmate, Dick Miller, along with Dick's wife and, most uncomfortably, their dog. Before that trip Bob had always liked Irish setters, in fact had been pro–Irish setter because he had gotten chummy with one in Shanghai. But he changed his mind after spending a few days sharing the backseat with that dog, becoming covered with red Irish setter hair, and making a toilet stop every fifty miles or so, expressly for the nervous canine. The group finally arrived in San Diego and Bob said goodbye to Dick Miller, his wife, and, with great relief, the dog. At nearby Camp Elliot, Bob began his final combat training before being sent to face the Imperial Japanese Army in the Pacific.

THREE

Combat Training: Camp Elliott, and
on to the Pacific, 1943

Though Bob went to California ostensibly for com-
bat training in early 1943, he also got a memorable introduction to Hollywood. This all started east of San Diego near the Camp Elliot Marine
Corps Base, at a place called Green's Farm, out in the desert.[1] It was summer, and Green's Farm was hot and dusty. Though the Marines later
questioned the wisdom of training for tropical Pacific island combat in a
desert environment, there was one element of Green's Farm that would
later become very familiar to Marines, and that was the sweating. But the
heat they experienced in Southern California was only the tip of the pro-
verbial iceberg compared to the sauna-like conditions that awaited them
in the Pacific.

Bob was dressed like all the other trainees, in green dungarees, camouflage cloth–covered steel helmets, shirts with "USMC" stenciled over
one pocket, and combat boots coated with a thin film of dust. Though he
was a highly trained language officer with valuable skills that few others
possessed, the philosophy of the Corps was that all Marines were inter-
changeable parts of the fighting machine. He was there for one purpose,
and that was to practice combat techniques and maneuvers.

This was not entirely new territory for Bob. From 1938–40 he served
as a private in the Marine Corps Reserve in Washington state. His training included combat doctrine, weapons use, tactics, field combat practice, and rifle-range competition. There were regular-duty sessions once
a week, on Thursday nights, which in those two years must have totaled

close to one hundred sessions. Then there was a month-long summer camp at the Navy base in Puget Sound, with field maneuvers and combat practice war games in the Olympic mountain range. He even earned a marksman medal. Most certainly he knew what was in store for him when he got to Green's Farm.

One day Bob was participating in an exercise that consisted of practicing how to coordinate tanks and infantry. The Marine trainees were first briefed on tactics. In combat, under fire, the Marines would theoretically work with tanks that led the way, thereby flushing out the Japanese defenders from their bunkers with fire from the cannons mounted in their turrets. The Marines would maneuver behind and alongside the tanks and gun down the enemy soldiers as they broke from cover. Bob learned later this rarely happened in actual combat, but they spent a lot of time on these types of exercises.

The group Bob was training with was no ordinary bunch of Marines. They were all officers, and a somewhat odd mixture at that. Some were fresh out of Officers' Candidate School, lieutenants, soon to be platoon commanders. They knew they had to get it right because they would lead Marines in combat, and they listened intently to the instructor. But then there were others who didn't quite fit. They looked to be a little older, maybe in their late twenties. They seemed more relaxed. Bob fell in with this group when they split up into smaller teams for the combat exercises. The instructor assigned five Marines to each of the three tanks that were waiting, their engines idling in low growls, the hot air turning acrid with diesel exhaust.

Standing up in the turret, the commander of the tank to which Bob's team was assigned yelled over the noise of the engine that they were the right flank, and the other two tanks were the center and left flank. He would angle the tank a little right and come around the bunker up ahead. It was constructed to simulate what they may face on a Pacific island. The tank commander said he would fire, move, fire, and move. Bob's group was to follow behind and shoot at the bunker. The Japanese defenders presumably would be scrambling out to get away from the tank fire. The Marines were to cover and move, shoot, cover and move, and so on. The tank commander then disappeared into the turret and closed the hatch with a metallic clang. Bob was standing close behind the left tread. He looked at the Marine next to him and saw his lips form silent curses as another on the far side yelled to just stay behind the tank and shoot. How hard could it be? At that moment the tank gunned its engine, a cloud of blue exhaust smoke was spewed in their faces, and the exercise began. Bob imagined Japanese snipers ready to pick him off if he weren't snuggled right up to the tank. The tank stopped and there was a sharp *wham* as it fired at the bunker up ahead, a hut-like log-and-earth emplacement embedded in the side of a hill. The tank started moving again, and Bob stayed close behind. Peeking around the side of the moving tank, he spotted muddy patches up ahead, the muck having been churned up by tanks plowing through the drainage furrows of Green's Farm.

The tank stopped again to fire. *Wham!* Then it moved forward and lurched to the left as it turned the flank. Bob was still close behind the left tread, but he was too close. The tank swerved, and too late Bob saw his right boot disappear under the tread. Panic surged through him as he expected an electric jolt of pain. But he felt nothing. As the tank clanked forward, Bob saw his foot emerge and he realized that he had stepped into one of the deep muddy spots. The tank tread had pressed his booted foot down into the soft, wet mud. The Marine next to Bob saw his boot go under the tread and expected to hear a scream. When he saw Bob's boot come out of the mud unscathed, he just shook his head.

When the training ended for the day, the Marines trudged back to the Spartan wooden barracks. Bob was walking with the two Marines who had been with him behind the tank. The Marine who had seen Bob's foot go under the tread was Sid Salkow. He always told anyone who would listen that he was not at Green's Farm to learn how to shoot anyone. Instead, he wanted to make movies. Sid was in his early thirties, had wavy black hair combed back, and a mischievous look in dark eyes that sparkled with good humor. He was a bit paunchy, like a man accustomed to good food served in expensive restaurants. The other Marine was Ed Marriott, billed as a munitions expert, not an infantry Marine. Ed was in his late twenties, clean-cut, thin, and sunburned. The three of them seemed out of place in combat training, but they were Marines now, and they were all in it together.

It turned out that Bob, being trained as an interpreter, was not the most unlikely Marine in this trio. Ed Marriott's middle name was Winchester, of the firearms Winchesters, and Sid was a Hollywood director.[2] Just a few months before, Ed had been attached to the Chinese military through the U.S. government. His family's company had been advising the Chinese on weapons and training in their bitter battles with the Imperial Japanese Army. It was painfully obvious that the Chinese were outgunned and out-trained. Ed told Bob he had joined the Marines so he could go back to China in a more official military capacity to advise the Chinese and hopefully help improve their combat capabilities.

Soon, Bob was scheduled to report to Marine captain Paul Dull, who was in charge of final language training.[3] Bob found Captain Dull in a classroom full of enlisted Marines, their heads buried in books. Captain Dull was thin to the point of emaciation, and he had the scholarly air of an academic. Bob glanced quickly at the class. A few of the trainees appeared to be Native Americans or Hispanics. He found out later that some were Navajos who were training to be code talkers. Bob followed Captain Dull to an office across the hall. He motioned for Bob to take a seat, went behind his cluttered desk, rummaged around for a few seconds, and finally pulled out a paper. He scanned it and confirmed that Bob was fresh from Japanese language training in Boulder. He then asked Bob if he knew the Japanese words for "mortar," "pack howitzer," and "torpedo." Bob shook his head and apologized, saying he had learned only a little military vocabulary, that most of their language training involved Japanese fables and classics.

Captain Dull leaned back in his chair with a resigned sigh, lamenting that Boulder graduates were learning Japanese literature well enough, but not enough military terms. He had been trying to tell the Navy the JLS needed to revise the curriculum to produce military interpreters, not academic linguists. He then asked Bob to do him a favor and write a letter requesting the JLS to teach more military terminology, the idea being that if they heard it from a former student, maybe it would be convincing enough to carry additional weight to reinforce what Captain Dull had been telling them. Bob readily agreed, since he and Otis and the others in the Boulder JLS had been concerned about this very issue. Back at his barracks that afternoon, he busily wrote page after page in longhand.

It turned out to be a very long letter. Later, Captain Dull used Bob's letter to help successfully convince the Navy to include more military vocabulary in the JLS course.[4]

And what about Bob's Hollywood experience? It all started when they got their first chance for a weekend leave. Sid was itching to head the short distance up the road to his old stomping grounds in Los Angeles. He was married and wanted either Bob or Ed to come along on a double date with him and his wife, the deal being that Sid would provide a female companion for the volunteer. As further inducement, as if any were needed, Sid said the girls in Hollywood liked men in uniform. He wasn't far off the mark. Ed was married and wasn't interested, so Bob took Sid up on his offer, and thus was able to sample the good life of Hollywood on weekends when they could get passes.

On the night of the first double date, Sid drove Bob up to Hollywood in his big, red Cadillac. It was a gleaming behemoth of a car, designed to impress, and it filled the bill. Bob and Sid wore their snappy, dress-green, wool Marine uniforms, shiny gold 2nd lieutenant bars glinting on their shoulders. It was a great way to head into Hollywood for a night out on the town in 1943.

Not only did Sid's Cadillac radiate affluence, but his residence in Hollywood was jaw dropping. It was a colonial-style mansion, with gardens full of roses and an elegant, carved wood-beam front door. As the car pulled into the driveway, two women emerged from the front door of the house, and one, a tall redhead, turned to lock it. She then joined a slender, dark-haired woman who appeared to be in her early twenties and walked toward the car where Bob and Sid were standing. Sid gave the redhead a hug and announced to Bob that she was his wife, Patricia. He introduced the other as Doris Dowling, Bob's date for the evening.

They all piled into Sid's Cadillac, and after a short drive they were soon seated in a nightclub at a primo table next to the dance floor. The waiter approached and greeted Sid by name with a smile. Obviously Sid was well connected in Hollywood and he was reveling in the attention, smiling, waving to friends. He acted like he owned the place, and for all Bob knew, perhaps he did. Sid ordered a round of drinks as the band cranked up, playing Benny Goodman and Glen Miller tunes. Couples crowded onto the dance floor, and Sid scooped his wife from her chair to join them. Suddenly alone at the table, Bob looked at Doris. She smiled warmly back at him and said almost apologetically that everyone in the club knew Sid because he had done a lot of films. Then she asked what Bob's duties were in the Marines. He explained that he had learned Japanese, was trained to be an intelligence officer, and would probably end up interrogating prisoners and translating documents. Doris was suitably impressed.

Bob asked her what she was doing in Hollywood, and she said she was on contract as a movie actress. She mentioned a few bit parts she'd had in New York on Broadway, and that her sister, Connie, was also in Hollywood acting and coaching actresses for a studio. Doris had been in the chorus line at Radio City Music Hall in New York, and she had appeared in a stage review called *New Faces*.[5]

Sid and his wife returned to the table as the drinks arrived. He raised his glass and made a toast to Harvard, of all places. Bob thought Sid had somehow found out he had been going to school there, but it turned out Sid himself had been admitted to Harvard Law before he got into the movie business.

More drinks were followed by dinner and dancing, and then Sid was checking his watch, suddenly impatient to leave. As they went outside and waited for Sid's car to be brought around, Bob nervously asked Doris what her plans were for the rest of the evening. She was agreeable to returning with Bob to his hotel room for a drink, and Bob was growing more thankful to Sid by the minute.

Soon, Sid and Bob got another weekend pass, and an encore Hollywood outing was in the offing. Doris had gone back to New York for a couple of weeks, but Sid had another date lined up for Bob. The drive up to L.A. was just like the previous weekend, but this time when Sid and Bob pulled up in front of Sid's mansion, his wife walked to the car with a softly beautiful, blue-eyed blonde. Sid was beaming as he introduced Bob to Virginia Mayo and said she was on her way to becoming a big star in Hollywood. Her handshake was firm and confident, and her flawless complexion had a natural golden glow.

The group went to a different club, but the scene was much the same as their previous Hollywood excursion. The drinks flowed, there was more dancing, and at some point in the evening Sid revealed his formula for making movies, mostly westerns: The good guys are living in peace. Bad guys come to town. The good guys rise up and fight the bad guys. There's gunfire, blood, death. The good guys win. Peace returns and everyone's happy again. He said he made basically the same movie over and over again, changing only the details of the plot, and shuffling the actors and actresses.

Later, outside the club while waiting for the valet to bring the car, Bob and Virginia agreed to return to his hotel for a drink, replaying the scenario from his previous Hollywood visit. Bob silently swore his eternal gratitude to Sid for these Hollywood jaunts.

For the rest of his training, Bob crammed military Japanese vocabulary between the requisite combat exercises during the weeks, and alternated dates between Doris and Virginia on the weekends. Doris was intelligent and funny. Virginia was affectionate and emotional. But it all came to an end when his combat training finished and Bob was shipped out of San Pedro Harbor as a 2nd Marine Division replacement officer on board the SS *Lurline*, bound for New Zealand, with stops first at the Pacific island territory of American Samoa, and then Australia.

After the war, Bob heard Doris ended up marrying big band leader Artie Shaw, and Virginia became modestly famous, making a name for herself in the movies just as Sid had predicted.[6] In spite of Sid's best efforts to avoid combat, Bob learned he actually got wounded during the war, hit by shrapnel while filming on an aircraft carrier. But he survived to return to postwar Hollywood, where he became known as "King of the B Movies."

On to the Pacific

The massive cruise ship SS *Lurline* loomed dockside in San Pedro Harbor. The ship's white, prewar paint scheme was now a dull, troopship gray. There was a long line of Marines boarding the vessel, fresh replacements for the casualties from Guadalcanal who had been killed, wounded, or disabled by malaria. Bob looked for the officers' line, shorter than the one for enlisted men. He gave his name to the uniformed Navy officer standing at the end of the gangway and was directed to a berth on the ship. Bob hefted his duffel bag over his shoulder and climbed up the steep ladder from the dock to the main deck. The luster of the old cruise ship still showed in places. The floors were elaborately tiled, and there was darkly finished woodwork along some of the passageways. He finally found the appointed door and entered a cavernous space filled with lattices of steel pipes that stretched from floor to ceiling. Within this network were stretched canvas bunks, each with its own steel frame. They were stacked like poker chips, one atop another, five bunks per stack, each with about two feet of head room. Looking around past the bunks, the vast space looked like it may have once been a ballroom or large dining room. A couple of other officers were sitting around, squeezed awkwardly into the cramped spaces. Bob dumped his duffel bag on his designated bunk, three up from the bottom. He immediately resolved to sleep somewhere up on the main deck if at all possible.

Soon the *Lurline* moved majestically from the dock, out from San Pedro Harbor, and into the open Pacific. Its decks were crammed with Marines getting their last look at California. Eventually the great ship was rolling on the ocean swells with all the elegance of a stomach-churning carnival ride. Bob felt woozy, which reinforced his determination to remain on deck. Looking at the horizon and breathing deeply of the salt air was the only thing that made shipboard existence tolerable. He found an empty refuge under one of the lifeboats. That became his alternate berth for the trip's duration. If it rained, he went to an interior space until it stopped, and then he returned to his spot. Only as a last resort would he sleep in his assigned bunk in the smelly, noisy sleeping quarters, where he felt like a piece of cargo crammed into the hold.

It was a long trip and the days passed drearily. The weather gradually got warmer, and the ocean turned a deeper shade of blue. No one knew exactly what their route was, though rumors, known as "scuttlebutt" in the Navy, swept the ship. They were only told they would eventually land in New Zealand.

One day someone yelled out that there was an island ahead. Bob rose from his spot on the deck. In the distance, the tops of a few emerald-green mountains were emerging mirage-like above the slate-blue ocean.

As they got closer, the mountains formed into a tropical island, steep sided, sprouting vibrant vegetation. The ship slowed and eased into a narrow bay, green-fringed mountains looming on all sides. There were a few buildings perched on the shore, and military jeeps and trucks slowly wound along the road that hugged the curving outlines of the bay. There was a dock ahead with several other identically gray Navy ships tied up, crewmembers busily unloading cargo. By now all the Marines were on deck, jammed like tourists along the railing. The island seemed incredibly green, startlingly so, since they had just spent two weeks looking at nothing but blue ocean. It was like an exotic, three-dimensional movie set built on a massive scale.

The *Lurline* pulled up slowly to the large steel dock. The cooling ocean breezes died down, and Bob was suddenly aware of the oppressive heat. A couple of sweating naval officers hustled past, heading down to where a gangplank had been dropped on the dock. Scuttlebutt said they'd docked at a place called Samoa, but to make sure, a Marine major standing next to Bob asked the officers where they were. One of them shouted back that they had arrived at Pago Pago, American Samoa, for a refueling stop of about twenty-four hours. The naval officer had pronounced it "Pongo Pongo." Bob certainly knew of American Samoa and had heard of Pago Pago. It was only his departure for Harvard that had kept him from being sent there before the war with the rest of the 14th Marine Corps Battalion of Spokane. Pago Pago did indeed sound exotic, like an island vacation destination. A disjointed voice rasped over the loudspeaker, its echoes washing over the ship, announcing shore leave assignments.

After a quick sandwich at the officers' mess, Bob headed down to where the gangplank stretched to the dock from a large, open door in the side of the ship. A uniformed Navy officer was there with a list, checking names as Marines filed past. Bob gave his name and started down the gangplank, eager to check out Pago Pago. The naval officer, a stocky ensign, appeared to be all of nineteen years old. He scanned the list, called Bob back, and informed him he had been assigned shore patrol duty. The ensign gave Bob a dark blue armband emblazoned with the large white letters "SP." He was instructed to patrol the dock and nearby areas, and to keep an eye out for trouble.

Bob helpfully pointed out that he had never been on shore patrol duty before, was therefore not qualified, and, by the way, what kind of trouble were they expecting? The ensign just smiled and told him not to worry. This was the Navy. He advised Bob to stay sober, break up drunken fights, and keep Marines away from the locals.

With that presumably comprehensive and not-too-reassuring advice, Bob would tour Pago Pago as a shore patrol officer. This wasn't what he had in mind for shore leave. As he stepped from the gangway onto the floating steel pier, he felt the heat from the sun-baked metal come up through the soles of his boots. It was like a huge pancake griddle. The dock was bustling with vehicles that had come to service the ship. American naval personnel mingled with sturdy Polynesian men wearing shorts and white singlets. Amazingly, the Samoans were all barefoot. The soles of their broad feet were thick and fleshy. They calmly walked around the searing hot steel pier as if it were cool wooden planking. Some were helping guide cargo nets filled with supplies into the ship's holds.

Bob dodged several trucks maneuvering on the pier and headed to the road that ran between several large warehouses toward "town," which appeared to consist of a few wood-framed buildings with verandas fronting the narrow street. On a pole at the road intersection were signs pointing in different directions to places like "Naval Hospital," "Marine Barracks," and "Naval Officers' Club." American Samoa was a U.S. territory and had been a naval coaling station for the previous half century, with the prerequisite American administrators stationed there for many years.[7] It turned out that Marines were also based on the island, and it occurred to Bob that training in the sultry heat and humidity of Pago Pago would seemingly better prepare them for combat on other tropical islands in the Pacific, a stark contrast to the dry, desert environment of Green's Farm.

He didn't know the details then, but the final preparation Bob would experience for island combat would be in chilly New Zealand during the Southern Hemisphere winter. This was not really a SNAFU, though it may have seemed so at first glance. New Zealand was a rest and recovery safe haven, a secure rear area perfect for planning and equipping for the next island campaign.

Having been cooped up on the *Lurline*, the Marines were eager to maximize their drinking during the short time allowed ashore. Though Pago Pago certainly did not offer the amenities of the most coveted port in the Pacific, Honolulu, it was invigorating to get off the ship and walk on solid ground. Marines were laughing as they hurried past Bob on their way to the handful of beer bars that would supply sufficient beverages in a timely manner.

But Bob had an assignment, and it didn't involve drinking. He figured he would go on patrol, keeping a wary eye out for trouble, emboldened by the official SP armband. He passed more wood-frame buildings, apparently shops of some kind. Samoans were strolling by in a relaxed, dignified way, upright, with a smooth gait, smiling and laughing and talking to each other in a language that seemed to consist mostly of vowels. Some of the men and women were dressed in brightly flowered wrap around skirts. Bob found out these were called "lavalavas," the standard mode of dress for Samoans.

Standing there in the sun, sweating for several moments, Bob realized he should keep moving, preferably toward some shade. Farther up the shore road was what looked like a native village sheltered by graceful, green-feathered palm trees bent overhead. He thought he should check the village to make sure no drunken Marines were bothering the Samoans.

On one side of the coast road was Pago Pago Bay, the deep, blue water reflecting the steep-sided, green-shrouded mountains. On the inland side of the road, thick tropical foliage pressed in like oversized house plants run amok. Ahead he could see the native houses, their rounded thatched roofs held up by wooden posts anchored around the perimeter in solid stone foundations. They reminded Bob of large, open-sided beach cabanas. He found out later they were Samoan "fales," pronounced "fawlays," with woven shutters tied up under the eaves during the day so that the breezes could waft right through each house. It seemed like an efficient way to air things out, though there appeared to be little privacy in a Samoan village. Groups of islanders were walking toward a particularly large fale. Bob could see many people inside sitting cross-legged on mats spread out over the coral stone floor. They were singing in forceful, melodic, four-part harmonies, accented by the booming bass baritones of the men, and electrified by the lilting sopranos of the women. One of the Samoan men seated inside motioned to Bob, so he took shelter from the relentless tropical sun in the shade of the fale and settled down to watch.

The singing soon stopped, and a tall, dignified Samoan man stood up. He was wearing what appeared to be a coarse skirt in a beige-and-brown pattern. Bob found out later it was a tapa bark–cloth lavalava. The Samoan was bare chested, and with his considerable girth he could have easily been a lineman on a football team. He began addressing the assembled crowd, his speech a cascade of fluid vowel sounds.

A Samoan elder seated next to Bob leaned over and explained in whispered English what was happening. It was something called a "taupo ceremony." The man speaking at the moment was a talking chief whose job it was to give speeches and remember Samoan history.

At this point, a lovely, tall, young girl entered the fale. She also was wearing a tapa bark–cloth lavalava, but hers was tucked up under her armpits. Her black hair was piled on her head in a large bun laced with pink hibiscus blossoms, and she wore a necklace of curved shells. The talking chief sat down, and a line of women at one end of the fale, sitting cross-legged like the men, started a low rhythmic chant, softly slapping their hands on their knees. The young girl at the center began moving slowly to the beat of the chant, her hands arcing gracefully, her head tipping from one side to the other, her feet stepping forward and back, all in time to the chanting. She had a natural sense of coordinated motion. Bob thought the Samoan dance was more restrained than the Hawaiian hula he'd seen in movies.

The elder whispered that the dancer was the taupo, the village maiden. She was the virgin daughter of the high chief, the man sitting next to the talking chief. The elder went on to explain that the taupo must remain a virgin until she is married to a high-ranking member of another *aiga* (pronounced "aye-inga"), or family. She had especially high status in her village, like a princess.[8]

Bob watched the supple, sinuous movements of the taupo as the melodious chanting continued. The voices carried out into the village of thatched-roof houses interspersed among the palm trees, the volcanic mountains towering above the bay nearby. The war with the Japanese seemed very far away. The ceremony finally ended and Bob thanked the elder for his commentary. The old man wished him luck, and Bob headed back toward Pago Pago. His shore patrol duty ended shortly thereafter without mishap, and soon he was back on board the *Lurline*, facing the rest of his trip to New Zealand.

FOUR

Adventures in Japanese Language: New Zealand and Noumea, New Caledonia, 1943

The *Lurline* finally sidled up to the dock in pleasantly temperate Melbourne, Australia, after plowing across almost the entire width of the vast, tropical South Pacific. Because most of the Marines on board were proceeding to New Zealand, it was unclear why they had been taken on a 1,500-mile detour through Australia. All they could do was shrug, blame it on the military, and concentrate on getting off the ship to enjoy a few days of shore leave. The Americans traipsed eagerly down the gangplank, and the trucks lined up at the dock hauled them to billets consisting of cots under the grandstand of a huge stadium called the Melbourne Cricket Ground, or, as the locals referred to it, the "MCG." As Bob and his fellow officers contemplated the grim accommodations, their dreams of an idyllic time ashore were transformed to a pleasing certainty that their Melbourne stay would be brief. Some would soon change their minds, though, after encountering what Melbourne had to offer young American Marines with cash to spend.

As it was already late afternoon, Bob wanted to waste no time getting into town. Quickly he dumped his barracks bag on a cot and hustled out of the stadium to a nearby street that was the main drag heading toward the center of the city. Evocative green streetcars clattered by, bells clanging seemingly at random, people jammed inside or hanging from brass rails while standing on steps above the wheels that sang with a metallic whine on tracks set into the pavement. From the roofs of the trams, masts sprouted at angles and pressed against the electric lines above the tracks. Sparks flew like fireworks as the pick-ups hit the couplings at each street intersection. Bob wedged onto a trolley that ran down the middle of a street evocatively named Wellington Parade. A while later he decided he was close to the city center and jumped off in front of the Flinders Street Station, an imposing, stone, Victorian-style train station that could have been found in almost any American city, except it was painted an exotic ochre yellow. The combination made it look at once familiar and pleasingly foreign. He nimbly dodged a couple of automobiles, suddenly mindful that they were driving on the "wrong" side of the road, and then walked up Swanston Street past the modern buildings, listening to conversations in twangy Australian accents. One after another, friendly Aussies greeted him with, "G'day Yank," as they recognized his U.S. Marine uniform. It was almost as if he had stepped ashore on a friendly foreign planet, with the added bonus of being able to understand, more or less, what the aliens were saying.

The U.S. military administration was putting on a big bash for the freshly arrived Marines in one of the downtown hotels that evening, supposedly not far from a building where MacArthur was running the campaign to take back the southwest Pacific from the Japanese.[1] Bob had no trouble finding the party because there was red-white-and-blue bunting hung over the entryway, and laughing Marines were streaming in from the street. Navigating through the crowded lobby, he entered a large ballroom also decorated with red-white-and-blue sashes. Marines were crowded around a bar set up at one end of the cavernous room, but what caught Bob's eye immediately was the large number of young, smiling Australian women amidst the sea of American uniforms. First things first, though, and Bob elbowed his way to the bar. A Marine major he recognized from the *Lurline* had planted himself nearby at a strategic location to size up the scene. Bob secured a beer and turned to watch as a band thumped out dance music from a stage at the other end of the ballroom. Uniformed American servicemen spun and twirled laughing Australian women in frenzied jitterbug dance moves. The place was literally jumping.

The major leaned toward Bob, having to shout above the noise of the band, and pointed out that all the Australian and New Zealand men had been away for the past two years fighting for Churchill in North Africa, and their women had been without men for a long time.[2] He didn't have to tell Bob what that meant; he was simply confirming the rumors running rampant on the *Lurline* that Australia was paradise on earth for American men in uniform. The women were attractive and friendly, their men were gone, and the Americans, in their stylish uniforms, had plenty of cash to spend. It was no contest.

Bob watched the noisy chaos on the dance floor, and then his attention turned to the crowds pressing into the ballroom. To his left a woman was talking to two Marines. She had brown wavy hair that cascaded over her shoulders and down the back of her brightly flowered dress. He caught her eye, she smiled, and then she turned back to the two Marines. Bob fortified himself with another beer and headed in her direction. As he approached, she looked at him and smiled again, and he asked her to dance. She glanced hesitatingly at the two Marines, who glowered at Bob, and then she grabbed his hand and led the way to the packed dance floor.

After a few dances that consisted mainly of being jostled around by the gyrating crowd, Bob motioned back to the bar and pulled her along. The two Marines she had been talking to were nowhere to be seen. The beer flowed and more dancing followed, but she soon had to head home. Bob helpfully offered to accompany her. They left the hotel and pushed past a boisterous crowd of Marines and Australian women out on the sidewalk waiting for taxis. They walked a block or two to a tram stop and boarded one of the distinctive streetcars. She told Bob it was only a short ride to where she lived with her parents. Like many of the urban Melbourne neighborhoods, hers was a self-contained residential district with its own set of local shops comfortably embedded in the larger urban mass of the city. They were soon standing in front of her parents' house, a modest, one-story, brick building with ornate ironwork fringing the front porch. It was winter in Melbourne, but the climate was warm enough for tropical-looking plants to grow in the small front yard. Still, it was chilly and Bob didn't relish returning to a cot under the stadium grandstand. She suggested they go to the garden, so they crept through the front gate and around to the back of the house where there was a small lawn surrounded by a darkened enclosure of trees, manicured plants, and flowers.

They sat down on the grass and, though it was brisk, agreed that it was nice to be outside under the stars. Bob looked up through the lattice of tree branches at the constellations and recognized the now-familiar Southern Cross, five stars that formed the shape of a kite. One thing led to another, and soon they were no longer aware of the chilly night air or the damp grass. A consequence of such activity in the great outdoors, Bob learned the next morning, was stubborn grass stains on his khaki trousers.

Most of the Marines agreed that their rustic accommodation under the grandstand at the MCG was more than worth it for the chance to experience the delights of Australian culture. After several frenetic but exhilarating days, the *Lurline* sailed for New Zealand.

A week of pitching and rolling back to the east across the Tasman Sea brought them to a large sheltered bay where the low buildings of Wellington, New Zealand's capital city, pressed down to the waterfront. It reminded Bob of a smaller version of San Francisco. But Wellington was not their final destination. After the *Lurline* edged up to the pier and docked, the Marines were loaded into trucks for an uncomfortable hour-long bouncing ride north to a small coastal town facing the Tasman Sea to the west. It had the tongue-twisting name of Paekakariki, soon to be shortened by the Marines to "Paekak" (pronounced "Pie-kak").[3]

When Bob's truck finally shuddered to a stop at the main gate of the military base, he saw an expanse of peaked, olive-drab tents in long rows. Bob and about ten other Marine officers piled out of the truck, stretching cramped legs. His immediate impression of New Zealand could be summed up by two words: "cold" and "wet." The Marines had arrived in the midst of the New Zealand winter, a seemingly incongruous setting to train for their next tropical island invasion. Bob was told later that New Zealand's climate was considered therapeutic for Marines who had come down with malaria during the Guadalcanal campaign, though he concluded the main reason for the location of the base was New Zealand's remoteness.[4] Consequently, it was probably safe from Japanese attack, but still relatively close to the Japanese-held islands targeted by the Americans.

Low overcast seemed to perpetually obscure the hills behind the camp that stretched along the shore of the formidable Tasman Sea. Frothing, wind-whipped waves crashed relentlessly on the forlorn beach. Massive bushy trees that Bob later learned were called "pohutakawa" lined the edges of the camp. It was another in a long list of linguistically challenging names from the native New Zealand Maori people, Polynesians who had originally sailed from the tropical islands to the north.[5]

The Marines in Bob's group reported to the headquarters building, were assigned to billets in the tents, and began training exercises. The days ahead were spent marching over the slippery, grass-covered hills above Paekakariki. The Americans universally griped and complained. They wanted to fight the Japanese, not the dripping, clammy New Zealand terrain. Bob wondered if he would ever get warm again. His wet feet were the consistency of refrigerated, raw steaks. Within a week he came down with a severe head cold.

He reported to sick bay, was immediately medicated, and was placed in a hospital ward in a wood-frame building warmed by glowing, potbellied, coal-burning stoves. His fever and sore throat finally subsided. Two weeks later, the doctor pronounced him almost cured. He then got a huge break. By a stroke of luck he was billeted in one of the few residential farmhouses on the base. He figured they didn't want him catching the flu again in one of the tents. One of his new roommates was Louis Hayward, the Hollywood actor. He was slim, with a narrow face, slicked-back brown hair, and a well-trimmed mustache. His assignment was to produce combat films that showed off the achievements of the Marines. Though Bob had briefly encountered the Hollywood scene through his Sid Salkow connection, he had to apologize that he wasn't familiar with any of Hayward's films. Louis shrugged it off and was quick to point out that he was mainly known for his wife, Ida Lupino, at the time a very popular actress.[6]

After Bob's Hollywood experiences, he could drop a couple of names. Louis responded that he knew Sid Salkow and had heard of the Dowling sisters and Virginia Mayo. He went on to add that, in his experience, the women in Hollywood were all crazy. He happily reported that Ida was the craziest of them all, which is why he married her. Bob wondered about Louis' marriage when, without prompting, he told Bob that Ida's idea of a good time was to have six or eight drinks, and then run around the house scantily clad with him chasing her and yelling in excruciating detail what he'd do when he caught her.

Bob's duties soon changed for the better, and there were no more forced marches across the chilly New Zealand hills. Captured Japanese documents had been brought in from the Solomon Islands, and they needed to be translated. Division headquarters told him to report to D-2, the intelligence section, currently headquartered in an office building in downtown Wellington. Bob caught a ride on a Marine jeep and, after an hour, they were weaving through the city that clung precariously to the shore, nestled below thickly forested green hills. Though at first glance Wellington had a lush, tropical appearance, it always seemed to be bone-chillingly damp with hurricane-force winds blowing. The jeep stopped in front of the appointed office building, and a sign on the door read, "2nd Mar. Div. D-2." Bob reported to a security guard and was directed to an office down a long hall. Inside were two Marine officers looking over maps. They introduced themselves as John Pelzel and Gene Boardman, the two senior Japanese language officers in the 2nd Marine Division. Bob would work closely with them for the next two years.

A Harvard graduate and Guadalcanal veteran, Pelzel was at least six feet tall, in his late twenties, and had rumpled brown hair and piercing brown eyes. He was rail thin with a drawn face yellowed by atabrine, the antimalaria drug he and the other Marines took on Guadalcanal. He had the air of a reserved academic, but with a subtle and sarcastic sense of humor that Bob found refreshing. Pelzel's parents were missionaries and he grew up in Korea speaking several Asian languages, including Japanese.[7] Boardman was older, a former professor of Asian studies at the University of Wisconsin, now incongruously a Japanese language officer in the Marine Corps. He was shorter than Pelzel, and he had thinning hair and a perpetual jovial, quizzical expression on a face that was framed by wire-rimmed glasses. As language officers, they were all working for the chief of D-2, Col. Jack Colley, and his second in command, Tom Dutton. Though neither Colley nor Dutton had any language training, they appreciated the important intelligence role the language officers played. Pelzel and Boardman were given almost free rein to do whatever they thought was necessary to supply intelligence information. Up until fairly recently, that had consisted mostly of analysis of Japanese documents captured at Guadalcanal.

Bob immediately felt comfortable with these two. They seemed more like academic colleagues than Marine officers. His first assignment was to sort through additional boxes of captured Japanese material. Pelzel and Boardman were now occupied with planning for the upcoming invasion of an island they could not yet reveal to Bob. It would become the site of the first U.S. amphibious invasion of a Pacific coral atoll. They couldn't have known it then, but what would become the invasion of Tarawa would be fraught with a series of unfortunate mishaps that resulted in the unpleasant consequence of a large number of dead Marines. Some of the miscues would be related to gaps in intelligence having to do with tides and the depth of water over the reef.[8]

Bob's assignments involved mostly sifting through reams of mundane paperwork generated by an enemy army. Tidbits of interest for intelligence were few and far between. Anything of obvious value had already been removed in the first screening by D-2 headquarters and sent off to the main intelligence and translating branch in Hawaii.

Meanwhile, among the civilian population of Wellington there was a certain sense of alarm that the Marines were taking over the young New Zealand women. The prime minister was said to have responded that New Zealand could have been occupied by the Americans or the Japanese—and they were spared that choice—but there was a price to be paid. If relationships and, in some cases, marriages of New Zealand women to American servicemen were part of that price, so be it. Though disconcerting to the New Zealanders, it was deemed to be better than having the Japanese army run the country. Second Marine Division headquarters passed the word around to all Marines that they were not there to rescue the New Zealanders, but were to act as their guests. Bob thought this was an overreaction. In his experience, Marines were generally well behaved overall. The overt friendliness of the New Zealand citizens, and the young women in particular, meant the Americans didn't need to force themselves on the locals. As it turned out, there were more than one thousand marriages of American Marines to New Zealand women before the war was over.[9]

Not being one to buck the trend, Bob soon became acquainted with several New Zealand girls. He met one at a "Tea Dance" sponsored by the Red Cross. Marine Corps officers were invited and local girls were there, usually accompanied by their mothers. It was all very proper. Her name was Patsy, and in Bob's memory she was very pretty, with English features, light brown hair and blue eyes, and a nice figure. She also danced well and was a good conversationalist. They kept a warm, "proper" friendship until he shipped out from New Zealand. He escaped from Paekakariki to go to Wellington to see her whenever he could get a ride, which was usually a jeep questionably requisitioned from the motor pool by fellow escapees. He was treated by her family not only as a VIP but also as a curiosity—they had never met an American before. Their gracious hospitality made him feel more like a long-lost son or brother than a potential suitor.

Despite being a young Marine, healthy and warm blooded, he didn't find it too much of a strain to behave properly with Patsy, mainly because he was rescued from propriety by another lovely, but quite different, New Zealand girl. She was half Maori, which surprised him because she did not look at all Polynesian, and she had the decidedly European name June Thompson. He met her at a dinner dance event for servicemen, attended by New Zealanders as well as Americans. She was in uniform and looked to Bob like she could pose for a recruiting poster. Much to his delight, she was unspoiled by her good looks and had an entertaining sense of humor.

June was in the New Zealand Army Defense Corps, the 71st Heavy Battery, based at Fort Dorset, Wellington. She wore her smartly tailored uniform with elegant style. Like Bob, she had to wangle time off for their meetings downtown. They had a favorite hotel that was just down the street from the building where the 2nd Marine Division headquarters, and D-2, was located. Much of the time Bob was nervous that John Pelzel or Gene Boardman might see him around town dining with this beautiful woman, thus exposing his phony excuse for staying in Wellington, allegedly working at the D-2 office, which he visited infrequently. When Bob eventually shipped out for the as-yet-unnamed invasion, their growing romance was cut short. It took him a while to get over her, and he consciously had to keep reminding himself how lucky he had been to meet and know both of those charming New Zealand women.

But before the upcoming island invasion, Bob had a detour that took him away from New Zealand on temporary duty with Admiral Halsey's headquarters, the Command of the South Pacific (COMSOPAC), in Noumea, New Caledonia. The exact nature of his assignment was unclear to him even as he boarded a ship at Wellington Harbor. After a week long ride north into the tropics on the small cargo freighter, Bob stepped onto the dock at Noumea. He had orders to report to Halsey's language people, but that was all he knew.

The harbor consisted of a large bay sheltered by tropical, green-clad hills, punctuated by a series of inlets. Waterfront wharfs were lined up in front of several large warehouses. The town of Noumea rose behind the docks as a series of low, wood-framed buildings in the characteristic colonial style of peaked, corrugated tin roofs and long, low verandas on all sides to provide shelter from the relentless tropical sun and sudden, heavy downpours. Noumea had the stereotypical look of a South Pacific port town. There were a number of U.S. naval vessels anchored in the harbor, and several destroyers were tied up near a larger warship, a cruiser, with obvious battle damage. The repairs were taking place out in the open, the surrealistic blue-white light of the acetylene torches sparking and glowing in the midday sun. The steel-gray ships loomed menacingly like hostile apparitions, oddly out of place in the otherwise idyllic South Pacific port. They were all-too-visible reminders of the shooting war going on not too far away.

The dock area was bustling with a curious mixture of U.S. Navy personnel and local dock hands, Melanesians who had much darker skin than the Polynesian Samoans Bob had seen in Pago Pago. They were barefoot, clad in shorts and T-shirts, and, because New Caledonia was a colony of France, they were all speaking French.

Bob caught a ride to COMSOPAC in a jeep that wound its way between the ramshackle buildings of Noumea, some with ornate French ironwork. Local Melanesian women strolled down the streets, chatting light-heartedly with each other and carrying baskets on their heads piled with clothes or food. They were wearing shapeless, ankle-length dresses splashed with bright, flowered patterns that had been introduced by European missionaries who had a preternatural obsession with the propriety of the local women.

The jeep emerged from town and pulled up in front of a series of large, corrugated-steel Quonset huts. The perimeter was fenced off and a guard was on duty at the gate. Seeing the American jeep, the guard waved them through. One of the huts had a large, white double door and was prominently positioned at the apex of the circle drive. Bob climbed out of the jeep, slung his barracks bag over his shoulder, and entered the hut. The clerk inside the door directed him to the intelligence section. As he entered the designated office, the first naval officer he saw, sitting at a desk and hunched over a stack of papers, was none other than his roommate from Harvard, Don Shively. This was to be the first of several small-world encounters Bob would have with former friends and Japanese language school graduates that were to take place on widely scattered islands in the Pacific.

They had a lot of catching up to do. Bob eagerly told him of his time at Green's Farm, the trip on the *Lurline* to New Zealand, and working for the 2nd Marine Division chief language officers Pelzel and Boardman. For his part, Don described how he had wended his way from Harvard to Noumea via a number of assignments, and how he was presently involved with translating documents that could provide clues to the next moves of the Japanese. They worked it out so that Bob was quartered in a tent with Don at the Marine camp, conveniently located near one of the best beaches on New Caledonia, called Anse Vata. It was Camp Goettge, named after a Marine intelligence officer who was killed tragically, along with nearly his entire twenty-five-man patrol, when they were cornered by attacking Japanese on a Guadalcanal beach the year before.[10]

Bob's assignment was to sort through fresh stacks of newly captured documents, including diaries taken from Japanese soldiers killed in the Solomon Islands. One set that needed urgent attention was a pile of waterlogged records, an aromatic stack of soggy papers that had been recovered from a sunken Japanese submarine.

The days passed at COMSOPAC, and Bob was making only slow headway in prying apart the damp pages of logbooks and diaries from the Japanese submarine. The documents smelled like a clogged drain. A couple of the pages had what appeared to be coded information, and that was immediately shipped off to Pearl Harbor for further analysis.

Early one morning before sunrise, Bob was awakened in his tent by someone from COMSOPAC and was told that survivors from a Japanese submarine had just landed at Noumea, and he was ordered to proceed to the POW camp to interrogate them. Finally, something interesting! Bob sprinted outside and jumped into the waiting jeep.

The Japanese POW camp held soldiers captured during the Solomon Islands campaign, hapless remnants of the defeated Imperial Japanese

Army. Some had surrendered by choice, and others were captured or wounded before they could commit suicide. Though their ultimate destination was the POW compound at Pearl, they had been staged through Noumea for a round of interrogations to quickly see if they had unique or useful knowledge. Most were labor battalion personnel who had little strategic information. The jeep carrying Bob skidded to a halt outside the gate of the POW stockade. He entered the interrogation tent, and there stood six rescued Japanese submariners who had been plucked from the ocean only a few hours earlier. They were being guarded by two Marines and an ethnic Japanese U.S. Army sergeant. He recognized Bob as a Marine officer, so he stood up and saluted and said his name was Sergeant Watanabe.[11] He had been assigned to help Bob interrogate the prisoners.

Bob knew the Army was training Japanese-American nisei to work as interpreters, but this was the first he had encountered in person. Watanabe told Bob that the POWs had been given medical attention, issued camp clothing, and fed a good meal. They'd been separated for the past two hours so they couldn't coordinate contrived stories, and they had been held in solitary confinement and kept away from the other Japanese POWs in the stockade. None of them seemed to be of high rank, and they stood silently in a ragged line, shoulder to shoulder.

Bob ordered the guards to take the POWs back to solitary confinement while he and Watanabe concocted a plan. They decided Bob would act the role of a high-ranking officer, and Watanabe would be his staff adjutant, thus mimicking the Japanese military style. The guards were then directed to bring the submariners to the interrogation tent one at a time. Bob sat at a desk and Sergeant Watanabe stood at his side. The first POW was brought to the entrance of the tent and, in Japanese, Watanabe barked, "Enter!" The prisoner came in, bowed, and Watanabe shouted, "Attention! Approach the Commander's desk!"[12] The young Japanese submariner bowed again and took a few steps to stand rigidly upright in front of Bob at the desk. This created a tense atmosphere familiar to all Japanese military personnel when questioned by persons of superior rank. The idea was to exploit the Japanese submariner's ingrained reflex of immediate, obedient reply to an officer. Though Bob's American background tempted him to be less severe, offer him a cigarette, and let the prisoner be seated, it was more effective to maintain a stern Japanese military atmosphere.

Bob began the interrogation by stating in a harsh tone, in the best Japanese he could muster, that he would ask questions to obtain what he referred to as normal, routine information. In fact, even seemingly routine information served military intelligence purposes. Bob then shouted in Japanese, "Name!" The sailor, at stiff attention, said his name. Bob yelled, "Rank!" and the sailor again replied with the information. This continued, with Bob sternly asking questions and Sergeant Watanabe screaming, "Answer!" every so often. They got the prisoner to state his unit, where he was assigned, and how long he had been at sea. He was an enlisted man in the Imperial Japanese Navy's submarine fleet, part of an elite group, rigorously selected from among the best-rated and most dedicated young volunteers. They received intense training and were imbued with nationalistic, militaristic Bushido ideals. He looked to be in his early twenties, healthy, and athletic. Though he tried to remain impassive, he exuded a kind of inner self-confidence that came from his pride in being a submariner, a breed apart, above the rest.[13]

More pointed questions followed, including details about military training, submarine service, combat experience, specialist duties, his vessel's performance capabilities, its armament, its navigation routes and refueling locations, and the identities of other Japanese submarines operating in nearby areas. After the first few questions, the sailor became evasive and claimed he didn't know much about what the submarine did or where it went. He was dismissed, and the second POW was marched in. A similar procedure followed, with Watanabe shouting at the prisoner to stand at attention and answer the questions, and Bob making more and more probing inquiries. During this first round of questioning, none of the six provided much more than their names and unit designations, though several mentioned they were from a submarine they called the I-17.

It soon became apparent that the Japanese submariners had never been briefed on how to conduct themselves as prisoners in the event of capture and interrogation. Japan's leaders emphasized that no member of the Japanese military would ever submit to capture, and no soldier or sailor could allow himself to be taken prisoner and remain alive. If faced with capture, suicide was mandatory. They could not become prisoners and remain Japanese citizens. Japan's military leaders also subscribed to the Bushido warrior creed of suicide rather than dishonor.[14]

While that kind of indoctrination no doubt reinforced morale and strengthened the suicidal resolve of most Japanese troops, it backfired to the advantage of American interrogators when dealing with captured Japanese military prisoners. Bob and Watanabe could point out logically that as surviving prisoners they now had nothing to lose by cooperating and providing "normal, routine information." Unexpectedly decent treatment by Americans often prompted the Japanese prisoners to question Japan's official propaganda and the doctrine of mandatory suicide.

After a couple more rounds of questioning, the first sailor was brought in again, and more information started to come out. He was a crewmember of the I-17, one of the I-15 class, with about one hundred crew. He described a large, beautiful submarine, two decks high inside, a 5-inch gun on the deck, and a waterproof hangar for a floatplane. It sounded to Bob like fiction—a huge submarine with a floatplane in a hangar on the deck?

Repeated questioning of the rest of the sailors revealed even more. The Japanese High Command had been very disappointed that the American aircraft carriers weren't sunk during the attack at Pearl Harbor. The U.S. carriers had been at sea, and it was just bad luck for the Japanese that they weren't caught in the harbor with the battleships. So the submarines received orders to chase the carriers and sink them. An American carrier was eventually found, and a Japanese submarine fired torpedoes, but they missed, and the carrier actually destroyed another of the enemy craft. The rest the Japanese subs were ordered to proceed immediately to the U.S. West Coast and sink any U.S. naval vessels departing for Pearl Harbor. They attacked any ships they could find, but they mostly came upon small tankers and freighters.[15]

The I-17 arrived off the California coast with the unusual mission of bombarding an oil refinery near Santa Barbara.[16] The crewman revealed that the purpose of that shelling wasn't to start big fires or destroy the refinery. Rather, it was to do something so unexpected and conspicuous that the U.S. Navy would have no choice but to order warships to steam toward Santa Barbara, and the I-17 could then sink them. But the tactic didn't work, and I-17 found no American vessels to sink.

The news that this huge submarine had attacked California was shocking in the extreme and of great intelligence value. The floatplane on the deck was particularly intriguing. During the course of the interrogations, Bob learned that each of these huge, long-range submarines carried a two-seat scouting floatplane housed in a watertight steel cylinder built so that it was streamlined on the deck. The launch procedure began with the aircraft being rolled out of its enclosure as the wings were deployed. Then it was shot from a bow ramp by compressed air catapult and retrieved by a deck-mounted crane after landing on the ocean surface and taxiing next to the sub. The vessel's armaments included a long-barreled 5.5-inch cannon, the same size gun as on a destroyer. There were also two 25-mm antiaircraft machine guns, and the submarine carried seventeen torpedoes.[17]

The prisoners later divulged more startling information. Their submarine, the I-17, possessed a previously unheard-of range of 16,000 miles. It was one of a number of such massive submarines, bigger than anything ever built before. The subs could easily span the Pacific to attack ships along America's West Coast. Other submarines, including its sister vessel, the I-25, had been in action all along the West Coast of America since the start of the war. The great range of these I-class submarines was especially disturbing information. The American coast was about five thousand miles from Japan, easily within range of the subs, and it was only half that distance from the Japanese naval bases in the tropical Pacific islands.

It was later established that the I-17, sunk on August 19, 1943, off Noumea, was one of the I-15 class of aircraft-equipped submarines completed in September 1940.[18] As large as destroyers, they were 356 feet long, displaced 2,548 tons submerged, and had a surface speed of 23 knots, a surface cruising range of 14,000 miles at 16 knots, and a dive depth of 325 feet. The crew of about one hundred men included a pilot and navigator for the aircraft. The I-17 had twice patrolled along the U.S. Pacific coast. On February 25, 1942, during its second war patrol, it was confirmed that the I-17 had indeed shelled a California oilfield facility and set it on fire. The location was later identified as Goleta, about ten miles northwest of Santa Barbara. Eight other I-class submarines had been patrolling strategic zones along the coasts of California, Oregon, and Washington on missions to sink ships, damage shore installations, and start forest fires.[19]

At the end of the day, Bob hurried to COMSOPAC and reported what he'd found out. The captain on duty immediately composed a message and sent it to the Commander in Chief Pacific (CINCPAC), Admiral Nimitz's headquarters at Pearl Harbor. Within forty-eight hours, a U.S. Navy admiral with experience in submarines was flown in from Hawaii. He spent several days supervising further interrogation of the Japanese sailors, as Bob and Sergeant Watanabe translated. The I-17 and others of its class represented a new threat, and news of this dangerous type of Japanese sub was relayed through classified channels back to Washington. The submarines' specifications, armaments, torpedoes, refueling stops, patrol routes, and other information were vital for U.S. antisubmarine warfare in the Pacific. Bob later learned the Navy sank another I-class sub, the I-25, assisted by information from the interrogation of the six Japanese submariners in Noumea.[20]

Days went by and Bob thought nothing else he could do in Noumea could top the submarine experience. Meanwhile, Don remained busy trying to untangle Japanese strategic intentions from his set of captured Japanese documents. Every day, Bob went from his tent in Camp Goettge to COMSOPAC and reported to the intelligence section for whatever odds and ends they had lined up for him to do, but he was getting antsy. There had been no time to do anything socially, or even get a jeep to drive around the island. He was just about to request a day off when the captain at Halsey's headquarters called him to his desk one morning. Bob figured he was about to get orders to return to his unit in New Zealand, but the captain informed him he was being assigned to a special covert operation. Bob's initial disappointment of not getting orders to go back to New Zealand was tempered by curiosity when he heard the words "special" and "covert." The captain said he was to help track down a reported Japanese secret agent in Noumea. According to local police, this agent was planning to blow up the nickel refinery located just outside of town.

Bob and everyone else in Noumea knew about the nickel mining and refining operations on New Caledonia because the smoke from the huge refinery enveloped Noumea in a thick haze if the wind was blowing from the wrong direction. New Caledonia, an island in the Pacific about the size of New Jersey, reportedly held an estimated 20 percent of the world's nickel reserves.[21]

The captain went on to summarize reports received by local police that a former Japanese resident of Noumea, a businessman who had been repatriated to Japan by the Free French authorities, had mysteriously reappeared in Noumea. He had contacted former friends, told them he had arrived by submarine, and tried to solicit their assistance. The police had passed this information to the U.S. military in Noumea and asked for help. Because a submarine was involved, it became a Navy matter.

Bob was intrigued—covert assignment, Japanese agent, secret mission. It was like he'd stepped into a movie, and he set off on his task with the zeal of a real secret agent. The first thing he did was to investigate how the nickel refinery might be sabotaged. He talked to the manager, an articulate Frenchman from the south of France who was glad not to be in his German-occupied home country at the moment. He was friendly and helpful and told Bob a lot about the nickel industry. Bob then spoke to the Noumea police. He learned where the agent had appeared, and whom he had contacted. Along with Sergeant Watanabe, he followed up leads, talked to people who knew the alleged agent, and investigated a shop where he had done business. Though Bob and Watanabe both spoke Japanese, neither knew French, and in New Caledonia that was a problem because it was a French colony and everyone spoke the language.

Eventually Bob pieced together a chain of information. The presumed agent had been a Japanese businessman and resident of Noumea for many years. He had mentioned his plans of blowing up the nickel refinery to some of his contacts. This scared a couple of his friends and that's why they'd talked to the police. But in spite of the best efforts of Bob and Sergeant Watanabe, the whereabouts of the agent were never determined. Bob suspected he was packed onto a Japanese submarine and taken back to Japan, but he couldn't know for sure. He gave up after a couple of weeks of sleuthing, glad to be getting back to translating documents.

As luck would have it, just then his orders came through to return to the 2nd Marine Division in New Zealand. When he got back to the D-2 office in Wellington, Pelzel and Boardman listened intently to Bob's stories from Noumea. At least they showed more interest than Bob's tentmate and old friend, Don Shively, back at Camp Goettge. Bob described the interrogation of the Japanese submariners and the startling revelation that the Japanese had massive airplane-launching submarines.

That information elicited genuine professional interest from Pelzel, but there were laughs all around when Bob described his awkward covert adventures and how he came up empty-handed while tracking down the elusive Japanese secret agent.

Then the conversation turned to the island invasion they had been helping to plan. The destination was still secret and wouldn't be announced until the task force had put to sea. But Pelzel revealed that the 2nd Marine Division likely would be shipping out fairly soon, first for a practice landing somewhere en route, and then the real show. That operation would soon be known to the rest of America as "Bloody Tarawa."

FIVE

First Combat: Japanese Surrender
Not an Option on Tarawa, 1943

It wasn't long after Bob returned to New Zealand from his adventures in Noumea that it was time to depart for the invasion of a still-unnamed tropical Pacific island. He was detached from the main D-2, the 2nd Marine Division intelligence section, and assigned temporarily to the 2nd Marine Division assistant commander, a general named Leo Hermle who, with his staff and combat teams of Marines, was loaded on the troop transport USS *Monrovia*.[1] Bob's Japanese language officer buddies from New Zealand, John Pelzel and Gene Boardman, were with the main D-2 group on the grand old battleship and Pearl Harbor survivor, the USS *Maryland*. It was flagship of the invasion fleet and carried the main command structure of the 2nd Marine Division.[2] Bob really didn't know anyone on the *Monrovia*, but as with Marines anywhere, everyone was congenial and there was an invigorating tension permeating the ship because they knew they were headed for combat. For Bob, the Tarawa operation would be his first direct contact with the armed forces of Imperial Japan since his childhood experiences in Shanghai.

After leaving New Zealand and heading north into the tropics, the task force tried a practice landing at the island of Efate in the New Hebrides group.[3] It was the final run-through of the boarding procedure and landing, and, as is often the case with dress rehearsals, there were a lot of glitches. Many of the Marines, eighteen- and nineteen-year-olds mostly, were replacements who, like Bob, had joined the combat veterans of the division in New Zealand. Though they had been thoroughly trained, the climb down thirty feet of cargo net into pitching "amtracs" or Higgins boats was not easy.[4] Bob was surprised to see a number of Marines injured trying to complete this procedure, some seriously. A few Marines fell from the nets into the landing craft; others plummeted into the water and were bashed between the amtracs and the troop ships. Later in the day, when the landing force returned to the ships, a head count revealed a few of them had gone AWOL, apparently thinking that finding liquor or women ashore was more appealing than going back to the fleet. Bob never heard what happened to the no-shows.

The imperative was to steam on because they had a schedule to keep. Their destination was only revealed to them when they were again at sea and well clear of the New Hebrides. The officers on the *Monrovia* were called into the wardroom for a briefing. General Hermle ran the meeting. To Bob's way of thinking, Hermle was probably the closest thing to a stereotypical Marine general you could get, with his tanned good looks, fit, lean physique, and close-trimmed brown hair slightly graying at the temples. He pulled a cloth covering from a map on the wall and announced that their island invasion target was Tarawa. This proclamation was greeted mostly with blank stares. Nobody had ever heard of the island before. Hermle said Tarawa was an atoll, a collection of tiny islands scattered on a coral reef with a huge circumference, the islands like beads in a necklace, with the reef itself roughly enclosing a considerable sheltered lagoon. The Japanese had built a coral airstrip on one of the little islands of Tarawa Atoll called Betio (pronounced "Bay-see-o"), and they had constructed fortifications suitable for a vigorous defense to ward off invasion. From the airstrip on Tarawa, Japanese aircraft could range far to the east and threaten Allied shipping.

To provide the overall context of the Tarawa invasion, Hermle then briefly summarized the American strategy to defeat Japan. It depended on capturing Japanese-held islands one by one in an ever-tightening noose. These far-flung bits of land stretched for thousands of miles across the tropical Pacific. The Allied strategy would be for these landings to take place in two separate thrusts. The southern route involved the ongoing combat in the Solomons leading toward the Philippines and eventually Japan. Tarawa would be the first island invasion on the path across the central Pacific in the more northerly push of this massive pincer movement. The goal would be for the two drives to converge on the Japanese home islands. The previous amphibious operations in the Solomons had involved landings on large mountainous islands. American Marines had never before invaded a fortified atoll, or had to deal with the complications introduced by a fringing coral reef covered by shallow water.[5] It would turn out to be the first of many such operations.

The officers listened with a professional interest born of hearing many military briefings. Hermle made it clear that the Tarawa invasion would have very little in common with the Guadalcanal operation the previous year, with the main difference being that Tarawa looked a lot easier. The roughly elongated, triangular islet of Betio, the only bit of land in Tarawa Atoll that the Japanese had fortified, was tiny, less than a half-mile wide and only a couple of miles long. It had no topography, no enervating jungles or mountain ranges like the Marines encountered on the miserable island of Guadalcanal. The entirety of little Betio's flat surface could be brought under fire from the war planes and big guns of the invasion fleet. According to Hermle, the operation would be straightforward. The entire island would be bombed and shelled intensively, wreaking havoc with the Japanese and their fortifications, and then the Marines would come ashore to clean up any dazed and battered defenders who had somehow managed to survive the deadly bombardment.[6]

Bob's particular role in the upcoming invasion was not specific. He was at the disposal of General Hermle and his staff for any intelligence needs that could be required of the assistant commander, and he was to act as liaison with D-2 on the main command ship. Consequently he did not have a particular combat assignment, so he really didn't know what he would end up doing in the Tarawa invasion. He assumed he would go ashore at some point and interrogate prisoners, and he would probably translate captured documents that could provide intelligence information.

Circumstances were conspiring to give Bob a unique perspective on the Tarawa invasion. Though he was trained for combat as all Marines were, he would be more or less a non-combatant, looking for opportunities to contribute to intelligence operations as they arose. Thus, his mental focus and preparation were quite different from the combat Marines on the *Monrovia*. He assumed he would come under enemy fire at some point in the operation, but the circumstances of how that could happen were hard to imagine beforehand.

The intelligence staff had put together big maps of the island showing all the known gun emplacements and fortifications. Bob realized Pelzel and Boardman had been working on these maps back in Wellington, together with the photo interpretation staff, headed by Lt. Joe Utz. Notes on the maps pointed out manmade mounds, apparently sand-covered bomb shelters of some kind, as well as several large concrete blockhouses.[7] The air photo interpreters had ingeniously determined the number of Japanese on the island by counting the outhouses built out over the ocean and multiplying by the average number of troops per toilet. It amounted to about five thousand Japanese outhouse users.

Bob sat in on lengthy discussions among the Marine officers as they hashed out strategies for how best to assault the Japanese positions. Much of the tiny island's surface was occupied by a packed coral airstrip that ran almost the entire length of Betio. The pre-invasion shelling would try to miss the airstrip because the Japanese couldn't build fortifications on it, and the objective of the invasion was to capture the airstrip intact for immediate use by American aircraft. The bombardment would be concentrated on the fortifications and gun emplacements built on the shores of the island and areas surrounding the airstrip.[8]

A prominent feature was a pier, several hundred yards long, extending over the shallow water out to the edge of the reef on the sheltered lagoon side of the island. The invasion beaches were designated on both sides of this pier. Some of the new amtracs had been brought along to cross the reef and deliver the first waves of Marines onto the beach.

But there weren't enough amtracs to carry the entire troop force, and many Marines would have to be taken ashore in plywood-hulled Higgins boats, with their drop-front steel ramps. They would become familiar to later generations of movie-goers as the landing craft featured prominently in the D-day invasion of Normandy. The catch was that they needed about four feet of water to float freely. Anything shallower and they were literally dead in the water. After extensive analysis of fragmented and incomplete information, the planners estimated that the water over the reef at Tarawa would be about five feet deep.[9] This turned out to be a flawed assumption with fatal consequences. The

Marines on the *Monrovia* and the other troop transports of the invasion fleet couldn't have known it at the time, but the seemingly innocuous detail as to whether they were assigned to an amtrac or to a Higgins boat would mean the difference between life and death for many of them.

Determining exactly how deep the water was over the reef at high tide, perhaps the most crucial piece of intelligence in the entire Tarawa operation, had been a particularly thorny problem for Pelzel, Boardman, and the rest of the high-level planners.[10] A couple of Europeans who had lived on Tarawa before the war were asked their opinions, and they thought the water would be about six feet deep, enough for the Higgins boats to make it all the way in over the reef to the beaches.[11] So why not just use more amtracs and forget about the problematic Higgins boats? The Marines would have liked nothing better. But the new amtracs were just then going into large-scale production in the United States, and quite literally all that were available at the time had been secured for the Tarawa operation.[12] So, about half the invasion force would have to be landed from Higgins boats, and the water depth was something that the planners continued to fret about. It was mentioned a number of times in the briefings on the *Monrovia*. The Marines had a plan for this eventuality, of course. If the water was too shallow for the Higgins boats, the amtracs would first unload at the beach, then retrace their steps back to the edge of the reef, transfer Marines from the Higgins boats grounded there, and ferry the troops to the beach in relays.[13] No one seriously believed that the Marines would have to unload from the Higgins boats and wade several hundred yards to the beach through chest-deep water, out in the open all the way in, a daunting prospect if there were still Japanese shooting at them from shore. Unfortunately, the unanticipated chaos of the landing would produce exactly this situation.

After several days at sea, the tension was building on the *Monrovia*. Bob heard a lot of "trash talk," to use a current saying, among the Marines as they psyched up for their battle with the Japanese. It reminded Bob of football players getting themselves pumped up before a big game.

The day of the invasion of Tarawa finally arrived, and Bob and the other officers on Hermle's staff were up early and out on deck to watch the start of the heralded pre-invasion bombardment. The *Monrovia* and the other ships of the invasion fleet came to a near stop in what appeared to be the middle of the ocean. It was still dark when suddenly a huge geyser of water shot into the air with a loud *whoom!* about two hundred yards from their ship. Before anyone could comment, two more fountains of white water and spray erupted near a troop ship starboard of the *Monrovia*. Along with every sailor and Marine of the invasion force, Bob suddenly realized with a start that, in spite of the terrific shellacking that had been inflicted on Betio by the pre-invasion bombing raids, the Japanese were shooting back. There were at least a few defenders who were not only alive, but also capable of firing at the American ships.

After a stunned pause, bright flashes from the naval guns on the battleships and cruisers around them seared the dim light, followed by concussions that slapped everyone on deck, and the deep cracking booms from the big guns echoed from ship to ship. As he stood on the darkened deck of the *Monrovia*, Bob could see the glowing paths of the shells streaking across the sky like huge tracer bullets until they exploded on the horizon with roiling, orange explosions. Bob and several officers from Hermle's staff agreed that surely nothing could survive such a concentration of high explosives focused on that small a space. As the sun rose, they could barely make out the low, flat island in the distance, essentially a smoking line on the horizon. There was a break in the shelling, and aircraft were dive-bombing.[14] Bob could hear the sound of distant explosions, a steady *boom—boom—boom*, accompanied by fountains of flame and black smoke. The whole display was mesmerizing.

Even as the bombardment continued, the amtracs and Higgins boats were launched and were driving in circles to keep their engines warmed up and ready. The treads of the amtracs were like inefficient paddlewheels propelling them slowly forward amidst a froth of white foam and spray. Cargo nets went over the side of the troop transports, just as they had in the practice landing. Memories of men falling off the nets during the rehearsal in the New Hebrides were still vivid in the minds of the Marines, so they deliberately made sure they had firm handholds on the rough ropes as they climbed down.

Unlike the practice at the New Hebrides, there were few mishaps this time as the *Monrovia* and the other troop transports unloaded the first waves of Marines. Meanwhile, the planes had ended their bombing and low-level strafing of Betio and returned to their home aircraft carriers. Just as the sun peeked over the horizon, the battleships and cruisers resumed their shelling.[15] Bob had secured a pair of binoculars and, even from his vantage point several miles away from the island, he could make out the silhouettes of the skeletal palm trees lining the shore as columns of black smoke billowed up behind them. He guessed that fuel stores and other flammable materials must have been ignited by the bombing and shelling.

The officers around him were commenting that the Japanese defenders should, by now, either be torn to pieces by the shellfire, or be stunned into a stupor by the concussions from the explosions. Hopefully the Marines could secure the devastated island in a few hours.

One of Hermle's staff ran up to him with a message. The timetable was being moved back because the landing craft were behind schedule.[16] The amtracs, full of Marines, plowed ahead in the choppy ocean, churning more slowly than anticipated toward the darkly ominous island.

Through his binoculars Bob could see the amtracs moving in excruciatingly slow motion. Suddenly, they started to draw fire from the beach and jets of water erupted among the craft. Incredibly, Japanese defenders manning antiboat and machine guns had lived through the seemingly totally destructive shelling and were firing on the amtracs as they came into range.[17]

Clearly evident through the binoculars was the long pier that stretched out from the island shore into the lagoon. It appeared to be crudely constructed, with what looked like a narrow avenue of planking and packed coral held about five feet out of the water by coconut log pilings driven into the reef. The amtracs parted and flowed to both sides of it. There were three designated landing beaches, each a couple of hundred yards wide, one to the left of the pier, and two to the right.[18] There was actually only one continuous shoreline and beach, but demarcation lines between the three landing beaches were drawn on maps for assignment of different assault sectors to keep various units together in selected locations as they landed.

The amtracs were finally reaching the beaches, but with his binoculars Bob could only see them faintly through a haze of smoke. The Higgins boats were several hundred yards behind the amtracs, and they also had been proceeding steadily toward Betio. But then Bob noticed something was wrong. One of the Higgins boats had stopped, still a good four hundred yards out from shore. Then another looked to be dead in the water, and then another. It suddenly dawned on Bob and the rest of Hermle's staff that the worst possible outcome for the Higgins boats was happening right before their eyes. The water over the reef was too shallow for the small craft, and they were stuck at the reef's edge. The backup plan was now supposed to kick in. Amtracs returning from the beaches after unloading were to stand by to transfer Marines from the Higgins boats and shuttle them to the beach. But there were no amtracs coming back out from shore yet. Left with little alternative, one by one the Higgins boats lowered their drop-front doors and the Marines stepped off the ramps, sinking into the water up to their necks.[19]

The view through the binoculars gave a certain sense of detachment as Bob watched the rows of Marines begin to move slowly toward Betio, holding their rifles over their heads. They would have to wade more than four hundred exposed yards in chest-deep water directly into Japanese machine-gun fire. Their only protection, if it could be called that, was the water they were struggling through. As they got closer to shore, the depth would get progressively shallower, and they would become gradually bigger and easier targets for the Japanese machine gunners.[20] A sense of dread swept over the Marine officers on the deck of the *Monrovia* as they watched the scene unfold.

The odds were now decidedly against those hundreds of Marines in the water. Little geysers from machine-gun bullets sprouted among them, relentlessly playing across the lines of men struggling toward the beach. They tried to stay as low in the water as possible and still move forward, but, one by one as they were hit, they dropped their rifles into the water, bodies limp. The officers on the *Monrovia* watched helplessly as the agonizing, slow-motion charge moved toward shore. As more Marines were hit, there were fewer targets. Still, the little spouts of water flicked around them. Incredibly, some made it all the way to the beach. For others, the pier, that seemingly innocuous feature on the maps, was like a magnet. It held out some hope of cover in their long wade in to the beach. Those that made it to the shelter of the coconut log structure disappeared from view, as they huddled under the stanchions in water up to their chests.[21] The bodies of those who were not so lucky now dotted the aquamarine water over the reef in dark, motionless clumps.

This was the first island invasion Bob had ever witnessed. The stupendous scale was awe inspiring and a bit overwhelming, but there was the depressing realization that the landings were clearly not going according to plan. The first wave of troops in the amtracs had been badly hit by the unexpected gunfire from Japanese defensive positions. It appeared the enemy troops had been relatively untouched by what had looked like such an impressive rain of destruction from the pre-invasion bombardment. The subsequent landings from the Higgins boats had been an unmitigated disaster. Bob walked over to look through the door to the wardroom just off the main deck, where General Hermle and his staff were now huddled around several radios. Maps of Tarawa surrounded them on the bulkheads. They were all extremely frustrated that so little information was coming in from the radios on shore. Occasionally a burst of static and a few shouted words from a couple of the battalion commanders, one named Dave Shoup, came over the speakers. About all they could make out was that there were heavy casualties, and the Marines needed more ammunition and drinking water.

Hermle was cursing the radios. Communication with the USS *Maryland* was working, but the Division command on that ship didn't have any better idea of what was going on than Hermle's staff on the *Monrovia*.[22] Bob returned to the deck and scanned the shoreline through his binoculars. He could see the tiny forms of the amtracs nosed up on the beach, and a line of Marines in front of a low, coconut log seawall. He knew that groups of Marines were huddled out of sight under the pier where they had been driven during their wade in to the beach. Up to this point, no amtracs or Higgins boats had come back from the island. There was a distant wall of noise, a continuous cacophony of artillery explosions, a staccato *pop-pop-pop* from machine guns, the snapping, flat sounds of mortars, and individual rifle shots.

Finally Bob saw a Higgins boat heading back toward the *Monrovia*. The driver at the control column near the rear of the boat was visible from the waist up. Peering out from under his helmet, he steered patiently toward the ship. As the boxy little craft got closer, Bob could see several Marines inside. One was sitting erect, intently holding a gauze compress against the side of his head. It was soaked in bright red blood. Another Marine had a tightly wound bandage around his right wrist where his hand should have been. It was startling to see Marine casualties, the first Bob had ever witnessed. His first thought was, *Well, this is combat, and that's what happens in combat.* Still, it was disturbing to see bloodied and disabled fellow Marines who just a short time ago had climbed down the cargo nets in top physical condition. From his experiences as a kid in China, he was able to rely on a familiar emotional distance to shield himself from such unpleasant sights. He kept telling himself he'd seen just as bad, or worse, in Shanghai. This was how Bob would make it through all the island combat he would endure, and it worked most of the time.

A couple of hours had passed since the first waves of Marines had gone in, and the situation was pure chaos. Not one of the carefully orchestrated stages of the landing had gone as planned. No one seemed to know exactly what was happening, what should be done, or even what could be done. Dave Shoup was one of the few regimental commanders ashore who could be heard over the poorly performing radios.[23]

The prospect of a failed landing now hung over the *Monrovia* like the ominous black smoke above Tarawa. Bob heard one of the officers whisper that he had heard a cryptic radio message stating, "Issue in doubt," a phrase used by the American defenders of Wake Island shortly before they surrendered to the Japanese.[24] Suddenly General Hermle emerged on deck and announced to Bob and the group of startled officers that the 2nd Marine Division commander on the *Maryland* had just ordered him to go ashore personally. He was to take a small group with him, along with a functioning radio, assess the situation, and communicate his findings to the main command ship.[25]

Bob couldn't believe his ears. A general leading his men in to the beach under fire? Generals usually commanded troops from a rear headquarters area, not in the middle of a train wreck of an amphibious landing. Hermle scanned the men in front of him and pointed at five or six who were to join the landing party. He then looked at Bob and, after confirming his status as the language and intelligence officer, motioned him to join as well.

This is what Bob had trained for, and now he would be making a landing under fire on a heavily defended enemy island. Energized, Bob ran down the ladder to his berth and grabbed his helmet, a poncho, a web belt with two canteens full of water, a couple of C-ration packs, his carbine, and a knapsack holding his two Japanese dictionaries. He then bounded back up to the main deck to join the squad forming around Hermle, who at that moment was in the process of hailing a passing Higgins boat. Did the general really think they could make it ashore in one of the ill-fated Higgins boats? Hadn't he just watched what happened to Marines who had been unloaded from Higgins boats at the edge of the reef?

There was no time to ask questions, and, with a sense of urgency, the shore party climbed down the rope nets into the craft as it heaved up and down in the swells, the *Monrovia* looming above them. As the last member of their group piled in, the landing craft pulled away from the ship and headed toward the island.

Two of Hermle's staff were operating the radio and were in contact with both the *Monrovia* and the *Maryland*. The coxswain stood upright at the back, behind the steering column, as he guided the pitching craft toward the island. Suddenly he shouted and grabbed his upper arm. He'd been shot, and blood was flowing onto his gray Mae West life jacket. Hermle urged him to return to the *Monrovia* for medical attention, but the coxswain shook his head determinedly and said he was all right. Blood was now running down his pants leg, and it was clear he was not in good enough shape to drive the boat. Hermle spotted an amtrac on its way back from the island and flagged it down. It splashed its way over to the Higgins boat. The coxswain kept saying he was OK, but the general firmly told him to go back to the *Monrovia* to get patched up.

Bob felt an immense sense of relief. Thank goodness they were now getting into an amtrac! They wouldn't have to wade ashore under fire, and the amtrac's steel sides afforded more protection than the plywood-hulled Higgins boat. As the landing party transferred to the amtrac, Hermle told the driver, who was hunched under a steel hood at the front of the vehicle with his hands on the control levers, to take them to the end of the pier. The driver nodded and engaged the gears, the engine roared, the treads spun in the warm water, and the machine started forward. It took a while to move slowly through the water toward the island, but finally they nosed up to the relative shelter of the end of the pier. From this much closer vantage point, the motionless amtracs Bob saw through binoculars from the *Monrovia* were now clearly visible on the shore just several hundred yards away. He could see also the huddled forms of Marines crouched behind the seawall. He glanced back toward the ships of the invasion fleet and noticed a destroyer close behind him. It slowly moved parallel to the island in the deeper water just off the edge of the reef. The two turrets of its forward 5-inch guns were turned toward the shoreline, the barrels lowered parallel to the water. There was a sudden sharp crack, and a puff of smoke was forced out of the barrel of one of those guns.[26] Bob followed its aim, and almost immediately an explosion erupted to the left of the pier, just behind a Japanese truck that was careening along the shore. Then *pow*, another round fired, and there was an explosion just ahead of the vehicle. The destroyer appeared to be sharpshooting the truck, using its 5-inch guns like rifles shooting at a target on a firing range. It made no sense whatsoever that anyone would be trying to drive anything on that chaotic shore, or that 5-inch rounds from a destroyer would be expended to try and hit it. Bob was transfixed by this bizarre scene. Another shot went wide. The truck continued to bounce along and then was hidden in smoke. It was impossible to tell whether or not it had been hit.

Though the volume of noise from the battle going on a short distance away was overwhelming, the landing party was relatively safe, crouched in the amtrac in the lee of the end of the pier. Bob was finally in combat under fire, sitting next to the general who was second in command of the entire operation. However, it was still unclear why Hermle had brought him along on this little expedition.

The radio operators were starting to have trouble. Their contact with the *Monrovia* was breaking up, and they could barely raise the main Division command on the *Maryland*. Hermle was peering over the steel wall of the amtrac, scanning the shore, straining to make sense of the scene. From the end of the pier it was impossible to tell what the combat situation was just a few hundred yards away. Then something happened that stunned Bob with its sheer incongruity. Hermle turned to him and shouted over the noise of the gunfire, "Sheeks, go in and see if you can get a prisoner and find out what's going on."[27] Bob automatically responded in the affirmative, but immediately he wondered how, exactly, he was going to "get a prisoner and find out what's going on." It seemed ludicrous, laughable even. But Hermle was a general, and lieutenants do not, as a rule, question a direct order from a general, no matter how strange the command.

Hermle motioned for an enlisted man to accompany Bob on his mission. The corporal, who seemed no older than eighteen, peered out anxiously from under his helmet. Bob glanced at him and then looked away quickly. He didn't want to betray his doubts about what he had just been ordered to do. Somehow he had to get to the island. He could either wade in the chest-deep water or traverse the pier. Neither avenue looked very promising, because enemy machine-gun fire was relentlessly sweeping both. Even if he could survive and make it to shore, he would have to join up with a combat team on the beach as they fought desperately to secure a toehold amidst a curtain of machine-gun bullets and mortar fire. In the chaos of combat, Bob would somehow have to take a prisoner, and then ask him what was going on. With the general watching, Bob motioned for the corporal to follow, and they climbed up from the amtrac onto the end of the pier. Bullets ripped the air above, and Bob jumped down immediately into the water, with the corporal right behind him. His feet hit the sandy bottom and the water was up to his chest. Quickly, both of them took shelter under the pier and started to make their way shoreward. Interspersed between hundreds of dead reef fish, killed by the concussions from shells exploding in the water and washing back and forth among the coconut log pilings, were wounded Marines huddled in the shelter the pier provided. They looked to Bob for instructions, since he was wearing a small, gold lieutenant bar on his lapel. Bob waved down an amtrac that was passing by on its way back out to the ships, and he and the corporal helped load some of wounded on board as bullets zipped by. But the mission was to get to the island and take a prisoner, so Bob resumed moving cautiously toward the shore, the corporal following close behind. It was slow going as they threaded between the jumbled pilings and stanchions under the pier. It seemed to be taking too long. If they could somehow make their way on top of the pier, it would be a lot quicker. Bob pulled himself up out of the water cautiously, and the corporal followed. They started to slither toward the shore as bullets whipped overhead. There were renewed bursts of machine-gun fire and ricochets showered them with wood splinters. They immediately dropped down again to take shelter beneath the pier. Though progress on top of the pier was quicker, it was far more likely to be fatal.

After more struggling to make their way through the pilings, they were nearly to the beach, but just ahead was a yawning gap in the pier only fifty yards from shore. It looked like a bomb or artillery shell had blown about twenty yards out of the structure, and that unsheltered distance had to be crossed almost directly in front of the Japanese machine gunners. Bob eyed this open space, and then glanced at the corporal behind him. He was staring back wide eyed, waiting for a decision. Bob's mind was racing. Even if, by some miracle, he and the corporal could cross this gap and make it to the beach, it was clear from the noise of the intense combat going on ahead of them that there was no way live prisoners were being captured. Bob motioned to the corporal to turn around, and they carefully picked their way back to the end of the pier. Bob climbed into the amtrac and Hermle looked up from the radio. Bob reported that there were intense firefights going on along the shore and just inland, with no chance of taking any prisoners at the moment. He suggested they could try again when the combat teams had made more progress. Hermle nodded and thanked Bob for his assessment, and he told him to try later.

What a relief! But now what? It was cramped in the amtrac, and Bob would have to bide his time until he had a better opportunity to make it to shore. Looking for a reasonably sheltered alternative, he spotted a ledge of wooden planking notched out of the coconut log stanchions at the end of the pier, and he quickly wedged onto that space. It was out of the water, out of the amtrac, and reasonably shielded from the various calibers of bullets ripping the air just above him.

Momentarily turned back into a spectator, Bob contemplated the scene around him. On either side of the pier, on Red Beach 3 to the left and Red Beach 2 to the right, there were the immobilized amtracs he had seen before. A couple of them were canted at odd angles, apparently knocked out of commission while trying to crawl over the roughly four-foot-high coconut log seawall. As far as Bob could see in either direction, Marines were huddled under the protection of that seawall. Occasionally, several would haul themselves over the roughly chest-high barrier of coconut logs and, laden with weapons and equipment, scurry short distances before diving for cover. There was almost continuous gunfire from intense combat as the Marines fought desperate, multiple, small-scale actions against the entrenched Japanese. Looking to the right of the pier, Bob's eyes followed the shoreline several hundred yards, until the beach curved away and then back out to a point that projected into the lagoon about one thousand yards away. The ragged stalks of the shredded palm trees on that smoke-shrouded promontory marked the western end of Betio and the far right boundary of Red Beach 1, the extreme right flank of the Marine beachhead. He shifted his gaze back to the Marines ahead of him on the shore on Red Beach 2. One after another, Marines were crawling over the seawall, past the wounded and dying men sprawled on the ten-yard-wide strip of sand between the sea-wall and the water. Others crouched motionless behind the wall. The living, the dead, and the dying were crowded closely together. Though some Marines were moving, it appeared to be a stalemate so far. The difficulties of simply getting off the beach and over the seawall indicated the Japanese seemed to be holding the upper hand.

Meanwhile, there was considerable activity going on around Bob. A Navy doctor who had been in the shore party with Hermle had crawled underneath the pier. He was flagging down the occasional passing amtrac to transfer wounded Marines back out to the ships in the lagoon.[28] Higgins boats filled with supplies were pulling up to the end of the pier next to the general's amtrac in a nearly constant procession. Marines were flinging boxes and crates up onto the wharf in a confused jumble. Some of the supplies in the boxes were undoubtedly being damaged, either by the rough handling or by the gunfire they were intercepting, but that was the only place on the island where anything could be offloaded. Somehow those supplies had to make it the rest of the way to shore, but it was unclear how that was going to happen any time soon.

Because he hadn't finished his assigned mission, Bob wanted to stay close to the island in case an opportunity presented itself to join a combat team to facilitate his assignment to take a prisoner. It was now evening, and if he had to spend the night on the island, his ledge on the end of the pier was as good a place as any, under cover, relatively safe from being shot.

Darkness finally enveloped Betio, but there was no letup in activity on the pier. It had become a kind of logistical focal point for the island invasion. If anything, even more Higgins boats pulled up to unload supplies in the darkness. The wounded were being brought continually to the empty boats and carried back out to the ships. Sometime during the night, Bob got word that General Hermle was leaving in his amtrac. The radio was still not functioning properly, so he was going out to a nearby destroyer to transmit his report directly to the USS *Maryland*. Bob got permission to stay on the end of the pier and maybe somehow get in to the island the next morning. The general's amtrac pulled away from the pier and trundled back out to the invasion fleet.[29] It was not until much later that Hermle found out about a radio transmission sent to him earlier that afternoon. The message was an order for him to take command of all Marine forces on Betio.[30] But the message never got through, and he was criticized later for not taking enough initiative. Instead, Dave Shoup remained in command on the island, and later was awarded the Medal of Honor for it.[31]

Bob's clothes hadn't fully dried from his wade under the pier that morning, and he was damp and sticky from the salt water. He hadn't eaten anything since breakfast on the *Monrovia*, so he made do with a cold C-ration package for dinner. His two canteens were almost empty, there was no way to get comfortable, and the ongoing commotion of loading and unloading Higgins boats from the end of the pier made it impossible to sleep, even though there had been a slackening of gunfire that came with the darkness. But he was still alive, and that was something, given the closeness of some of those Japanese machine-gun bullets. He'd survived his first day of combat, though he hadn't set foot on the actual island or fired his carbine. A language officer was not really expected to shoot anyone, and his rifle probably wouldn't fire anyway because it had been dunked repeatedly in the warm waters of the lagoon under the pier. It looked to Bob like the Marines had penetrated only a short distance inland, and the Japanese showed no signs of giving up. Occasionally, sporadic firing erupted from somewhere on the darkened island. Tracers flew wildly into the sky like Roman candles, and then died down again. Bob heard a few shots from close by and figured one of the other Marines on the end of the pier was firing at something.

The long night finally started to give way to day two on Tarawa. As the sky lightened, Bob noticed there were quite a few Marines around him. They had taken shelter in the jumble of wooden packing crates stacked haphazardly on the end of the pier. One of them was grumbling about somebody nearby who was shooting randomly during the night. Hadn't they been taught fire control in basic training, he wondered? Suddenly, another Marine shouted something about a Japanese infiltrator inside a big steel buoy sitting up on the pier. Incredibly, a Japanese sniper had crawled all the way out to the end of the pier during the night, and had climbed into the buoy through a shell hole that had been blasted in its side. He was firing at Marines on the beach. Bob watched as a Marine aimed his rifle into an aperture in the top of the buoy and let loose an entire eight-shot clip in rapid succession. Bullets went pinging around inside, and that was the end of the Japanese sniper in the buoy. Several other Japanese had crawled out in shallow water to the hulk of a small, wrecked Japanese freighter on the reef to the right of the pier, and firing was coming from it, as well.[32] There was nothing the Marines around Bob could do about that.

Amidst this activity, the sun rose on D+1 on Betio. Still on the pier, Bob contemplated his chances of getting onto the island. He was on his own. The corporal who had been with him the day before had left with the general's party during the night. His mission, to find a prisoner to interrogate, seemed as questionable as ever.

As Bob turned once again to look for developments seaward, to the right of the pier he noticed a group of Higgins boats in the process of grounding on the edge of the reef. Then, their steel doors dropped open to disgorge Marines. Immediately the Japanese on shore opened fire, the staccato popping from multiple machine guns merging to one continuous blast of sound. It was a sickening replay of the previous morning. All eyes on the end of the pier turned to look to their right, as the unfortunate Marines struggled in the neck-deep water. One after another they were shot and went limp. It was as if no one had seen what had happened twenty-four hours earlier to those who tried to wade the hundreds of yards from the edge of the reef to the beach. Marines on the pier were incredulous and angry. What kind of screwup was this? Didn't the high command realize the Japanese were still alive in their bunkers and machine-gun nests? Bob found out later that a tragic miscommunication between General Hermle and the command ship just before dawn had inadvertently caused a last-minute diversion of the Marine reinforcements. Originally, they were meant to land farther to the left and out of the most direct fire of the Japanese. But there was a misunderstanding in the chaos of the previous afternoon and night, compounded by the chronic breakdowns of radio communications at key times, and the Marine reinforcements were disgorged helplessly from the landing craft directly in front of one of the strongest Japanese defensive positions on the boundary between Red Beach 1 and Red Beach 2 to the right of the pier. And, as had happened the day before, many Marines were gunned down while struggling to wade to the beach. Their lifeless forms floated in the shimmering blue-green water, still several hundred yards short of their objective, an island they would never set foot on. Others, against all odds, made it all the way to the beach, while some stragglers and wounded made their way to the shelter of the pier.[33]

After watching this terrible debacle, some of the disgusted Marines around Bob turned their attention to organizing the piles of supplies on the pier, using the stacks of boxes and crates as shelter from the fire coming from shore. Others climbed down into the water beneath the structure and helped the wounded make their way to the Higgins boat shuttles that were once again bringing in more supplies.

It was becoming clear that the chances of actually getting to the island and finding a prisoner on either Red Beach 2 or 3 were pretty much nonexistent. Since Bob didn't know where General Hermle had gone, he decided to try to get back out to the USS *Maryland* and find the commanding officer of D-2 to receive further instructions. Around midmorning he hopped into an amtrac idling along the pier, picking up the wounded stranded below. About an hour later, after transferring several times between landing craft, Sheeks arrived at the battleship USS *Maryland*. He had to report on what he'd been up to, see if D-2 wanted him to find Hermle again, and check if they had any other assignments for him. He searched the huge ship and learned that the D-2 commanding officer, Colonel Colley, and Bob's immediate superiors, John Pelzel and Gene Boardman, had all gone ashore a short time earlier, but no one seemed to know where they were.

Now what? He checked into the wardroom and, similar to the scene on the *Monrovia*, the 2nd Marine Division leadership was trying to figure out what was happening on shore. Bob saw a grizzled Marine colonel with thinning red hair standing against the back wall smoking a cigarette, apparently taking a break from the general hubbub in the room. Bob recognized him immediately. He was Col. Merritt Edson, known to the Marines as "Red Mike." He had become a legend for his exploits on Guadalcanal, and everyone knew his story. Edson had called Marine artillery fire in on his own positions during a last-ditch stand on Bloody Ridge, thereby holding the line and blocking the Japanese from taking the Guadalcanal airfield. For that action he was awarded the Medal of Honor.[34] Red Mike was referred to in reverential terms when Bob was training at Green's Farm. Edson had been a China Marine and was rumored to have sympathies with Mao Tse-tung and the Chinese Communists who were fighting the Japanese. Though most thought his nickname came from his younger days when he had a red beard, Bob thought there could be another political interpretation. Edson was now chief of staff for the 2nd Marine Division.

Bob went in, reported to Edson, and explained what he had been doing for the past twenty-four hours. He added that he was trying to find Colonel Colley, and he asked if there was any information as to where D-2 was located on the island. Edson replied that they were still waiting to hear a report from D-2. For now, no one knew exactly where they were, and he suggested that Bob should stand by on the *Maryland* until more was known as to their whereabouts. Bob then took the liberty of mentioning his own connection to China, and Red Mike seemed interested. They talked briefly about prewar Shanghai, both welcoming the chance for a diversion, even momentarily, from the chaos of the Tarawa landing.

Bob felt listless and an overwhelming urge to sleep was overtaking him. It was as if gravity had suddenly become stronger, and he was almost being pulled down physically to the deck. His need for sleep was like craving water, dominating his consciousness almost to the exclusion of all else. Edson had turned his attention back to the immediate, frantic problems of the invasion gone bad. Without any immediate assignment, Bob made his way back out on deck and curled up to take a nap in the shade beneath one of the battleship's big guns.

After two hours, Bob woke up sore and stiff from lying on *Maryland*'s deck and wondered where he was. First, he heard distant explosions and gunfire. Then his eyes slowly focused, he propped himself on one elbow to look at the smoking island in the distance, and everything came back to him quickly. He dragged himself into the wardroom to see if there was any new information about the location of D-2. Headquarters had learned they had gone in on Green Beach on the west side of the island and had set up just inland from the shore. It was around the western corner of the island, beyond the right flank of Red Beach 1, and the word was that the Marines had made headway over there.[35]

Bob felt groggy, grimy, and in a daze, but he knew that Green Beach would be his best chance to get ashore. A Higgins boat had pulled up to the *Maryland* and was being loaded with supplies, mostly ammunition and water. The coxswain said he was going back in to Green Beach, so Bob hopped on board. The craft pulled away from the giant battleship and churned toward the west end of the island, to the right of the initial invasion beaches. Some Marines were visible along the shoreline, but many had moved inland by that time. The landing craft wove among the dark shapes of Marine bodies bobbing in the shallow water. Some had been killed attempting to wade in, and others had drifted out from the invasion beaches on the tide. The Higgins boat drove to where the water shallowed on the reef and scraped to a stop. Bob thanked the coxswain for the ride, hopped out into the knee-deep water, and waded about one hundred yards to the beach. The Marines had pushed the Japanese inland in this sector, so thankfully no one was shooting at him.

He plodded out of the sea, water squishing out of his boots onto the white coral sand, and headed inland through an explosives-blasted landscape. The coral gravel of the island was churned up as if a giant steam shovel had run amok. He picked his way past shell holes and gaunt, blackened palm trees, asked a lieutenant if he knew where to find D-2, and went to where the officer pointed. Even though the actual fighting was taking place a few hundred yards inland, stray bullets zipped through the air above him. Finally, he found Pelzel and Boardman. They were standing in a five-foot-deep taro pit, about ten feet by ten feet square, and looking at a captured Japanese document.

Gilbertese natives who had lived on Betio before the Japanese arrived had grown a starchy root bog plant called taro in pits about four feet deep. The taro thrived on the brackish water that seeped into the pits. Taro, also known locally as "pulaka," was an essential food source for the Gilbertese, and the pits dotted the island.[36] For the Japanese defenders, they had been ready-made trenches. For the Marines, they were pre-dug foxhole-like shelters. They were wet at the bottom but cool, a pleasant respite from the baking daytime heat.

Bob slid down into the pit and was greeted by Pelzel, who immediately warned him that there was a Japanese sniper somewhere in the nearby palm trees, and the Marines had been having trouble finding him. Pelzel motioned in the direction of the open ground Bob had just walked across on the way to the taro pit. He had been almost certainly in the sights of the sniper. Marines nearby were hunkered down behind the slender trunks of palm trees and were looking furtively at the tree tops. A shot rang out and a bullet pinged off the ground near the pit where the language officers were sheltered. The Marines all started yelling and pointing to where they thought the shot came from. Simultaneously they started shooting at the tops of several nearby palm trees. Finally a cheer went up. At the top of a fifty-foot palm not twenty yards from them, the lifeless form of the Japanese sniper suddenly appeared, dangling limply from a strap he had used to tie himself up in the fronds of the tree. He appeared to be wearing makeshift, wire climbing cleats strapped to his sneakers. Apparently he had climbed up the tree like a telephone lineman the night before, waited all morning until there were numerous Marines around, and had carefully chosen his targets. He'd gone undiscovered for so long because it wasn't easy to pinpoint a particular shot in the midst of the profusion of explosions and gunfire on Betio. Knowing he could not survive and had no means of escape, his goal was to kill as many Marines as possible before he was killed. And he wasn't alone. Pelzel said that the Marines had already dealt with a number of these treetop shooters.

Relieved the sniper had been eliminated, Bob told Pelzel the story of Hermle's order for him to get to the beach, take a prisoner, and find out what was going on. Pelzel shook his head and said Hermle should have known better. Few Japanese prisoners had ever been taken alive in combat situations, and, given the chaos of the Tarawa invasion, there was virtually no chance of capturing any alive on the first day of the battle.

The tropical heat and humidity were terrific, with meager shade found only in small patches under the splintered and shattered palm trees. Bob had refilled his two canteens when he was out on the *Maryland*, and he had nearly emptied one of them already. Drinking water was essential to keep functioning. On the first day some of the most urgent messages that got through over the minimally operative radios had been requests for water. Bob wondered how the Marines doing the fighting could drink enough to keep going. The adrenaline-infused, heart-pounding rush of combat only accentuated the dehydration from the heat.

Pelzel pointed to his left and noted that Colonel Colley and Dutton were in a taro pit in that direction. D-2 had been limited in their actions by the extreme difficulties of the landing and subsequent combat at close quarters. About all they'd been doing since they came ashore several hours earlier was looking for documents and code books in the bunkers and fortifications that had been cleared of Japanese. No prisoners had been taken yet, and they'd only seen a few Japanese bodies out in the open. Most were dying inside their bunkers and fortified positions as the Marines overran them.

After a pause in the conversation, Pelzel brought up a topic that would weigh heavily on D-2 for months after the battle for Tarawa ended. He noted that they didn't get the water depth over the reef right. That led directly to Higgins boats not being able to make it in to the beaches, resulting in the deaths of hundreds of Marines who were machine-gunned in the shallow water as they waded ashore. It wasn't all D-2's fault, though. They had been provided incomplete intelligence from the Australian expatriates and the U.S. Navy.[37]

Another fundamental problem was the failure of the pre-invasion bombardment to disable the Japanese defenses. This had led to most of the subsequent difficulties, but it profoundly affected the amtrac shuttle system, the fall-back option if the Higgins boats couldn't get to the beach. That plan failed because so many amtracs had been knocked out by the Japanese antiboat guns on their way to the beaches. The language officers all agreed that one of the main tasks of D-2 would be to document the construction of the Japanese fortifications, so they could be more effectively put out of commission before future island landings. As it turned out, that documentation process, still two days away, ended up being the most important assignment Bob would have during the entire Tarawa operation. The radio communication screwup also was inexcusable and caused additional Marine casualties owing to the ensuing confusion and chaos. And, of course, future atoll and tropical island invasions would need more amtracs that could crawl up over the shallow reefs and deposit Marines directly on the invasion beaches.

Pelzel told Bob to head over to D-2, report to Colonel Colley, and see if there was anything that needed to be done. Bob jumped up out of the taro pit and ran over to a larger pit holding several Marine officers. He recognized Colonel Colley and his aide, Tom Dutton. As Bob climbed into the pit, Dutton was recounting a harrowing trip to the beach he had made the previous evening. Unbeknownst to Bob, Dutton also had received an assignment from Hermle, except instead of taking a prisoner, he was to find Shoup's command post and report the situation. He and another officer made their way to the beach under cover of darkness and eventually found Shoup. Then, they returned to Hermle in his amtrac at the end of the pier and reported that Shoup needed reinforcements.[38] Bob never saw Dutton, so he must have passed unseen underneath the pier during the night. Unfortunately, Hermle couldn't relay that information to the Division commander on the *Maryland* because of the faulty radios. That is why he left in the middle of the night from the end of the pier. He went back out to one of the destroyers patrolling near the reef edge and tried to make his report from there, only to be frustrated yet again when his message was misinterpreted to mean that Shoup wanted the reinforcements landed specifically on Red Beach 2, leading to the tragic slaughter of the Marines Bob saw on the morning of the second day.[39]

Colonel Colley told Bob to report back to Pelzel and Boardman, and as Bob was trotting back to their taro pit he heard a shout, followed by a muffled explosion and a flurry of rifle fire. The firing stopped and one of the Marines close to the shooting yelled for an interpreter. Bob went over to where a small group of Marines was crouched around a half-dozen prone and motionless Japanese bodies. A sergeant saw him approach and told him the Japanese came running out after they threw a satchel explosive charge into the small concrete bunker next to them. A couple of the Japanese were still alive.

Bob crouched down over the shattered enemy soldiers. Several were dead, their uniforms scorched from the explosion, their bodies riddled by shrapnel. Thick, scarlet blood had oozed from the holes torn into their uniforms and was seeping into the white coral gravel. One was lying on his back, his eyes open and his mouth trying silently to form words. He didn't appear to have any obvious wounds, but the concussion from the explosion had clearly stunned him into near unconsciousness. Another lying face down next to him was moaning intermittently. He was alive, barely. Here were the first Japanese ground troops Bob had encountered in the Pacific. The POWs he had interrogated in Noumea had been navy submariners, a different breed from the combat infantrymen lying in front of him. Though their uniforms were in tatters, Bob recognized they were Imperial Marines, reputed to be the best troops the Japanese had. Some of the Japanese forces he'd seen in Shanghai had been Imperial Marines. He looked at the four dead bodies and the two living Japanese. He didn't have time to reflect on the meaning of that moment, how he had come full circle from his experiences in Shanghai to again face the tangible military incarnations of Imperial Japan. Instead, he focused on the opportunity to ask them questions and obtain intelligence information as quickly as possible.

He moved over to the one who seemed the least injured and asked him in Japanese if there were other soldiers in the bunker. Bob had the odd sensation of doing language triage, picking the least injured in the hope that he would live long enough to respond to questions. The Japanese marine stared straight up, his chest heaving in agonized twitches, and he responded with short gasping answers. Bob didn't think he even realized he was being interrogated by an American. He was just hearing a voice speaking in Japanese and answering. He mentioned there were more troops nearby, but he couldn't say where, and then he lapsed into unconsciousness. The other one was barely alive and mostly unresponsive. The MPs had been called, and they took charge of the two survivors. There was another call for an interpreter from off to the left. More Japanese bodies had been found. Bob took a final look at the Imperial Marines who had come such a long way to die on an island in the middle of the Pacific. For them, and many more young Japanese and Americans, their lives had come to an end on a speck of land no one had ever heard of, in a battle future generations would scarcely remember.

As the afternoon wore on, Bob was able to recover a number of documents from the bodies of dead Japanese. He had come across a few Japanese military survivors, all wounded or shell-shocked from explosives detonated in their bunkers. Many more Korean laborers were eager to surrender, having tired of their treatment by the Japanese. As the fighting subsided on the second day, it was clear that the operation would be successful, but there was still a lot of fighting left.[40] After the sun set it seemed to cool only slightly. That second night, Bob huddled in the taro pit with Pelzel and Boardman. They ate some C-rations, mostly in silence. No one had slept much since the battle had begun.

Discussion finally turned to how difficult it was to take prisoners. It appeared that the Japanese didn't actually know how to surrender. Bob wondered if, given the option, more would elect to give up and come out of the bunkers, rather than die where they fought. This was an idea that Bob would pursue in earnest when he got back to Hawaii after the Tarawa operation ended.

Meanwhile, it was another long and nervous night. A number of Japanese soldiers were creeping around, a tactic the Marines called infiltration, trying to search out individual Americans to attack silently with knives. Every now and then a nervous Marine would fire several shots, thinking he'd seen an infiltrator in the shadows. When the sun finally came up on the third day of the battle, the Marines breathed a little easier. Better to be killed in daylight than to be knifed in silence in the middle of the night.

Pelzel suggested that Bob should try to find Dave Shoup's command post and see if they had taken any POWs or found any Japanese documents that could be of use to intelligence. Bob hopped out of the taro pit and took off in a low trot, running parallel to Red Beach 2. He kept asking Marines he encountered where Shoup's CP was, and finally he came across a group of Marines sheltered behind a concrete bunker just inland from Red Beach 2. Bob recognized Red Mike Edson in the group. As it turned out, on the previous afternoon after Bob left the USS *Maryland*, Red Mike had been ordered to make his way to the island and take command of the entire Tarawa operation.[41] He was looking at a map that was spread out on the sand and held by two other officers.

Edson had taken his helmet off and was mopping his forehead with a handkerchief. As he looked up, he noticed Bob and nodded as if to say, "I told you it would be tough." A stocky Marine officer was crouched nearby next to a radioman, speaking loudly into the handheld microphone. Bob recognized him as Dave Shoup and could hear him describing the current situation in measured, though shouted, tones. Shoup was telling Division where his front lines were and was asking for artillery support on the eastern end of the island. He put down the handset and turned to scrutinize the map with Edson. Shoup looked like a linebacker, short, stocky, barrel chested, and bull necked. There was an air of efficient competence surrounding Shoup and Edson as they plotted the next advance amidst the almost-constant din of rifle and machine-gun fire, and the occasional mortar going off near the runway. Dave Shoup looked up and Bob heard him say in a tired voice, "God, how can a man think with all this noise?"[42]

Bob asked one of the officers near Shoup if they had taken any prisoners or found anything of intelligence value. The answer was negative, so Bob headed back to Pelzel and Boardman's taro pit. After helping Pelzel sort through some captured documents, word came over from Colonel Colley that a large command bunker would be attacked shortly, and maybe there could be POWs or documents to be found. Bob headed off in that direction and was soon creeping up to a group of Marines crouched behind a coconut log wall that had been built as a tank trap by the Japanese. Ahead was a huge, rectangular blockhouse of reinforced concrete two stories high, nearly one hundred feet long, and seventy-five feet wide. Two huge concrete arches protected iron doors on the inland side, and concrete stairs led up to the roof. There didn't seem to be any firing ports, but Japanese retreating from surrounding positions had been seen ducking into the blockhouse. A Marine lieutenant shouted orders to sequence an attack from different sides. No firing came from inside the massive structure, but there were Japanese trenches and small, coconut log bunkers to each side, and occasional bursts of machine-gun fire kept the Marines under cover. Then, a command was shouted and the Marines went to work methodically taking out the various Japanese defenses. It was an amazing thing to watch, just what Bob would have expected from well-trained Marines. He was reminded of the 4th Marines he'd admired as a boy in China—professional, thorough, competent.

After about an hour, all that remained in Japanese hands was the massive concrete blockhouse itself. But how were the Marines to get into the thing? The lieutenant huddled with a couple of squad leaders, and they called for flamethrowers and explosives. Their strategy was to blow in one of the big steel doors, and then have flamethrowers shoot through the gap.[43] Several Marines with flamethrower tanks strapped to their backs crept closer, and a few others with explosive charges moved slowly and carefully up to the massive steel doors in one of the concrete-covered entrances. They set the charges and ran back to shelter right before the resulting massive explosion. Through the smoke Bob could see there was a gap blown between the two steel doors. A Marine with a flamethrower ran forward and immediately emptied a stream of fire into the opening. There were muffled noises from inside, and suddenly Japanese began to run out through the gap. Some of their uniforms were on fire, and most of them were screaming in pain and fright. The surrounding Marines opened fire immediately and cut them down. Several of the Japanese were wearing ammunition bandoleers. As the flames consumed their uniforms, the ammunition in the bandoleers started cooking off, and they were killed by a combination of the flames, their own exploding ammunition, and gunfire from the Marines.

Maybe fifty or sixty Japanese had fled the blockhouse and all were dead before they had gone twenty feet. The hail of fire from the Marines was so noisy that Bob's eardrums hurt. All of the shots were coming from within thirty feet of where he was crouched behind a pile of scrap wood and corrugated iron. The Marines were relentless and they fired without stopping, even as the last Japanese fell in a heap, black smoke pouring out of the buckled steel doors of the blockhouse behind them. The Marines seemed to be getting some measure of revenge for seeing their buddies mowed down as they had waded in helplessly to the beach. It was a rare event to actually witness such a large number of live Japanese in the open where they could be easily shot. Most of the time they were deep in their bunkers, killed invisibly by flamethrowers or satchel charges when the Marines could get close enough.

122 ★ Chapter Five

The shooting stopped and the Marines picked their way forward slowly, their rifles trained cautiously on the heap of smoldering Japanese bodies. Bob moved up with them, thinking perhaps a couple would still be alive to interrogate. But the Marine fire had been efficient. The Japanese were all dead. Once again Bob wondered if any of them would have come out voluntarily if they had somehow been given that option. He turned to go back as the Marines called up a bulldozer to push sand over the entrances to the blockhouse. If, by some miracle, any Japanese had survived inside, the bulldozer would make sure they wouldn't emerge later to kill Marines.

Bob found Pelzel, Colley, and Dutton packing up to move to the other side of the airstrip, where most of the fighting was now taking place. They wanted to stay close in case there were any prisoners. Still clutching his carbine, Bob grabbed his knapsack from the taro pit and joined the little group as they trotted another couple of hundred yards forward to get closer to the edge of the runway. The sound of combat was just on the other side of the large, open, packed-coral expanse, and the familiar tearing sound of bullets passing overhead kept them in a low crouch, moving from one shrapnel-pocked palm tree to another. It wasn't long before they stopped at the edge of the sun-dazzled white airstrip. Colonel Colley motioned ahead and started across. Bob, Pelzel, and Boardman followed.

They made it to the other side and immediately started digging foxholes. They were just off to the side of the hard packed coral surface of the runway, and there wasn't much loose material to dig into. All Marines carried a short-handled, folding shovel called an entrenching tool. Colley and Boardman broke theirs out and began digging one foxhole. Pelzel and Bob worked on another. As they took turns digging shallow depressions for cover, Bob heard a different sound over the shooting going on nearby. It was the drone of an airplane engine. He wondered if the Marines had called in air support from the Navy. He looked up and, to his surprise, saw an olive-green Japanese Zero, the bright red rising sun on its wings, banking low over the runway and turning to make a strafing run. Bob yelled out something about a Japanese plane. The rest of them looked up and immediately dropped down to press themselves into the shallow foxholes they had managed to scrape out of the hardened coral. Bob lay flat on his back in the little foxhole, so he could see what was happening, and peered up at the plane as it turned to come in low over the island. It appeared to be heading straight for them. A bomb dropped from the plane at the far end of the runway, and it exploded with a loud *bang!* Bob could see bright flashes of light on the leading edges of the wings as the Japanese pilot strafed the full length of the runway. A trail of white bursts of coral was kicked up as the bullets stitched straight toward their foxholes. This was going to be close. Bob could hear the pounding of the bullets hitting coral only feet away. The plane roared by just over-head, pulled up quickly, and banked steeply to the right to get away from the island.

After a few moments, the four of them stood up and saw the line of pockmarks in the packed coral that were three feet to one side of their little foxholes. Without saying a word, they all looked at each other and realized they had survived a very close call. Then, without miss-ing a beat, they were digging in earnest to deepen their fox holes and wondering aloud where that plane must have come from. The consen-sus was that it had flown down from the Marshalls, Japanese-occupied islands several hundred miles away. Their earlier intelligence analyses estimated that it was unlikely there would be very many enemy planes over Tarawa because it was such a long flight. The Zero must have had to use an auxiliary fuel drop-tank to get all the way to Betio.[44]

The Marines up ahead were moving more quickly and taking very few prisoners. After they reached the far side of the little island, only a couple of hundred feet from the edge of the runway, they turned to the east and pushed toward that end of the island. Bob and Pelzel were able to collect a few documents from inside the bunkers, but there were no code books. They inspected Japanese bodies to recover diaries and other personal effects. A few more shell-shocked prisoners were cap-tured alive. Many could not hear, their eardrums shattered by the noise and concussions from the intense American bombing and shelling. In some of the bunkers they entered, all the Japanese had killed themselves. A preferred technique was to remove a rubber-soled shoe, hook the big toe around the trigger of the rifle, place the upturned end of the bar-rel under the chin, and pull the trigger with the toe. Finding Japanese marines in this state was unpleasant to say the least, but Bob had little reaction. He kept reminding himself that he'd seen worse before.

That evening, Bob came across a sergeant named Shaw. He'd gone through the enlisted language program at Camp Elliott and was assisting D-2 and the language officers. Sergeant Shaw had set up what he called his "office" in a large shell hole. It was partially covered with a sheet of corrugated iron that had been blasted from the roof of one of the Japanese structures on the island, and he was collecting Japanese documents that were being brought in by Bob and the other JLOs. Shaw had handwritten a sign posted outside the little shelter. It read, "ADC [Assistant Division Commander] D-2 Language Section." A few Marines had seen the sign and had actually brought Japanese documents there.

As the darkness of the third night of battle enveloped the tiny island, Pelzel, Boardman, and Bob returned to their foxholes near the edge of the airstrip and ate C-rations. The fighting had moved farther to the east, so it was relatively quiet. Green Beach wasn't far from them, and they could hear soft splashing in the water just offshore. Boardman had just about emptied the C-ration can of cheese and crackers and wondered aloud what the splashing was.

Without looking up, Pelzel explained in a matter-of-fact tone that it was reef fish, scavengers, feeding on dead human bodies in the water. They had witnessed plenty of shocking carnage in the past three days—men blown to pieces, Marines with hideous wounds, dead Japanese killed in almost every conceivable way by various and sundry types of high explosives—but the thought of reef fish feeding on dead Marines was almost too much to take.

The next morning, the fourth day of the battle, it was apparent that the struggle for Betio Island and Tarawa Atoll was almost over.[45] Although some of the few remaining Japanese were fighting at the eastern tip of the island, the intensity of the gunfire had decreased noticeably. Marine MPs watched over 17 military prisoners being held near the pier, awaiting transport off the island. There were also 127 Korean captives, laborers brought to Betio by the Japanese to construct fortifications. A number of them were standing around on the beach under guard, and a few were wounded and had been laid out on the sand. Bob tried to interrogate them. The Koreans spoke Japanese and were willing to talk, but they didn't know much about the military situation. The Japanese marines who were still alive were badly wounded. They had intended to die at their posts. In retrospect, even if Bob could have captured a POW on that first day somehow, he wouldn't have found out much of "what was going on" for General Hermle.

Colonel Colley approached Bob and gave him an assignment, his first substantive task since he arrived at Tarawa, and one that Pelzel and Boardman had anticipated two days earlier. He was told to accompany one of the Marine combat photographers and document all the Japanese fortifications on the island. The idea was to make an intelligence estimate of the construction techniques used by the Japanese, and what it would take to destroy the structures. It was clear that the colonel didn't want a replay of the ineffectual pre-invasion bombardment on the next island landing.

The photographer was standing there ready to go, along with Joe Utz, a member of D-2 whose job was "API" (aerial photo interpretation). They got started right away. As they walked toward the big gun emplacements on the west side of the island, they passed Sergeant Shaw's "office." The photographer saw it and wanted to take a photo. Bob shrugged and jumped down into the hole with Sergeant Shaw. They both looked up from under the corrugated iron sheet, smiled, and the camera clicked. Then Bob, Utz, and the photographer went off to document every Japanese fortification they could find. It took most of two days to cover the island, and they took multiple photos of all the Japanese guns and fortifications.

Bob was surprised at the variety and ingenuity of the Japanese construction techniques. Many of the large concrete bunkers had been covered with sand to deaden the force of U.S. bombs and artillery. They had appeared as odd-looking hills in the pre-invasion aerial reconnaissance photos. The most lethal bunkers along the shoreline, the source of the machine-gun fire that had cut down hundreds of Marines as they had waded to shore, were emplacements made from double walls of coconut logs with a two-foot-thick layer of coral-sand filling and layered over with coconut logs and sand roofs. Then everything was covered over with sand, allowing small firing ports to open from the sides. Nothing but a direct hit from an artillery or naval shell could destroy such bunkers, and there were many of them along the shore. Most survived almost intact. Bob was also surprised to see a wrecked radar station, and he wondered if the Japanese had gotten it to work effectively. Huge coastal defense guns were housed in gigantic sand-covered, concrete bunkers at the corners of the atoll. These had been more obvious from the aerial photos and had been shelled heavily. It was unclear if they had been able to fire many shots before being destroyed. One had taken a direct hit on the steel barrel, and it was only a jagged stump sticking up from the steel housing.

Bob, Utz, and the photographer hurried around the island in the relentless heat and blazing equatorial sun, scrambling for hours over fortifications. After the photography was finally finished, Bob reported back to Colonel Colley, who looked pale and wrung out but was still issuing orders enthusiastically and organizing various tasks for the intelligence officers. Bob's next assignment was to return to Hawaii and write up a report on the Japanese fortifications, using the photos that had just been taken as illustrations. In the meantime, he was ordered to board the *Monrovia* and accompany the POWs back to the stockade in Hawaii. On the way, he was supposed to interrogate them and see what he could find out.

The trip to Pearl Harbor would take more than a week, so Bob would have a lot of time to do the interrogations. It seemed fairly pointless because he didn't think he could get much more out of the miserable Japanese military POWs. They seemed surly and uncommunicative, and most of them were suffering from wounds. The captured Korean laborers would talk cheerfully, but they knew almost nothing of military value.

The MPs had assembled all the POWs on the beach in a group as they waited for transport to one of the ships offshore. One Japanese noncommissioned officer was hunched glumly to one side, a large bandage around his chest and another wrapped around one leg. Bob sat down beside him. It was apparent they would be there for a while, so Bob offered him a cigarette and tried to liven him up a little bit with small talk—where was he from, how long had he been in the military, any family back home? Bob got only perfunctory, gruff replies. Several American Marines stood nearby. It was surprising and somewhat disconcerting to them to see a fellow Marine speaking Japanese casually to an enemy prisoner.

After several minutes of unsuccessful attempts at getting the Japanese POW to respond, Bob gave up and contemplated how to come up with better ways of trying to get the Japanese to surrender. The few Japanese and Koreans who had been pulled out of the bunkers had to be told repeatedly to raise their hands. It was obvious they didn't realize that raising their hands or using white flags were accepted ways of giving up. In the language course in Boulder, Bob had learned that surrender had never been part of their culture. It could explain at least part of their determination to fight to the death. Maybe if they knew there were alternatives, some of them may consider surrender as an option. If even a handful came out, it would save Marine lives because fewer Americans would have to risk going out in the open to rush the bunkers. Bob would have a long time to ponder this possibility on the trip back to Pearl Harbor.

White smoke from an enemy mortar shell, exploding at that moment, rises in the brush behind a startled Bob Sheeks, interrupting his broadcast surrender appeals using a portable amplified megaphone to his right. The involuntary reflex from the shell explosion caused the Marine combat photographer to snap the picture. Note the tin can in foreground that contains drinking water to supplement canteens. (Robert Sheeks photo)

Bob Sheeks (center) instructs Korean POWs to broadcast surrender appeals to Japanese defenders holed up in caves in cliffs up ahead. (Robert Sheeks photo)

The Sheeks family, Shanghai, circa 1928: parents Malkah and George Sr., with Bob (left) and George (right). (Sheeks family photograph)

Bob Sheeks and his Chinese amah, Shanghai, circa 1933. (Robert Sheeks photo)

Bob's lifelong friend and fellow Marine Japanese Language Officer in WWII, Dan Williams, with their bikes near the Shanghai American School. A farm owned by the Culty Dairy is in the background. Photo was taken on an outing to the countryside outside Shanghai, circa 1931. (George Sheeks photo)

George Sheeks took this photo of Japanese soldiers patrolling a neighborhood that had recently seen combat during the Shanghai Incident near the North Station in Shanghai, 1932. (George Sheeks photo)

This very unusual 1932 photo was taken by George Sheeks at the urging of the Japanese officers pictured with Bob Sheeks (center front), their father (right), and a couple of his father's friends. Bob's father was often accompanied on his hikes around the battlefields by other friends as well as Bob and George, and this photo was taken during one of those outings. This was an uncomfortable situation given the notoriously barbaric behavior of the Japanese military in Shanghai, and the uneasy relationship between the Japanese military and the American expatriate community. Bob's next close encounter with the troops of Imperial Japan came on the Pacific island battlefield of Tarawa eleven years later. (George Sheeks photo)

The man who recruited Bob and most of his classmates to be members of the Japanese Language School, Cdr. A.E. Hindmarsh, speaking at a graduation ceremony for one of the JLS classes at the University of Colorado. (University of Colorado at Boulder, University Archives, Roger Pineau Collection, Box 6, Folder 4)

Nakamura Susumu, chief instructor at the U.S. Navy Japanese Language School, instructing a class at Boulder. (University of Colorado at Boulder, University Archives, Roger Pineau Collection, Box 6, Folder 5)

Group photo of Boulder JLS sensei and families on an outing to Chautauqua Park near the University of Colorado campus, September 1942. Director Florence Walne is at center of second row from bottom in light dress; Ida Inouye is behind Florence Walne's right shoulder, and directly behind her is her husband Ari Inouye; Ashikaga sensei, who taught Bob Japanese calligraphy, is at far left in second row from bottom; Nakamura sensei is third from right bottom row. (University of Colorado at Boulder, University Archives, Roger Pineau Collection, Box 6, Folder 5)

In the JLS class that graduated a couple months after Bob's was his brother George (bottom right) and childhood friend Dan Williams (top right). Others in the photo, standing at back left is Jim DiCrocco, center back row unknown; front row far left is Arthur Dornheim, front row middle is Walt Williams. Note Dan and Walt are in Marine Corps uniforms, and the others are wearing Navy uniforms indicating the service in which they were commissioned. (University of Colorado at Boulder, University Archives, Roger Pineau Collection, Box 10, Folder 6a)

Graduation day for Bob's JLS class, January 15, 1943. Some members of the class are pictured here, from left to right, Donald Keene, Dave Osbourne, William DeBary, Frank Turner, Bill Allman (one of Bob's childhood friends from Shanghai), Sam Houston Brock, Marshall Green, Royal Ward, Sherwood "Sherry" Moran, Bob Sheeks, John Ashmead, Vincent Canzonari, and, partially visible at extreme far right, Otis Cary. (University of Colorado at Boulder, University Archives, Roger Pineau Collection, Box 6, Folder 4)

Betio Island at Tarawa Atoll, scene of the U.S. Marine landing in November 1943. The Japanese-built coral airstrip, the objective of the attack, is clearly visible at center. Bob Sheeks and other D-2 officers were strafed by a Japanese aircraft as they attempted to dig in at the right edge of the airstrip. The invasion beaches are at left on either side of the pier that extends to the edge of the reef at the left edge of the photo. Bob Sheeks spent the first night of the invasion at the end of that pier, and ended up coming ashore on the second day on Green Beach in the foreground. (National Archives, B-6514A.C.)

Bob Sheeks (left) and Segeant Shaw in an improvised document collection point in the combat area on Betio Island at Tarawa. The sign in front of this roughly covered fox hole is meant to be a humorous take on what should have been a much more secure post for the Assistant Division Commander (ADC) D-2 Language Section. (National Archives, U.S. Marine Corps 64312)

Some of the very few surrendered POWs on the beach at Tarawa near the end of the battle. Most of the POWs in the photo are Korean laborers. Bob Sheeks (kneeling at right) tries to comfort and question a mortally wounded captive before he died. (Robert Sheeks photo)

Surrender leaflet composed by Bob Sheeks and John Pelzel, printed in Honolulu and used in the Saipan and Tinian campaigns. Actual size is 5'x10", or a little larger than a business envelope. It is a simulated personal letter from a Japanese prisoner in U.S. hands attempting to convince his countrymen to give up rather than die. (Robert Sheeks collection)

Below: "Patrol Card" put together by Bob Sheeks and D-2 intelligence officers in Hawaii before the Saipan invasion to be distributed to U.S. Marines prior to the invasion. It was designed to encourage the Americans to take prisoners. (Robert Sheeks collection)

LOCATIONS OF OTHERS
てぃつに所る居の間人るゐてれくか
요데 어온곳은인이들랃사는잇머수

NUMBER OF PERSONS ?
か人幾は間人るゐてれくか
요이 명멋은랃사는 잇머수

WHO ARE THEY ?

요이정병본일 TROOPS	か 隊兵本日
요이랃사는사에섬 CIVILIANS	か 民通普
요이인도 NATIVES	か 人土
요이랃사선조 KOREANS	か 人鮮朝

APP. DISTANCE FROM HERE (FEET) ?
かる丙尺幾近所る居の間人るゐてれくか
사너됨나자멋지 써곳은 인 머수

YOU HAVE ···· MINUTES TO GET BACK
い來てっ歸れ連を間人の其に内以分 ····
요시오고리데을들랃사는인머수 에버이분 ····

45ʰ 40ʰ 35ʰ 30ʰ 25ʰ 20ʰ 15ʰ 10ʰ 5ʰ

PATROL CARD

On this card are instructions to Japanese and to Koreans. It directs them to show you on a map or by some other way where there are others hiding or in a position. If you show this man how you want him to approach the position, after he tells you where it is, he will go forward and call to the others to come out unarmed, with hands up. They are to return in single file when you motion them to return. He is directed to make no suspicious motions. Beware of trickery, but make every effort to capture as many prisoners as possible.

(Remember that some prisoners will not be able to read; some will not know where there are others.)

EVERY PRISONER TURNED IN MEANS THE SAVING OF AMERICAN LIVES, TIME, MATERIEL

CONFIDENTIAL   7 May, 1944.

TRANSLATION OF PROPAGANDA TEXTS

1.   The four propaganda leaflets, of which the following is a translation, are supplementary to those which will have been disseminated by Corps. They are on call through D-2 to be dropped by 2d MarDiv observers in carrier-based planes, and to be spread by means of 60mm mortar illuminating shells.

Format: Two large red characters meaning "common sense" or "intelligence" form the background for the text.

Theme: Use comon sense; do not die uselessly.

TRANSLATION:

Let us use common sense and examine our respective situations. Let us speak only of actualities. On land, you know that all roads are blocked. In the air, our planes are without opposition. Try as your navy would like to, it cannot hope to bring help. Every avenue of escape is denied you.

You have fought well; no one could do more, or be expected to do more. Our artillery, mortars, bombers, ships, all await only the signal to completely anihilate you. But before the lives of brave are exchanged for a few cheap shells -- let us use common sense.

Are all those who have fought as well as possible to die as animals? Are all Japanese to die for the mistakes of others? What can dead men do? "Does the dead blossom bear fruit?" - (A Japanese Proverb).
          Let the men of intelligence come forth!
          Come during daylight, singly, with hands up.
          Food, water, tobacco, and medical care await you.

Act now! There is no time for waiting!

✠ ✠

Format: Simulated Japanese personal letter, written in letter style.

Theme: A letter from a Japanese prisoner in U. S. Hands.

TRANSLATION:
To you troops who have fought bravely, it is my hope that you are well. I am a soldier just as you are, and am writing from an American camp among a great many others whose message is the same as mine.

Some of us come from the MARSHALLS, others from the GILBERTS. Many are from the ALEUTIANS or NEW GUINEA. We are what is left of units which were all over the PACIFIC.

Our life is good. Those who wish to work are paid a fair wage. Everyone receives excellent and healthful foods, and medical care. There is recreation and study.

Just as crumbling Germany or Italy we can see that Japan is being encircled and is fighting a losing battle. Are those who have fought as well as humanly possible to die? Is every Japanese to die because the fleet and our forces can no longer fight back?

What part in culture or progress can dead men play? The food, drink, rest, and good living conditions await.

As the Second Marine Division prepared for the invasion of Saipan while on the Big Island of Hawaii in the spring of 1944, Bob Sheeks and John Pelzel planned to broadcast amplified surrender appeals during the upcoming campaign. They composed four possible "P/A Directives" using words and phrases they imagined could be effective in convincing Japanese military and civilians to come out and give up. (Robert Sheeks collection)

Second Marine Division troops pinned down on the beach at Saipan, June 15, 1944. Remains of the ironwood trees that lined the shoreline can be seen at upper right. Bob Sheeks landed in this vicinity and was in much the same situation as the Marines in this photo. Note amtracs ferrying to and from the beach under fire in the background. (National Archives Marine Corps 89471)

John Pelzel, Bob's immediate superior and senior Second Marine Division Japanese Language Officer, pictured in the latter stages of the Saipan campaign holding a Japanese sign, Charan Kanoa, South Saipan, July 1944. (Robert Sheeks photo)

Marine language officers and U.S. naval intelligence officers on Saipan during the campaign. Bob Sheeks is far left back row, Otis Cary in beard next to Bob in back row, John Decker standing at upper right, Reed Irvine seated in front row third from left. (University of Colorado at Boulder, University Archives, Roger Pineau Collection, Box 10, Folder 6)

Second Marine Division D-2 headquarters in a damaged building near Garapan, Saipan. Bob Sheeks (at back) listens to radio transmissions and determines that an English-speaking Japanese is attempting to direct Marine artillery strikes on American positions. At left is D-2 commander, Colonel Colley, and his assistant, Capt. Tom Dutton, is seated at right. (Robert Sheeks photo).

Second Marine Division forces advance northward across the coastal plain on Saipan. The inland limestone cliffs in background are typical of those that contained caves sheltering Japanese military and civilians. Shortly after this photo was taken, the tank hit a mine and small arms fire opened up from caves in cliffs in background. (Robert Sheeks photo)

Moment of truth on Saipan. Bob Sheeks uses his jeep-mounted loudspeaker system for the first time. Note Marines in background have their weapons slung to appear less threatening to the surrendering Japanese. Second Marine Division sector on Saipan, June 1944. (Robert Sheeks photo)

A Japanese civilian, dressed in a Japanese army uniform and carrying an injured girl, has just come out from a cave after hearing surrender appeals broadcast by Bob Sheeks from his jeep-mounted loudspeakers. North Saipan, June 1944. (Robert Sheeks photo)

Bob Sheeks broadcasts surrender appeals toward caves in the distance from his jeep-mounted loudspeakers. Central West plain, North Saipan, July 1944. (Robert Sheeks photo)

A Japanese girl broadcasts appeals for her parents to come out of caves in the distance. Bob Sheeks is holding the amplified megaphone. Marines on truck in background, anxious to return to their lines, watch impatiently. Man in pith helmet at left front is a Japanese civilian from Saipan who has volunteered to help with surrenders. (Robert Sheeks photo)

This squad of Marines watches as Bob Sheeks, unarmed and out of the photo to the left, approaches a cave on Saipan. Shortly after this photo was taken, Bob accepted the surrender of a group of about ten Japanese soldiers in a sword presentation ceremony. (Robert Sheeks photo)

Bob Sheeks uses a portable amplifier powered by a truck battery (on pole behind Bob) to broadcast surrender appeals to hold-outs in caves on Saipan in Col. Bill Jones sector, July 1944. (Robert Sheeks photo)

A Japanese civilian climbs down from a cave on Saipan while Bob Sheeks (top) tries to convince more civilians to come out. (Robert Sheeks photo)

Marines in background watch as Japanese civilians jump to their deaths from cliffs above ocean at Marpi Point, Saipan. Note Japanese civilian in pith helmet in foreground who was assigned by Civil Affairs to assist Bob Sheeks. For safety he is wearing an arm band indicating, in English and Japanese, that he is officially assisting the Americans. (Robert Sheeks photo)

The beginning of a difficult day during the mopping-up phase of the Saipan campaign. Bob Sheeks (center, holding megaphone) prepares to accompany a squad of Marines down to a ledge below their position to locate Japanese hold-outs. The sergeant in charge of the squad (just to the right of Bob) explains the operation to a couple of the Marines. Shortly after this photo was taken, they discovered a Japanese encampment, and one of the Marines was horribly wounded by "friendly fire," receiving a rifle bullet through his left hip joint into his groin. Bob rushed him to the field hospital to undergo emergency surgery. (Robert Sheeks photo)

On Saipan, one of several excavated tunnel entrances to a Japanese Army communications center. Radio transmitting equipment shown in this photo had been tossed outside by Marines. (Robert Sheeks photo)

Bob Sheeks at the end of the Saipan campaign standing before a Japanese flag near the headquarters of Vice Admiral Chuichi Nagumo. Nagumo had been in command of the Japanese naval force that attacked Pearl Harbor, as well as the armada that later tried to invade Midway Island in June of 1942. Blamed for the disastrous Japanese defeat at Midway, he was assigned to Saipan to take charge of sea, land, and air defense of the Mariana Islands. When it became clear that the battle for Saipan was lost, Nagumo and Army General Yoshitsugu Saito issued the order for the final banzai charge on July 7, 1944. Without waiting to see the outcome, Nagumo and Saito committed suicide shortly thereafter. U.S. admiral Turner announced on July 9 that the island was officially "secured," though mopping-up operations continued for weeks. Nagumo's giant Japanese navy flag was the size of those used on large ships. Saipan, July 1944. (Robert Sheeks photo)

UNITED STATES MARINE CORPS

HEADQUARTERS
FLEET MARINE FORCE, PACIFIC
C/O FLEET POST OFFICE, SAN FRANCISCO

In the name of the President of the United States, the Commanding General, Fleet Marine Force, Pacific, takes pleasure in awarding the BRONZE STAR MEDAL to

FIRST LIEUTENANT ROBERT B. SHEEKS,
UNITED STATES MARINE CORPS RESERVE

for service as set forth in the following
CITATION:

"For heroic achievement in action against the enemy while serving as a Japanese interpreter with the intelligence section of a Marine division on SAIPAN and TINIAN, MARIANAS ISLANDS, from 15 June to 1 August, 1944. Prior to the MARIANAS campaign, First Lieutenant SHEEKS did pioneer service in devising methods of directing combat propaganda at the Japanese. With outstanding initiative and energy he prepared several means of propaganda that were used extensively and with good results by two Marine divisions. During the latter stages of the operations on both SAIPAN and TINIAN, when large numbers of civilians were driven into hiding by our advance, First Lieutenant SHEEKS was constantly, and at considerable personal danger, with front line units utilizing public address systems to call civilians and soldiers out of hiding. By effecting the surrender, alive and safe, of large numbers of these civilians, First Lieutenant SHEEKS aided the tactical mission of his division and assisted in the saving of many hundreds of non-combatant lives. His display of loyalty, outstanding service, and devotion to duty was in keeping with the highest traditions of the United States Naval Service."

H. M. SMITH,
Lieutenant General,
U. S. Marine Corps.

Above: Bob Sheeks is awarded the Bronze Star by General Watson, commander of the Second Marine Division, for his actions on Saipan, August 1944. (Robert Sheeks photo)

Below: Bob Sheeks' Bronze Star citation. (Robert Sheeks collection)

Second Marine Division D-2 headquarters set up in a railroad cut on Tinian shortly after the landing. The man in the foreground hoisting a tent pole is Frank Turner, Boulder JLO and a close friend of Bob and Otis Cary. Frank lived in the Manoa Valley house with Bob, Otis, and the other JLOs in Honolulu before the Saipan campaign. (Robert Sheeks photo)

A Korean civilian on Tinian, wearing white clothing for surrender as instructed in the surrender leaflets, assists Bob Sheeks in broadcasting surrender appeals in Japanese and Korean using Bob's improvised jeep-mounted loudspeaker and amplifier rig, including its own gasoline-powered electrical generator. (Robert Sheeks photo)

An Okinawan farmer (lower left, holding child), who has just surrendered, has identified the man at center front (without shirt) as a Japanese soldier who was pretending to be a civilian. Bob Sheeks (center, with camouflage shirt) and fellow Marine JLO Reed Irvine (in helmet and open shirt to right of Sheeks) translate as the two argue. Tinian Island, August 1944. (Robert Sheeks photo)

Bob Sheeks interrogates two Japanese civilians during the Tinian operation, August 1944. (Robert Sheeks photo)

A welcoming delegation, including Bob Sheeks of the Asia Foundation (far left), greets newly elected Vice President Richard Nixon (far right) and his wife Pat (center, receiving a floral bouquet). The photo was taken on their arrival in Malaya during their fact-finding tour. Standing behind is Mr. Eric Kocher, American Consul General in Malaya. Kuala Lumpur Airport, October 1953. (Robert Sheeks photo)

Bob Sheeks (left) and Jerry Meehl, 2009, Santa Rosa. (Photo by Marla Meehl)

SIX
Between Campaigns: Hawaii, 1943–44

The *Monrovia*, direct from Tarawa, pulled through a break in the reef marked by buoys and into the channel leading to Pearl Harbor. Homes with newly planted trees around them lined the shore on the right. Those were the houses of Army Air Corps officers based at Hickam Field. The airfield and hangars located just behind had been bombed during the Japanese attack. Straight ahead, Bob could see the remains of what had been Battleship Row on December 7. He recalled the Pearl Harbor survivors telling him their vivid stories when he was in the hospital in Denver with his broken leg the previous year. A number of cranes and repair ships clustered around what looked like a massive, steel turtle shell next to Ford Island. It was actually the capsized hull of the USS *Oklahoma*. Workers scrambled over the wreck in their ongoing efforts to salvage the remains of the ship. The forlorn and abandoned wreckage of the USS *Arizona* lay farther along. By late 1943 it was a familiar image. Bob had seen photos in the newspaper, the forward mast and crow's nest canted forward at an angle, the ship settled down into the water. The Navy crew on the *Monrovia* had mustered on the main deck and stood silently at attention along the port-side railing. They saluted as they glided slowly past the already iconic remains of the sunken ship. Most of the Arizona's crew was still below decks, entombed there on December 7. The ship would never be salvaged.

After the *Monrovia* tied up to the dock, Bob helped the MPs usher the captured Japanese and Koreans from Tarawa to the POW stockade at the naval base. As they filed in to a fenced enclosure, a short, vaguely Asian-looking naval officer came hustling over. It was none other than Frank

Huggins, the most fluent Japanese language student in the class ahead of Bob at Berkeley. They shook hands and perfunctorily reconfirmed their JLS connection. Frank seemed distracted, just like the first day Bob met him at Berkeley. Motioning to the Tarawa POWs, Bob said he didn't get much useful intelligence information from the Japanese marines on their ride to Pearl, and the larger number of Korean laborers, though cooperative, had little to tell. Frank was unimpressed and pointed out that some of the POWs had opened up a little once they got settled in the compound, implying he had his own ways of getting information out of POWs.

Bob's impression of Frank was that he had an aloofness that made it difficult to get along with him. He still had his tough attitude toward the Japanese. Bob wondered if Frank, being half Japanese, was struggling to distance his own heritage from the POWs. Huggins casually waved the Tarawa prisoners into the camp to join the Japanese captured at Guadalcanal, who eyed the newcomers with passive, blank stares.

As Bob was about to leave and look for CINCPAC, the headquarters of Adm. Chester Nimitz, another familiar but much more welcome figure approached from inside the compound. It was Otis Cary, Bob's roommate in Berkeley and classmate in Boulder. After a warm greeting, Bob gave him an update on the prisoners he had brought in and expressed his reservations about Huggins' methods. Otis shrugged and admitted Frank still had issues, but he quickly changed the subject to Bob's accommodation situation. He invited Bob to move in to a house that Otis and some of their JLS colleagues had rented close to the university in the Manoa Valley. Though on the far side of downtown Honolulu, and thus quite a distance from Pearl Harbor, Otis said they usually took the local buses to work. But on this particular day he happened to have a car from the motor pool and offered to give Bob a ride to the house. He could get away in about an hour.

In the meantime, Bob caught a jeep to Nimitz's Aiea headquarters building, which was a short ride away at Makalapa Hill overlooking Pearl Harbor. A sign that read "CINCPAC" confirmed that Bob had found the right place. He made his way through the door, brushing against naval officers as they hustled in and out. The orderly on duty found Bob's name on one of those mysterious lists that always seemed to precede people wherever they went in the military. He wordlessly handed Bob a typewritten sheet of paper. It was signed by Colonel Colley, with a note from John Pelzel handwritten at the top. It confirmed in writing the instructions he had received on Tarawa, that he was to prepare a report on Japanese fortifications he had helped photograph. A draftsman had been assigned to come up with detailed drawings based on the photographs and measurements they had made of some of the structures. In the crisp words of the orders, he was given permission to request any further assistance needed in documenting all relevant aspects of the fortifications to assist in future interpretation of aerial reconnaissance photos. The orderly directed him to his assigned workspace. He soon found the office, and standing at the door at the end of the hallway was a Marine guard. Bob noticed the letters "FRUPAC" on the door behind the guard. This was the Fleet Radio Unit Pacific, the code breakers. It was top secret, and Bob couldn't get anywhere near it. The documents he would prepare on Japanese fortifications were also meant to be secret and classified, though far below the security level of the code-breaking operation and not connected in any way to FRUPAC.

This was day one of Bob's nearly six-month Hawaiian idyll, a kind of suspended animation between bouts of island combat. The rest of the 2nd Marine Division had been shipped to Kamuela on the Big Island of Hawaii to train for what would become the invasion of Saipan, though they didn't know it yet. Meanwhile, Bob would work mainly on the summary and analysis of the Japanese fortifications on Betio. In addition to the pictures he'd directed the photographer to take at the end of the Tarawa battle, he also included captured maps, photos, diagrams and other material in the document. In his spare time he worked on improving his Japanese.

Bob soon met up with Otis for the drive from the CINCPAC building in Aiea to the house in Manoa. It was a scenic traverse through southern Oahu and Honolulu. Stunning green mountains formed the spine of the island and rose dramatically behind the city. The car windows were open to the soft, warm, Hawaiian breezes carrying the scents of flowers and lush tropical vegetation. Otis pointed out the sights as they drove past the red-light district of downtown Honolulu. Bob heard later that brothels in this area, with their huge lines of American servicemen, rivaled the "Pink House" in Noumea. The remarkable assembly-line efficiency of those mass-production operations was astounding to contemplate.[1]

The car turned onto Kalakaua Avenue, the main drag of Waikiki. Otis noted the elegant Royal Hawaiian and Moana Hotels as they drove past, both set near to each other on the ocean side of Kalakaua, amid palm trees and immaculately manicured grounds. Newspapers in the 1930s routinely featured Hollywood stars lounging on the famous golden sands of Waikiki Beach in front of these storied establishments. Bob was surprised when Otis told him the Navy had taken over the Royal Hawaiian as a rest and recreation facility, and had it reserved mainly for submarine crews.

The car finally turned inland, wound through a series of quiet, residential neighborhoods, and pulled up in front of an unassuming bungalow. A palm tree graced the neatly trimmed lawn, and red hibiscus flowers sprouted from a bush in the front yard. Bob climbed out of the car, walked up to the front porch and into the house, and suddenly it was like old-home week. Inside he was greeted by his friends from the language school in Boulder, including Sherwood "Sherry" Moran, Bob Boyd, and Frank Turner. He hadn't seen them since they had graduated earlier that year, only about ten months before, though their language studies at the University of Colorado already seemed like ages ago.

For the rest of the afternoon, Otis and the other language officers in the house insisted that Bob tell them about his Tarawa experiences. Though Otis had been present for the Attu and Kiska operations in the North Pacific, none of them had been in actual combat.[2] Bob's stories seemed quite exotic to his fellow JLS graduates. They shook their heads in amazement at the ludicrous order from General Hermle to capture a prisoner and "find out what's going on," and they listened with rapt attention to his tale of trying to make his way to Betio Island on the pier under fire.

That evening, shortly after the sunset lit the soft, trade wind cumulus clouds over Honolulu vivid shades of orange and purple, Otis suggested they go for a walk around the neighborhood. Walks at dusk soon became a part of their daily routine. Their stroll took them over to the University of Hawaii. The broad, grassy expanses of the tropical campus were dotted with exotic, leafy trees and flowering plumeria. It was quite a contrast to the pine trees and mountains of Colorado where they had been classmates just months earlier.

Their discussion turned to friends they knew from the JLS in Boulder. Otis told Bob that his classmates and childhood friends from Shanghai, Bill Allman and Bucky Freeman, were also working in Honolulu for naval intelligence and had rented a house in the exclusive neighborhood of Black Point, near Diamond Head. They lived almost next door to the mansion of world-famous heiress Doris Duke.

Otis described his duties in naval intelligence and civil affairs. He thought he'd probably be sent out to the Pacific to continue the work he'd been doing in Honolulu interrogating Japanese POWs. He was in a reflective mood, as he often was, and still worried about his role in the war. He was interrogating POWs and translating documents with the ultimate goal of getting information that would help to kill more Japanese. He knew this was what he had been trained to do, and he had agreed to do it, but he continued to fret that his duties would negatively impact his plan of traveling to Japan after the war to do missionary work. He was worried that if the Japanese found out he'd helped kill their countrymen, it would sour their attitude toward him, thereby ruining his effectiveness as a missionary and teacher.

Otis had confided some of these feelings before in Boulder. While Bob understood his point, it still exasperated him. It had always been an irritant between them. Bob tried to point out again, patiently, that the United States was at war with Japan, and how could Otis expect a war to be fought without killing? The Japanese military was vicious, and the rumors about them fighting to the death were true. Bob had seen it up close on Tarawa. The Marines were going to have to kill a lot of them before it was over.

Bob still had little empathy for the Japanese military. The nisei instructors in Boulder, as well as the nisei sergeant who had helped him with the interrogations in Noumea, had made him realize the problem was not with the Japanese civilians. But there was no doubt in his mind the Japanese military was unfathomably and brutally dedicated to death and destruction. It seemed to Bob that the whole of Japanese society had gone off the rails under the influence of the Bushido military doctrine. Otis was less critical, more conciliatory, and with his missionary attitude, he had greater concerns about his future working with the Japanese than the present direction of the nation of Japan.

Bob soon adjusted to the somewhat unusual habits of his housemates. Being academics as well as language officers, they probably exhibited more than the usual set of personality quirks that could be expected in a group of males. As a case in point, Bob noted that Frank Turner had a unique way of starting the day. He would rise, head to the kitchen, light a cigarette, open the fridge, take out a beer, open it and take a large gulp, and let out a resounding belch that echoed through every room in the house. He did this every morning right on schedule. It seemed to have an alarm-clock-like effect on the rest of the roommates because it was hard to sleep through. When they heard Frank going through his morning ritual, they knew it was time to get up.

The next week several of the roommates from the Manoa house headed to Waikiki to try to learn how to surf. They rented massive, long surfboards and soon were exhausted trying to paddle out and catch the waves. Bob finally gave up and dragged himself up on the beach to catch his breath. He started talking to a group of rookie surfers who were also trying to regain their strength. One introduced himself as Richard, a half-British, half-Chinese professor from Shanghai. He was living in Honolulu near the UH campus in Manoa and was to be married on February 11, 1944, to a woman named Iris. Given their common Shanghai background, they hit it off, and Bob was invited to the small wedding ceremony and reception to be held at the house of a female faculty member from the university.

On the appointed day, Bob made his way to the Kahala neighborhood, near Diamond Head, in the vicinity of Black Point where Bucky and Bill were billeted. The ceremony was held at a bungalow surrounded by lush, tropical vegetation. It featured an enclosed, grassy backyard ringed by flowering plants that gave the space an exotic greenhouse-like feel. Bob arrived in his Marine uniform, surveyed the guests, and noted they were all civilians. There were several Chinese, and some friends of Richard and Iris from the university where he taught. Richard welcomed Bob and eagerly introduced him to his bride-to-be. Bob had barely congratulated Iris on her impending wedding when it was time for the ceremony to start. The guests, totaling about twenty, gathered in a semicircle in the shade under the lanai, a covered porch. Richard was wearing a black tuxedo, and Iris was resplendent in a white satin wedding dress. For the ceremony they stood under an archway of vines and plants sprinkled with bright-red hibiscus flowers.

Bob was trying to pay attention to the ceremony but was distracted by one of the women in the wedding party. She was wearing a form-fitting flowered dress and was strikingly attractive, with long black hair and a pink plumeria blossom over one ear. She looked faintly Polynesian but appeared to be a lovely mixture of European, Asian, and Hawaiian. Her exotic features were accentuated by dark eyebrows arched over shining brown eyes. Bob thought she looked like a fashion model. He remained focused on her slender figure, barely aware there was a wedding going on.

After a mercifully simple and straightforward exchange of vows, the wedding party led the guests to the garden, where a white tablecloth covered a long table with drinks at one end and food at the other. Bob edged closer to the woman who had distracted him from the ceremony and introduced himself. She was immediately friendly, said her name was Makanui, and asked about his duties in the Marines. Bob tried to carry on a conversation but he couldn't stop staring at her. She was possibly the most beautiful woman he had ever spoken to, even counting the Hollywood actresses he'd dated courtesy of Sid Salkow back in California.

It turned out she was a hula dancer in a nightclub restaurant in Waikiki. Bob asked if he could see her dance some time, and she invited him to her next performance at a place called La Hula Rhumba in Waikiki. With a name like that, Bob wondered what kind of nightclub it was. He promised to show up there some night soon to watch her dance.

One evening the following week, Bob made his way to La Hula Rhumba. It was within walking distance from the Moana and the Royal Hawaiian and the other top hotels in Waikiki. The nightclub was in a huge, theater-like building. On his way in, he noticed a number of expensive cars and limousines parked outside. Bob was shown to a table, and he ordered a drink and waited for the show to start. The club was a real showplace, like a tropical version of Radio City Music Hall, exuding class and elegance, with a large stage and orchestra. The diners were well dressed, definitely not Waikiki beach-bum types as Bob had feared when Makanui had told him the name of the place.

There were a series of musical and dance numbers, one after another, with a group of Hawaiian singers and their guitars adding a more traditional local flavor to the large orchestra behind them. As a finale, the lights dimmed, and off to the side of the stage Makanui appeared, bathed in a spotlight. She was dramatically dressed in a floor-length, tropical-flower-patterned dress. Her shining, long, black hair was set off by a lei of white plumeria blossoms draped around her slender neck and over her shoulders. The orchestra music swelled, and the Hawaiian singers' harmonies washed out over the hushed audience. Makanui began to move to the rhythms of the music, her feet slowly stepping from side to side, arms extended in fluid motion, hands arching gracefully in the ancient hula dance style that expressed the meanings of the song. Bob was awestruck. He thought her supple, graceful movements were sheer poetry. When her dance ended, the audience applauded so enthusiastically she had to return to the stage several times, waving and bowing to her admirers.

Bob motioned to a waiter and asked him to take Makanui a message. It was an invitation to join him at his table. A few moments later she walked over and sat next to him. Bob was almost speechless, overwhelmed by her mesmerizing performance. He finally complimented her dancing. She smiled and said the missionaries had tried to stamp out the hula, but it had survived somehow, and she had been studying and practicing and innovating for several years. She had two more performances that evening, and she asked him to stick around until she got off work.

After her final dance, they walked to Waikiki Beach and made their way to the beach in front of the landmark pink stucco Royal Hawaiian Hotel. An orchestra was playing in the hotel ballroom. Faint strains of big band music could be heard above the soft, lapping sounds of small waves washing on the golden sand. They meandered slowly along the seashore, past the other stately main hotel on Waikiki, the Moana. Its Victorian wood-frame outline was silhouetted against the stars. The hotel's form was an open U shape facing the ocean. A huge banyan tree dominated the courtyard in the middle of the U. A band was playing there, too, a smaller one, with Hawaiian instruments and guitars accompanying singers. The Hawaiian harmonies blended softly under the spreading canopy of limbs overhead. Laughter and clinking glasses sounded from under the lattice of the tangled branches.

They continued to walk and talk, and soon they were past the end of the beach and out into Kapiolani Park. Its grassy expanse, dotted with palms and other tropical trees, was dominated by the imposing backdrop of Diamond Head. The dark outline of the extinct volcano loomed behind the park in the moonlight. Bob felt like he was in a movie, strolling in Hawaii with a beautiful South Seas girl under the moon and stars and palm trees. Ahead on the shoreline they could see the outline of the Natatorium, an ornately decorated concrete grandstand at the water's edge, built as a memorial to the veterans of World War I. Its low concrete walls enclosed part of the ocean to create a calm, seawater swimming pool. Makanui explained that Johnny Weissmuller and local Hawaiian surfing legend Duke Kahanamoku had swum in competitions there. Bob remarked that when his parents visited Honolulu in the early 1920s, his father had met Duke. Then, much too soon for Bob, Makanui said it was late and she had better head for home. They ambled back to Waikiki, and Bob flagged down a taxi that would take her to a house near Hickam Field, where she said she resided with her mother and aunts.

Bob's days became a mix of work on the Tarawa fortifications document during the day, and dates with Makanui, sometimes for lunch, and other times after she got off work at night. She always met Bob somewhere in Honolulu and took a taxi to and from her home. This was convenient for Bob, so he didn't think too much about the fact he had never seen where she lived. He figured she didn't want her mother and aunts to know she was dating a Marine.

Pleasant thoughts of Makanui made concentrating on the Tarawa document a challenge. Bob also had something else on his mind: how to convince the Japanese to surrender. This thought process had started on Tarawa and continued after he had returned and checked in at Kamuela on the Big Island of Hawaii. The 2nd Marine Division was stationed there to recuperate for the next island invasion. This involved not only rest, but also taking on and training replacements for those killed and wounded on Tarawa. Kamuela was the home of the Parker Ranch, a sprawling, world-famous cattle operation. The Big Island was located within the latitudes of the tropics, but the desiccated brown tufts of grass, crumbled black lava, and cactus on the dry side of the Big Island reminded Bob of Arizona or Green's Farm outside San Diego. The vegetation was not very tropical, and the altitude of Kamuela, high on the flanks of the Mauna Kea volcano, kept the weather surprisingly cool. Though the Marines were living in tents much like their previous camp at Paekakariki in New Zealand, the drier climate of Kamuela was a welcome improvement.

During his visits to Kamuela, Bob talked to Pelzel and Boardman about what specific methods they could use to take more prisoners. There were several obstacles they had to surmount, and they had already identified some of those on Tarawa while the battle still raged. Near the top of the list was how to actually communicate surrender instructions to Japanese who were holed up in fortified positions. It was very difficult for anyone to hear anything over the noise of combat, least of all potential POWs in concrete bunkers. They agreed that amplified megaphones or loudspeakers could be the answer.

Though Pelzel couldn't tell Bob which island was the upcoming target for their next operation, he indicated there would likely be a big civilian population, and that made the issue of surrenders even more urgent. Bob proposed dropping leaflets printed with basic surrender information, and then using amplified sound systems to broadcast surrender appeals through loudspeakers to civilians or Japanese military in fortified positions. They also discussed how they could use portable megaphones, as well as larger speakers mounted on a jeep, with a gas-powered generator to run an amplifier. Pelzel agreed to promote the ideas to Colonel Colley, and Bob would take the lead in organizing the surrender leaflets and securing the megaphones, amplifiers, and speakers that would be required to make their plan work.

Then the scheming began as to how to acquire the equipment. At the start, Bob had no funds with which to buy anything, but then he got help. Pelzel not only obtained the support for the effort from Colonel Colley, but he asked the colonel if Division recreation equipment and even some cash from the recreation fund could be made available for Bob's project. He argued that the Division wouldn't be doing much in the way of recreation in the midst of preparing for the upcoming campaign, and Colonel Colley agreed. Using those funds, Bob was able to buy some of the larger pieces of equipment, including big speakers. He also scrounged some Navy battery-operated megaphones usually used for directing beach operations during a landing.

Then there was the matter of the leaflets with instructions in Japanese describing how to surrender. Bob came up with a draft "Surrender Pass," treating surrender as normal and honorable, with directions on how to surrender safely without being killed. Pass holders were instructed to come forward, wave a white flag or cloth of some kind, and hold their hands above their heads. He also composed four different surrender leaflets, three in Japanese and one to be translated into Korean. Because Otis was the most fluent of the language officers, Bob ran the Japanese texts by him, and he made some grammatical corrections. Then they took the drafts to the Pearl Harbor POW camp, where Otis and Frank Huggins got a few of the Japanese POWs to read them. When the POWs looked at the texts and didn't break out laughing, it was Bob's first clue that he may be on to something. A few of the Japanese prisoners went a step further and actually made constructive suggestions to help improve the style and clarity of the wording. As a final check, two of the other language officers at the Manoa house read over the leaflets and agreed it was worth a try.

D-2 also put together something they called a "patrol card." This was intended to be a kind of "how-to" guide for American Marines. After taking prisoners, they could read English language versions of various key questions and point to translated subtitles in Japanese and Korean, asking "locations of others," "number of persons," "who are they," "approximate distance from here (feet)," and "you have X minutes to get back." The idea was to encourage Marines to actually take prisoners, and then use the patrol card to find out additional information. The final instruction in English was, "Every prisoner turned in means the saving of American lives, time, materiel."[3]

But then there was a snag. Bob had run out of resources, having exhausted the Division recreation budget to buy the megaphones, loudspeakers, and amplifiers. There was nothing left to pay for printing the leaflets. Because the cheapest paper available was newsprint, Bob went down to the office of the local newspaper, the *Honolulu Advertiser*. After hearing his pitch and the emphasis on helping the war effort, it didn't take any additional convincing. The newspaper agreed to print the leaflets in color, on newsprint, free of charge. Thousands of copies were printed, each about 5"x10", a little larger than a business envelope.

Two of the Japanese-language leaflets included red as well as black characters. One had the characters for "Common Sense" splashed in bright red across the face of the leaflet. The black print underneath reviewed what the Japanese defenders were presumably experiencing, namely defeat. They had fought well, so why die needlessly "for the mistakes of others?" The text of this leaflet ended with the words, "Let the men of intelligence come forth! Come during daylight, singly, with hands up. Food, water, tobacco and medical care await you. Act now! There is no time for waiting!"[4]

Another was a simulated personal letter, written as if it were an actual message from a Japanese soldier addressed to his countrymen. The salutation read, "To you troops who have fought bravely." The text described a good life for a POW. The "letter" ended with, "What part in culture or progress can dead men play? The food, drink, rest and good living conditions await. We are all hoping that you will save your life." It was signed, "A comrade in America."[5]

The third also had colored print as well as black. It had the characters for "Military Secret" in bright red in the upper right-hand corner, and it was written in field order style. The theme was that Japan was losing the war, and this fact had been a well-kept "military secret" from Japanese troops in the islands. The final line read, "Do not waste your lives for lies."[6]

The Korean-language leaflet stressed the theme of Korean independence. The text attempted to exploit the resentment the Koreans felt for the Japanese as a result of the brutal occupation of their country and exploitation of their citizens. One of the lines read, "Strike a blow now for Korean freedom! You have a chance now to free yourselves," and ended, "For Korean independence the time is now!"[7] While the leaflets were being printed, the translated texts were recorded later in a confidential document signed by John Pelzel, the assistant D-2 for the 2nd Marine Division "in the field," actually on the Big Island of Hawaii.[8]

Having solved the documentation and printing problems, next was the logistical issue of delivery. The initial idea was to fire artillery shells filled with leaflets at the enemy lines, or to use U.S. carrier planes to drop the flyers. But then Pelzel suggested, and then arranged for, artillery spotter planes assigned to the 2nd Marine Division to drop the leaflets over enemy troops and civilians during the upcoming operation. But how would the pilots make the drops? Bob devised a simple method of release that involved first wrapping bundles of about a hundred leaflets in brown paper, then tying each bundle with a string that was easy to break. Attached to the string was a strong cord about fifteen feet long, and the end of that cord was to be tied to the frame of the plane inside the cockpit. When the bundle was dropped and the cord played out to its fifteen-foot length, the string would snap, thus releasing the leaflets that would be scattered by the plane's prop wash and flutter to the ground. The pilots of the artillery spotter planes could be directed to specific map coordinates over Japanese positions to make the drops.

The portable amplified megaphones were light enough to be carried by hand and would probably be adequate for close-in appeals, but a jeep would be required to handle the large loudspeakers and motorized generator to run the amplifier. This setup would be used at a distance when it was too dangerous to get in close to Japanese positions, or in situations where amplified appeals needed to be broadcast in areas of inaccessible terrain. The generator was relatively easy to requisition because the Division was planning on bringing some along to run radios and other equipment. But the sergeant at the motor pool was less than enthusiastic about mounting the equipment on a jeep. He was a grizzled Marine combat veteran from Guadalcanal, and he thought he'd seen just about everything, until the young lieutenant standing in front of him started talking about getting the Japanese to surrender. He tried to be polite and, as respectfully as possible, pointed out to Bob that he was wasting his time because the Japanese on Guadalcanal never surrendered. In spite of his skepticism, the sergeant helped Bob fill out the paperwork, and his request for a jeep was usefully labeled "POW intelligence cost." He arranged for the vehicle and all its equipment to be combat-loaded on an attack transport, so that it would come off early in the invasion and be ready for use as soon as possible.

Bob and John Pelzel composed a number of "P/A Directive Texts" designed to provide guidance for possible appeals to be broadcast with the amplified sound devices. They spent time trying to imagine the phrases that could be used most effectively to convince Japanese civilians and military to come out of hiding. They specifically did not use the word "surrender," which had negative connotations for the Japanese, but "come out" was a more palatable choice.[9]

There was one last obstacle to face, and it was probably the toughest nut to crack. It was the attitude and actions of the Marines themselves. They would have to be convinced that it was worth giving the Japanese a chance to give up. For the surrender passes, patrol cards, and leaflets to work, Bob would need time to broadcast amplified surrender appeals before the Marines moved in with the overwhelming firepower necessary to snuff out recalcitrant Japanese. The tools of this trade typically involved grenades, flamethrowers and high-explosive satchel charges. Colonel Colley, using his authority as head of D-2, arranged for Bob to give lectures to combat units of the Division to persuade them the surrender business was worth a try. It was a tough sell.

The first group consisted of squad sergeants and their combat teams. They were gathered in an open, natural amphitheater on a slope of the volcano on a warm, breezy evening just after sunset. Bob explained the basic problem, and that it was important to take prisoners. The response was probably predictable. From the back, one of the sergeants, a Tarawa veteran, yelled, "With all due respect, lieutenant, are you out of your fucking mind?"[10] This was met with a roar of laughter from the rest of them.

Bob stood his ground and patiently made his case. He argued that if they could get some of the Japanese to surrender, it would mean fewer of the enemy shooting and killing Marines. Additionally, the prisoners could then be interrogated to reveal where others were hiding, especially snipers. The idea was to save Marine lives. From live prisoners they could get information. It would be better to know where fortified and camouflaged emplacements were located, and where the enemy was holed up, instead of finding out the hard way by sacrificing Marines. Another voice yelled out, "It's our job to kill the bastards. We prefer to shoot them!" More laughter. It wasn't going well. Bob could see it was going to be an uphill battle.

At each of the units he talked to, he usually got a similar reaction. It was like force-feeding a person who just finished a big dinner—it just wouldn't go down. But most officers were only minimally hostile to the idea, and Bob thought the Marines would give him a chance to try and talk some Japanese into surrendering if the situation were right.

To Bob, it simply made sense to use the leaflets, surrender passes, and loudspeaker gear to save civilian lives and perhaps even some military. He would rather have the Japanese surrender than get in the way or shoot at Marines. But he was aware that it wasn't just about saving Marine lives. It really was about saving lives, period, American and Japanese. The pointless death of anyone simply didn't make sense to him, especially after what he saw in Shanghai and Tarawa.

After Bob returned to Honolulu from his difficult lecture tour on the Big Island, he concentrated on putting the finishing touches on the Tarawa report. It had turned into a three-volume set and, though the bulk of the work had been completed in late 1943 and early 1944, there were inevitable loose ends involved with the final publication. The three volumes constituted an impressive compilation of descriptions, photos, and maps of the Japanese fortifications and facilities on Betio.[11] The phone rang in his office, and he guessed it was Pelzel calling to ask how the lectures to the 2nd Marine Division went. But on the other end of the line was a female voice. It was Makanui, and she had to talk to him. It was urgent. He was to meet her at a café in Waikiki for lunch.

Given her distraught tone, his first thought was one that would spring into the feverish minds of most other healthy young men in a similar situation—she must be pregnant. If so, what should he do? The honorable thing would be to marry her. But that was out of the question because he was most certainly going to be leaving very soon for combat. Getting married was the last thing he wanted to think about.

As lunchtime rolled around, he took a Navy shuttle bus to Waikiki to meet with her at the appointed place and time. Bob sat down across from her, and she started to speak quickly. Right off the bat she said she had three things to tell him: first, she was married; second, her husband had found out about their affair; and third, he had sworn to find Bob and kill him. They looked at each other silently. Bob's initial reaction was relief— she wasn't pregnant—but then her husband's threat quickly sunk in, and relief changed to shock. She guessed Bob's next question would be why she didn't tell him she was married. What Bob actually wanted to know was how her husband found out.

She shook her head and, cool as a cucumber, said she herself had told him. She went on to describe a terrible fight she'd had with her husband,

and how she wanted to hurt him. He was already suspicious. One time he had seen them together and later asked her about it. She had explained it away, saying they were just friends, that they had met at Richard and Iris' wedding, and they had run into each other and were just having a cup of coffee. But the husband didn't really buy it, and now his worst fears had been confirmed—she and Bob were indeed having an affair.

Makanui explained that her husband was an American academic. He'd started out at a university on the West Coast, and then came to Honolulu for a teaching job at the University of Hawaii. One night he showed up at La Hula Rhumba and bought her a drink. They started dating and soon were married. Through her husband, she met Richard and Iris at a university party. Makanui got to be good friends with Iris but still felt awkward around the well-educated university people. In her mind, she was just a hula dancer. How could she ever hope to keep up with these intellectuals? Her husband wanted to help her improve her education, so he taught her about history and literature. But he knew how attractive she was, and given the huge numbers of single males on Oahu looking for female companionship, he was extremely jealous of almost anyone who could be a potential threat to his marriage.

So what to do now? It was clear they could no longer see each other. Her husband didn't know where Bob lived or worked, Richard and Iris hadn't told him anything, so if he found Bob it would only be by chance. About all he knew was that Bob was in the Marines, but there were Marines all over Honolulu. Their conversation trailed off into silence. There wasn't much more to say. They got up to leave, and on the sidewalk outside the restaurant they looked at each other silently one last time and walked away in opposite directions.

Bob's mind was racing. Now he was facing the very real prospect of being murdered by an angry husband. It seemed somehow unfair because, in his mind, he was innocent. He had assumed Makanui was single, and she had never indicated otherwise. But to an enraged husband with mayhem on his mind, that was beside the point. It was also clear why Makanui always met Bob somewhere and never let him pick her up for their dates. She was living with her husband, not her mother and aunts. Luckily, their house was out by Hickam and Pearl Harbor, far from Bob's house in the Manoa Valley near the university. But her husband was a professor at the university. Hopefully Bob wouldn't run into him accidentally somewhere near campus.

Two days later, while Bob was still trying to come to grips with the situation, he received an alert from 2nd Marine Division headquarters. He was to return to Kamuela on the Big Island immediately. Something was up, and indeed the time had come to ship out for the next island campaign. Feeling he'd dodged a bullet, quite literally, Bob took the opportunity to put some distance between himself and Honolulu and caught a ride on a cargo plane to the Big Island. When he got there, he found the Division in the midst of final preparations for departure. Within two days he was on a troop ship in the middle of a convoy heading for some unnamed tropical island far to the west.

Safely on the ship for the time being, Bob contemplated his fate. He figured it was inevitable he would have to go back through Honolulu on his way home. Even though he would soon land under fire on an enemy-held island, where he would again face the inevitable dangers posed by combat with the Japanese, the prospect of being confronted eventually by an angry husband bent on killing him loomed large in his mind. In spite of the life-threatening events he was about to experience, his fear of the husband's murderous intentions would stick with him until the end of the war.

SEVEN

They All Didn't Commit Suicide: Saipan, 1944

Bob Sheeks was crammed into an amtrac with about twenty other Marines like commuters in a crowded bus. It was June 15, 1944, the morning of D-day on Saipan, and the amphibious vehicle was churning its way toward the beach. He could look up at the deep-blue, early morning, tropical sky flecked with puffs of white cumulus clouds. Over the roar of the engine, the Marines heard the thumping of the heavy artillery from the U.S. battleships and cruisers behind them. After his Tarawa experience, Bob knew what they were in for. The pre-invasion bombardment was never able to destroy all the enemy gun emplacements. And just like Tarawa, the Japanese were shooting back. An occasional *boom* of a shell exploding in the water near their amtrac sent a jolting vibration through the steel hull. The Marines were all trying to steady themselves as the amtrac swayed and bounced in the choppy waves. A few were making offhand comments about how this was easier than their practice landings. For most, this would be their first time in combat. They were replacements who had joined the 2nd Marine Division after Tarawa. Not wanting to appear nervous in front of the combat veterans in their midst, they came off as casual, cool, and not particularly worried. Bob knew from personal experience this was mostly an act. They were all scared.

As they got close to the beach, the metallic ping of bullets hitting the front and sides of the vehicle added to the general din of the shelling. The Marines around him were now silent, anticipating the order to climb over the side. Just then, there was a sudden lurch as the treads found the edge of the shallow reef and the amtrac pulled itself up onto the rough surface. The driver was hunched under a steel hood in the front part of the vehicle, peering ahead through a slit in the armor plating. He struggled with the levers and pedals to maneuver the vehicle through the three-foot-deep water over the irregular contours of the reef. It was a rough ride as the amtrac pitched and bumped along, now riding higher on the reef with only a few feet of water for protection. Pieces of shrapnel from exploding artillery shells slapped the amtrac's metallic sides like rocks being thrown against a corrugated iron building. Suddenly the ride got smoother—the treads had found the sand of the beach—and they came to a sudden stop. The driver turned and yelled, "Everyone out!"

That was their cue, and there was no wasted time as the Marines scrambled over the sides. It was a long drop to the beach, about seven feet, made clumsier by the weight of the gear they were carrying. But they had practiced this many times in training and they all leapt down onto the pale coral sand without hesitation, moving forward quickly once they gathered themselves and their equipment and weapons.

Bob was carrying a lighter load than the other Marines. His carbine was slung across his back, and around his waist was a web belt with two canteens of water. He wore a small canvas backpack like he had at Tarawa. It contained a few personal items, including an extra pair of socks. Also in the pack was essential equipment for all JLOs: two small Japanese-English dictionaries that he had been issued in Boulder. Inside the front cover of one was an ominous warning that the book had to be returned to the Navy as soon as the course was finished. He had ignored that advice and would carry these two small, worn volumes with him in every one of his combat operations.

As he jumped down from the amtrac to the beach, he was aware of explosions close by, the now familiar popping of small arms fire, and the tearing sounds of artillery shells streaking overhead. Almost immediately the amtrac driver gunned the engine, spun the machine around in a cloud of acrid, bluish-gray exhaust, and headed back out to the ships for another load. Bob looked around to get his bearings. Some Marines had made their way across the beach and were nowhere to be seen. A few laid flat on the wet sand, peering inland. They were under fire and trying to figure out the best thing to do next. A mortar shell hit close by, and the sharp explosion showered wet sand down on them. A sergeant who had jumped out of the amtrac with Bob was yelling something about getting off the beach. The Marines around him began to scuttle forward like crabs. The white sand strip was narrow, less than thirty feet wide. It sloped to a low, five-foot-high bluff that backed the beach. A few wispy ironwood trees fringed the beach, most of them splintered by shellfire. A few appeared undamaged, their long needles, like shaggy pines, waving in the morning breeze. Bob crawled to the shelter of the sand embankment and laid flat. His assigned objective was to find the whereabouts of D-2 and report to Colonel Colley for duty. But the trick was figuring out where D-2 would most likely set up. Artillery and mortar explosions were blanketing the area, and bullets zipped menacingly just feet above his head.

As he tried to decide the best course of action, he heard the roar of an incoming amtrac gunning its engine. Over his shoulder, he saw a cluster of Marines jumping down onto the sand. Bob noticed three figures without weapons and recognized one of them. It was Otis Cary, his roommate at Boulder and, more recently, Honolulu. In one of those unfathomably incongruous coincidences that occur in life, amidst the thousands of Americans pouring ashore on Saipan that morning, it was none other than Bob's old friend and former roommate who suddenly materialized not twenty feet from him.

Bob waved him over to where he was huddled in the lee of the sand embankment. Otis motioned to the two who were with him, and all three crawled to where Bob was crouched. They were breathing hard, and sweat was pouring down their faces. Bob recognized John Decker, a tall gangly JLO whom he had met at Boulder. After graduating from the JLS, John had ended up in the Navy, like Otis. The third person was a middle-aged Asian man who had a look of stark terror on his face. Otis anticipated the question and shouted to Bob over the noise of the explosions that they were assigned to civil affairs, and that the Asian man was Father Cho from the Korean Anglican Church in Honolulu. There was a Korean community on Saipan, and Father Cho had been recruited to minister to them and also act as a Korean language interpreter.

Bob couldn't believe his ears. Civil affairs people were supposed to arrive *after* the fighting stopped. Their job was to help interrogate and organize civilians who surrendered. Inexplicably, two unarmed naval officers and a civilian Korean padre had been thrown into the middle of a chaotic live-fire situation, something they had never been trained for.

Father Cho was trying to make himself as small a target as possible. He was curled up in the fetal position in a shallow depression. Decker pressed himself grimly into the sand and didn't say anything. Bob's first thought was that these guys should have come in days after the beachhead was secured, because clearly there wouldn't be any civilians to talk to until after the combat troops had moved inland. But here they were, and Bob felt he should look out for them because he was the only one in the group with combat experience.

They had landed in the 2nd Marine Division sector at the northernmost end of the invasion beaches. The 4th Marine Division had landed farther south. The plan was for the 2nd to wheel left and drive up the coast to the north end of the island. The 4th was to penetrate further inland before turning north. The Army's 27th Infantry Division was initially held in reserve and later landed to fight with the Marines.[1] As Bob was trying to figure out what to do next, he looked to his left up the beach and saw a group of about fifty Marines sprinting toward him, away from the northern front. Obviously it was not a tactical move, but terrorized flight. Bob was shocked and angry to see Marines running away from a fight, but he gave them the benefit of the doubt, figuring they must have been hit by a Japanese counterattack. Reacting instinctively, his officer training and indoctrination kicking in, Bob stood up, ran to the middle of the beach directly in the path of the onrushing Marines, stretched out his arms, and yelled at them to stop, to go back and take cover. Without missing a beat, the Marines ran right past him. One of them paused briefly, shouted that the Japanese had broken through, and then he was gone, following the others in their sprint down the beach. Bob was left standing in the open with bullets zipping by. He scrambled back to where Otis and the others were lying flat on the sand. They were all incredulous at what they had just seen, but if the Japanese had broken through, maybe they should reconsider their position and follow the fleeing Marines.

From their relative shelter, they continued to watch the retreating Americans in their flight down the beach to the south. Just then, a few suddenly veered left and dove into the shelter of the sand embankment under some ironwood trees, and the rest did the same. Then, just as quickly, many of them, the same troops who moments before had been fleeing in seeming panic, started moving forward in small groups. The retreat had been temporary. Their training had reasserted itself, and they soon blended in with the other Marines moving inland.[2]

There was a large shell crater about ten feet ahead of Bob's group, and two Marines advancing inland ran past and dove into it. Just then there was a huge explosion, and they were showered with sand. They looked up cautiously and saw that an artillery or mortar shell had landed directly in the crater. There was no sign of the two Marines who had just taken cover in it. The explosion had vaporized them as surely as if they had never been there. It was a shocking thing to witness, but Bob reminded himself he had experienced worse on Tarawa, and he had steeled himself to such sights in combat. It was quite a different matter for Otis, John, and Father Cho. Their eyes were wide open and filled with horror at what they had just seen. Bob realized this was no place for them. Close explosions showered them with more dirt and debris, and they pressed down as deep as possible into the sand depression sheltering them. The amtracs were still coming in, disgorging their human cargo and then backing around to return to the ships. Bob had turned to watch the amtracs and was contemplating the possibility of getting his friends off the island. Otis followed Bob's gaze, thought the same thing, and without hesitating yelled something about taking Father Cho back to the ship and coming back later. Bob nodded and Otis motioned to Decker and Father Cho. He joined the three as they ran in a low sprint back across the beach. An amtrac had just unloaded Marines, and Bob flagged it down. He then directed Father Cho to climb up the footholds in the steel side. Decker and Otis followed. The amtrac gunned its engine, turned around, and bounced its way back over the reef and out toward the ships offshore, its treads churning the shallow water and leaving a boiling white froth in its wake.

Immensely relieved that Otis and the others had been able to get off the beach before they were wounded, or worse, Bob turned his attention back to his more immediate problem of finding D-2. Just then there was a lull in the firing, and he crawled out of the sandy depression and started running inland. Forty or fifty Marines who had taken shelter nearby were doing the same thing, using the opportunity of the relative quiet to move forward. It didn't last long, and Bob heard first one mortar and then several others exploding, both in front of and behind him. He came to an antitank ditch and jumped in.

Bob glanced to his right and looked down the trench. Its sandy sides had begun to collapse, and about five yards away he saw a partially covered head, shoulder, and arm. It was a dead Japanese soldier. Bob automatically crawled past several Marines to get to the body. Scooping the sand away from the torso, he searched for maps or other documents. The dead soldier was wearing the typical Japanese army–issue helmet—a flared steel pot with string mesh stretched over the top, a single red star on the front. There was a gaping hole in his chest, and the wound was still wet. Bob quickly unbuttoned what was left of the front of the tunic to search for any documents the soldier may have been carrying. He pulled out a small, soft leather–covered book, opened it, and saw it was a diary. Inside the front cover of the diary were two black-and-white snapshots. One showed a stern soldier in uniform standing at attention in front of a tropical scene, probably taken after he arrived on Saipan so he could send it home to relatives. Another photo was of a smiling, attractive, young Japanese woman in a traditional kimono, posed in front of a backdrop of a Japanese village scene. Bob turned the photo over and, inscribed in kanji characters, was the phrase, "To my sweetheart far away." He quickly paged to the first entry in the diary and started doing a quick translation to judge its strategic importance. It was a description of the soldier's arrival at Saipan. He complained of having to do construction work on fortifications instead of training for combat. He also didn't like the poorly prepared food. It was pretty mundane and of little interest for intelligence purposes.

In the early stages of the invasion Bob would have to do a lot more of that sort of thing, sifting through diaries, documents, and maps collected from the bodies of Japanese defenders, looking for any information that would have military intelligence value. It would be a while before he would have access to his improvised jeep-mounted loudspeakers and portable battery-powered megaphones. The equipment was "combat-loaded" so that, in theory, it should come off the ships relatively early in the invasion. In the meantime, he would have to do the conventional work of a Marine intelligence officer. But first he had to find D-2. He knew it should be somewhere nearby, but locating individuals in the whirlwind of combat was not easy.

There was another pause in the shelling, so he climbed out of the tank ditch and made his way forward. Finally, he entered a patch of pandanus trees amidst a jumble of coral rocks that had been relatively untouched by shell fire. As Bob approached he could see several Marines studying maps spread on the ground. He recognized John Pelzel and realized he'd found D-2. Pelzel looked up and nodded as Bob squeezed into the sheltered space. The D-2 chief officer, Col. Jack Colley, glanced at Bob, said something about being glad to see him, and then went back to inspecting the map on the ground. It was a Japanese sketch showing some defensive positions.

Pelzel turned to Bob and wanted to know if anything interesting had happened so far. Bob told him about his unarmed friends from naval intelligence and civil affairs who went back out to the ships before they got killed on shore. Pelzel shook his head and marveled at the SNAFU that produced such a potentially tragic situation.

The day wore on, and by evening Marines had brought in more captured documents for D-2 to inspect. Colonel Colley and his staff were using shaded flashlights to look at several more Japanese maps that had been recovered. Just then a flurry of mortar shells exploded ahead of them in the twilight. The Marines had formed a perimeter and were dug in, expecting counterattacks in the darkness. Bob and the others looked out from their sheltering coral rocks and saw the flashes of tracers lighting up the darkened sky. Incoming Japanese artillery shells started exploding nearby. It was a counterattack, but soon it was repulsed and the firing died down. There would be a couple more that first night, but they were poorly organized and the Marine lines held.[3]

Pelzel turned to Bob and said they had better try and get some sleep. Sheeks slapped at mosquitoes that were biting his neck and looked for a sheltered spot to lie down. He found one among some of the larger coral boulders and curled up under his poncho. This was not for warmth, but to keep the mosquitoes at bay. He took a ration pack of chewing tobacco from his pocket, wetted a bit of it in his mouth, and then squeezed tobacco juice on the mosquito bites on his neck to stop the itching. It was a useful trick he had learned from Marines who had fought on Guadalcanal.

Bob was exhausted and tried to sleep, but adrenaline was still coursing through his system, and the sputtering of occasional gunfire kept him awake. He tried to close his poncho around his body, but mosquitoes were getting inside, and he could hear their high-pitched whines, like tiny dentist drills, as they circled his ears.

The next morning at daylight the Marines in the vicinity of D-2 expanded and consolidated their positions along the narrow coastal plain.[4] There were a couple of dozen Japanese bodies scattered in front of their positions, evidence of the failed counterattacks the night before. It appeared that the village of Garapan, north of the Marine positions, was being used as a collection point for Japanese counterattacks. Prior to the invasion it had been a picturesque Japanese sugarcane town.[5] After U.S. bombing and shelling, Garapan was turned into a pathetic collection of debris, with only the partial remains of a few buildings left standing.

Bob was still assigned to document duty. Anyone who came across anything written in Japanese was supposed to turn it in to D-2, and he was to collect whatever was found and determine if there was any intelligence value in the bits and pieces. He also organized the drops of the surrender leaflets, the ones he had had printed in Honolulu, from the artillery spotter planes. There was no indication they would work, but it was worth a try.

On the second night the Japanese were able to muster a better-organized counterattack.[6] The Marine lines were buttoned down at sunset, and Bob was back at D-2 with Pelzel and the rest of the staff. In the darkness there was a flurry of shooting and explosions, and enemy mortars started raining down on the front lines ahead of the D-2 position. Someone yelled something about tanks, and over the firing they could hear the rumble of engines. A shell exploded about one hundred yards from their shelter. They all crouched lower among the rocks; it was difficult to tell what was going on. The usual confusion of combat during daylight became compounded and amplified into a terrifying chaos at night. Before long Marines ahead of the D-2 position were shooting at something. A star shell from one of the ships offshore went off with a *pop* several hundred feet above the front lines and illuminated the terrain in the distance with a garish, yellowish-green flickering light. Suddenly, like a flash of lightening, a brilliant blue-white light lit up the terrain for an instant, and a huge orange fireball from a massive explosion roiled skyward from the direction of the diesel engines they had heard. Pelzel said someone must have hit a tank. There were more explosions, but they didn't seem to be getting any closer. The Marines had fended off the enemy attack. After a time, the firing died down until there was only the occasional *pop pop* of rifle fire.

A Marine runner scurried in to report what had just happened. He paused for breath and said that it looked like about twenty-five Japanese tanks and some supporting troops had counterattacked.[7] Most of the tanks had been destroyed. Marines had killed a lot of Japanese soldiers, but some had retreated. And with that, the runner disappeared into the darkness to find Division HQ command, which was nearby in a similar patch of coral outcrop rocks and pandanus and ironwood trees. The excitement died down, but Bob again found it difficult to sleep, the prospect of being overrun by counterattacking Japanese still fresh in his mind. He finally dozed off, once again wrapped in his poncho for protection from the incessant mosquitoes.

During the next few days, D-2 stayed in its temporary headquarters. As the front-leading elements of the 2nd Marine Division surged north toward the remains of Garapan like an onrushing tsunami, Bob had to range farther and farther afield to collect documents.[8] On one trip to the front lines he came across a battered Japanese truck pushed to the side of the road. It had bullet holes and dents from shrapnel, but miraculously all the tires were still inflated and there was a starter switch in place of an ignition key. He climbed in and pressed the switch. The engine turned over a few times, and then sputtered to life. Attempts to shift gears produced alarming grinding noises of protest from the vehicle, seemingly still loyal to the previous owners. Finally Bob got the vehicle to move, but the only gear that would engage was reverse. He ended up driving backward for the rest of the day, shuttling from the front lines to the D-2 headquarters.

The next morning, Bob's neck was stiff and sore from looking over his shoulder to drive the Japanese truck. He brought a load of documents to D-2, and Pelzel watched him carefully back the truck toward the jumble of coral boulders. Bob emerged, bringing an armload of documents and dumping them on a board laid across two rocks that served as the D-2 "inbox." As Bob stretched and rubbed his sore neck, Pelzel wondered aloud if there was a Marine Corps record for number of miles driven in reverse. If so, Bob had certainly broken it.

A few days later, D-2 moved into a partially damaged wood-frame building in a valley east of Garapan. Shortly after the move, Colonel Colley called Bob inside and asked him to listen to a strange conversation on the radio. The Marines on the front lines had been complaining about enemy interference with calls for artillery strikes. Sure enough, Bob confirmed at least one English-speaking Japanese soldier was on the Marines' frequency, trying to confuse the Americans into shelling their own positions. Much later, Bob met one of the Japanese who surrendered, an enemy counterpart to the Marine Japanese language officers. He was an Imperial Japanese Army English language officer who had been involved in a variety of activities aimed at disrupting Marine operations, including broadcasting phony artillery requests.

A portable amplifier-loudspeaker set, as well as a handheld electric megaphone, had been packed in one of the crates unloaded at the D-2 headquarters within hours of the landing. As Bob was backing his battered Japanese truck to and from the front lines, he brought them along in case the opportunity presented itself to talk some Japanese into surrendering. He was anxious to get his combat-loaded jeep with the amplifier and big loudspeakers. Not only would he have more options to use amplified sound for surrenders, but also a vehicle with forward gears that worked would be a godsend for his aching neck.

The Marines had already captured a few civilian refugees found wandering around, and they had been collected in a camp that civil affairs had set up in the southern part of the island, away from the fighting. Otis, Decker, and Father Cho had finally made it back in to the beach without incident a couple of days after Bob saw them, and they were hard at work at the camp. Harris Martin, nicknamed "Jish," a tall, rangy JLO, was assisting them at the civilian camp. Like Otis, Jish had been born in Japan to American missionary parents. The day he was born an earthquake struck, and this event prompted his parents to nickname their new son "Jishin," the Japanese word for earthquake. He was well suited for the task of dealing with the refugee civilians. His reassuring air and congenial personality complemented his excellent command of the Japanese language. He transferred Korean civilians brought into the camp to Father Cho, who then organized them into what came to be known to all the Japanese language officers as "Father Cho's Flock."[9]

Before too long the moment came when Bob had his big chance to try out the portable megaphone. There were reports of civilians hiding near the edge of the 2nd Marine Division perimeter on a rocky, wooded hillside. Sounds of firing could be heard in the distance as Bob passed through the front line, clutching the battery-powered handheld megaphone. He hadn't gotten far up the hill when the terrain became very rough, and forward progress was difficult holding the megaphone and battery pack. Crouched down low in case there were any armed military left in the area, he turned the device on, and pointed the megaphone up the hill toward the scrub brush. This would be the first test of what he envisioned on Tarawa. The big question was, would his scheme actually work? Bob started speaking in Japanese into the megaphone.

His amplified words blared up the hill, the rocky terrain acting as an echo chamber. He used simple Japanese phrases and words of reassurance: it was safe to come down, there was food and water available, there were other civilians already in a camp, and they were being treated well.[10] He paused. Nothing happened. Maybe there weren't people hiding up on the hillside after all. He tried again, doing his best to sound calm, reassuring, soothing. Still nothing. Then he noticed movement further up the hill in a fractured formation of limestone rocks. He could see a man, a woman, and two children. Bob kept talking over the megaphone. They were coming down. His appeals seemed to be working.

As they worked their way cautiously down through the rough terrain, Bob could see they were a native Chamorro family. When they got close enough, Bob motioned them forward and held out a canteen.

They looked scared to death but seemed resigned to their fate in a dazed, detached kind of way. Exhausted and disheveled, they were also very thirsty. The woman took the canteen and drank one quick gulp without hesitating. Then she paused and looked at the canteen, and then at her husband, silently trying to determine if the water was safe. It seemed to be, so she immediately had the two children drink, and then her husband took a gulp. In Japanese, Bob thanked her for coming out. She said the Japanese soldiers had told them the Americans would kill everyone on the island. She seemed relieved, but numb, like someone with a terminal illness being told they had a temporary reprieve.

Bob accompanied the family back through the Marine lines and secured a ride for them to the rear area. After a brief but bumpy ride, the truck pulled up in front of the civilian camp, a fenced compound that had been set up just behind one of the invasion beaches. Bob jumped down and was met by Jish Martin, who peered into the back of the truck. The civilians looked back out at him apprehensively. Jish used a steadying tone in his fluent Japanese to tell them to come on out and they'd be given more water and food.

On his way back to D-2, Bob was elated as well as gratified. He'd proven that the concept of using amplified sound could be successful in convincing people caught in the maelstrom of combat to come out. And he would find out just how well it could work in the coming weeks.

The next day, Bob went to the improvised vehicle motor pool to see if he could find his jeep. It should have been off-loaded in the first few days. The ordnance section had helped him put it together back at Kamuela in Hawaii, so they were going to take delivery of it for him on Saipan. The combat loading priority, and thus the sequence for unloading supplies from the ships clustered offshore, had been determined back in Hawaii.[11] First off was ammunition, weapons, fresh water, medical supplies, and food in the form of crates of C-rations. All of this was distributed to designated areas, each set up to receive specific types of supplies. The ordnance section was where ammunition was being stockpiled, along with weapons and explosives. They had a small fleet of vehicles to make deliveries to the frontline troops. There was a motor pool with jeeps and trucks lined up in several rows. This marvel of organization provided a reassuring semblance of order to the general havoc of speeding vehicles and men rushing around. Bob arrived to find Marines busily loading boxes of ammunition onto trucks. As each one was filled, the driver would jump behind the wheel and roar off in a cloud of coral dust, heading north toward the front.

Approaching an officer who seemed to be in charge, Bob asked if the jeep with the loudspeakers had come in. Without hesitating, the officer pointed to the end of the line of vehicles. There was his jeep, loudspeakers bolted to the hood where the windshield once was, generator in the back with the amplifier next to it. The officer peeled back a few pages on his clipboard and pointed to a space on a list labeled "vehicles." Bob signed and then went over to look at his jeep. It had come off the ship with almost no damage. One of the loudspeakers had been knocked a bit askew, and all the fittings needed to be tightened, but otherwise it looked good.

After all the effort to get the equipment in one piece to Saipan, Bob now wondered how successful this ad hoc set-up would be. Given his initial luck with the amplified megaphone, the additional volume and range of the jeep-mounted equipment provided the potential to reach even more people from much greater distances.

Bob drove his new jeep back to D-2, peering around the speakers on the hood, grateful for not having to drive in reverse. Pelzel came out to meet him, nodded approvingly, and then said there was a situation in a walled valley just inland where the loudspeakers could come in handy. Bob knew exactly what John was talking about. He'd driven his Japanese truck backward through that little valley a few times and had been fired on. The area had been bypassed as the Marines rushed north, and Japanese soldiers and possibly some civilians were in the caves.

The drive to the little valley in question was only a few minutes up a rough coral road that passed through sugarcane fields torn up by shellfire. Ahead Bob could see the limestone walls of a small crease in the ridge that formed the backdrop to the coastal plain. He parked the jeep near a group of Marines peering tensely at the cliffs above them. Bob climbed out and a lieutenant asked him if he was the language officer. He nodded, and the lieutenant told him there were some people in the caves above them. The Marines really didn't want to climb up there with satchel charges to blast them out unless absolutely necessary. Next to the lieutenant were a few of his squad sergeants, all eager to find an alternative to risking their necks in getting up to the caves.

Bob wasted no time. He jumped out of the jeep and started up the little gas generator. As it popped and sputtered, Bob picked up the microphone and was about to start his surrender appeals, when he noticed some of the Marines around him had their rifles aimed toward the caves in the cliff face. Bob motioned to the lieutenant and asked him to have the Marines sling their weapons so that the barrels pointed at the ground. He figured the Japanese wouldn't come out if they saw guns pointed at them. The Marines grudgingly did as ordered.

Gripping the microphone to test the speakers, Bob said a few words and there was an immediate squawking feedback, like fingernails scratched across a blackboard. The Marines all winced at the awful racket. He turned down the volume and fiddled with a few of the connections. The screeching subsided, and he turned up the volume again. Everything was ready.

Bob started broadcasting his appeals in Japanese, as he had done with the portable megaphone—water, food, and medicine were available if they came down; many others had already come out and were living in a camp; no one would be harmed. The generator-powered amplifier projected the sound of his voice easily among the distant caves in the cliff face. As he continued talking over the loudspeakers, nothing happened. He repeated the appeals over and over. Still nothing. The lieutenant shrugged, motioned to his men, and they trudged off back down the valley, leaving a couple of Marines to stay behind with Bob and the jeep. Still, he continued his pleas. Maybe no one was up there. Maybe the appeals wouldn't work from this greater distance.

Finally Bob gave up. Before he turned off the generator, in the most polite Japanese he could muster, he said, "Goodbye," got behind the wheel, and started to drive away slowly. Just then he noticed movement among the caves. He hadn't turned off the generator yet, so he stopped and began his appeals again. He could see a few women and children had emerged cautiously from one of the caves and had started to climb down. Behind them were several men. The pathetic refugee group approached the jeep slowly, and Bob motioned them to come closer and talk. He handed them his canteen, and a couple of the Marines who had stayed behind gave them theirs as well. After they took eager gulps, Bob asked a few more questions and determined they were Okinawan Japanese.

One of the men took out a crumpled piece of paper from his shirt pocket, smoothed it, and held it up. It was one of the surrender leaflets printed back in Honolulu and dropped over Saipan from the artillery spotter planes. Bob asked the man if the surrender leaflet had played a role in his decision to give up. After hesitating a minute, the man said it was dangerous, that if the Japanese military caught anyone with a surrender leaflet, they would be killed.[12] He said he kept the one he found and concealed it in his shirt. It seemed to Bob that perhaps some of the message had gotten through. Over the coming weeks a number of civilians who came out of the caves were carrying the leaflets, invariably concealed in their clothing. The man went on to add that Japanese soldiers in another cave nearby had been shooting at passing Americans, but the soldiers had all committed suicide earlier that day.

The few Marines who had remained behind with Bob were now relaxed, and they even offered the women and children candy bars. They were trained to kill, but they showed kindness to the civilians readily. It was almost like a switch they could turn on and off.

Over the next couple of weeks, as the fighting moved farther north, Bob kept rounding up civilians from the caves and delivering them to Jish Martin at the civilian camp. July Fourth came and went with no visible celebration. The Marines and U.S. Army units by this time were relentlessly driving the remnants of the Japanese army, as well as thousands of civilians, toward the northern tip of Saipan. Everyone on the island, Americans as well as Japanese, knew the end was near. Early in the morning of July 7, Bob heard that something big was happening in the vicinity of the devastated coastal village of Tanapag, an area that had been overrun a couple of days earlier. Bob set out in his jeep to hook up with a unit in that area. He couldn't have known that thousands of Japanese, constituting the largest last-ditch banzai charge of the Pacific war, had overrun the American frontline positions several hours earlier, and by then were fighting rear area troops.

Bob tried to make his way toward Tanapag, but it was slow going as the narrow coastal track was crowded with Marine and Army vehicles.

At this point there were three American divisions, two Marine and one Army, stretched in a nearly continuous front across Saipan, all pushing northward. What they did not realize was that, a couple of days earlier, they had reached what the Japanese had designated as their final line of defense. The enemy commanders, General Saito and Admiral Nagumo— the same Admiral Nagumo who had commanded the Japanese attack on Pearl Harbor and the failed invasion of Midway—had decided a massive banzai charge was the only option left to them. The unacceptable alternative would be a humiliating retreat and ultimate annihilation at the cliffs on the northern end of the island.[13]

As Bob got closer, he could hear an increase of gunfire in the distance. A unit of Marines was trudging along the road heading to the front, and as he passed them there was a shout from their radio man that he'd heard calls for reinforcements, that huge numbers of Japanese had broken through the front lines several hours ago and were now in the American rear area. As Bob would learn later, in the predawn darkness that morning, human waves of Japanese had hurled themselves headlong into the direct fire of Marine and U.S. Army machine guns and artillery. American units had been overwhelmed and rear echelon personnel were suddenly confronted with screaming Japanese soldiers running through their positions. But as Bob attempted to get closer to the action, it was unclear exactly what was happening or where.

Still in his jeep, Bob's northward movement had slowed to a crawl with the real prospect of running head-on into the charging Japanese. It was early afternoon when he finally reached Tanapag, and the main part of the banzai charge was over. What greeted him was the aftermath, and it was awful.

He began discovering Japanese bodies scattered over a large area, his first indication of the massive scale of the banzai charge. He was appalled to find enemy dead piled in heaps, stretching inland from the beach at Tanapag and covering the area of several city blocks. The attackers had overwhelmed the American frontline units by the sheer force of numbers, even as they were being cut down by opposing fire. He could still hear the sounds of gunfire from farther inland, as the last remnants of the charge were wiped out.

Many of the dead Japanese had no weapons and apparently were attacking with whatever they could lay their hands on. He saw some who were holding only sharpened sticks. It was pathetic and sickening. Groups of Marines were already moving among the corpses, looking for souvenirs. Bob went to work and started picking his way across the wide area covered by the banzai charge, searching Japanese bodies for documents or maps, and talking to Marines and some U.S. Army soldiers about what they had seen. The final body count was hard to guess. Bob thought it could have been something like several thousand, a banzai charge unmatched in deadly magnitude either before or after Saipan, and the biggest of the Pacific war. Some later estimates put the number of Japanese dead at more than four thousand.[14] It was a colossal but ultimately failed final desperate assault, and it effectively ended coordinated resistance on Saipan. But it didn't end the fighting, because there were still many hundreds of Japanese troops holed up in caves as the remnants of their army and unknown numbers of civilians retreated to the northern part of the island.

Photos taken of the aftermath at Tanapag show a scene of appalling slaughter. Thousands of Japanese bodies lay sprawled across the coastal plain, from the beach to the hills and inland cliffs. As a kid Bob had seen dead Chinese soldiers on the battlefields around Shanghai, and then he saw the Japanese and American bodies on Tarawa, blasted by high explosives or torn up by gunfire. But he had never seen corpses in these numbers. In his mind, a familiar numbness took over. This seemingly callous emotional distance, first cultivated when faced with Japanese brutality in Shanghai and reinforced by the bloodshed at Tarawa, was how he had come to deal with such scenes of gut-wrenching carnage.

Captured Korean laborers were pressed into service to help drag the bodies into trenches gouged hastily in the sandy ground by bulldozers.[15] Ropes and bamboo poles were used to haul and slide the bodies into the trenches. The sheer number of corpses to be buried made it a big job. As the bulldozers pushed sand over the bodies, Marines tried to make estimates of how many went into each trench. Time was of the essence, as the rising heat dictated the bodies must be disposed of quickly. An accurate accounting of how many and where the bodies were buried was of secondary importance under such conditions. Decades later on Saipan, the remains of the Japanese killed in the Tanapag banzai charge were still being unearthed whenever new foundations were dug in that area.[16]

When Bob finally made his way back to D-2, Pelzel and the rest of the intelligence officers were buzzing about the incredible scale of the banzai charge. Reports of ongoing combat kept coming in over the radio, and Marines were still fighting and dying. Tanapag was not the last gasp of a defeated enemy, because there were still plenty of Japanese combatants willing to fight. But it was clear now that it was just a matter of time before the battle ended.

After Tanapag, most of the remaining Japanese soldiers and civilians were compressed into the far north end of the island. Bob was having more and more success with the portable amplified megaphones and the jeep-mounted loudspeakers. Another JLO from the 4th Marine Division, Chuck Cross, heard of the positive results Bob was producing with the loudspeaker jeep. Known as "Chuckie" to his fellow JLS students in Boulder, on Saipan he had been humorously promoting a new nickname for himself, "Satchel Charge" Cross, or just "Satchel" for short. He showed up at the 2nd Marine Division D-2 one day and wanted to know where he could get his own loudspeaker jeep, or if he could borrow Bob's. Explaining that the jeep was not standard issue, Bob said it had been put together as a personal initiative with the support of D-2, and John Pelzel in particular. Chuck persisted and tried for quite a while to convince Bob to lend him the loudspeaker jeep. By this time Bob was using the equipment nonstop and had to turn Chuck down. Later on, the 4th Division got its own loudspeaker equipment, probably from the Seabees, and Chuck put it to good use.

For the next couple of days, Bob helped groups of Marines clear caves in the north part of the island. On one of those excursions, while assigned to Colonel Jones, he was able to convince a young Japanese soldier to surrender. The boy then volunteered to return to the cave and blow up his former comrades. Another day, Bob came across a group of Marines eyeing a prominent cavern visible in the distance. The sergeant in charge complained about the enemy fire they'd been receiving from the cave.

Bob hoisted the truck battery by a sling on a pole and lugged the megaphone up the slope to get in position. The Marines followed behind him at a distance. There were shots from the direction of the cave, and they ducked behind the shelter of some fractured gray limestone rocks. Bob turned on the megaphone and broadcast his usual appeals. Suddenly there was a shout from inside the cave and a large explosion. Bob and the rest of the Marines ducked instinctively, though they were still many yards away. A cloud of black smoke billowed out of the cave. The Japanese holed up inside had detonated a large explosive charge of some kind. The sergeant and the rest of his squad got up silently and trudged away. Just like that, the standoff was over, at least for that cave. Though Bob was always hopeful of a more positive outcome, many of his cave encounters ended with some kind of variation on that same theme.

A little further along there was an eight-foot-high limestone outcrop. One of the Marines in the squad said there was a Japanese soldier behind the rocks. Bob approached carefully and from a distance of about fifty yards used the portable megaphone to attempt to call out to anyone hiding there. There was no response. Suddenly there was a loud *boom* and a body flew into the air, cartwheeling as if in slow motion, catapulted up about twenty feet higher than the rocks. As the corpse fell back behind the limestone outcrop, Bob and the Marines approached cautiously. The enemy soldier must have crouched with his chest to his knees, held two grenades to his stomach, and detonated them to blow himself up. The Marines looked at the dead enemy soldier impassively, and then a couple of them knelt over the body to look for souvenirs.

At another cave, Bob was using his battery-powered megaphone and, after the usual appeals, he heard a voice shouting from inside the cave. He couldn't make out all the words, but the message was that those inside refused to come out. Bob replied in his most soothing Japanese that they would be given water, that they would not be harmed, that many Japanese soldiers were living safely in a camp with food and water and medicines, and so on—all of the familiar refrains. After a few moments of silence, there was movement at the mouth of the cave and he could see two Japanese soldiers crawling out. Bob crept closer to the cave and paused to make a few more reassurances on the megaphone. It seemed to be working. The soldiers continued crawling forward slowly and hesitantly. The Marines working with Bob, a sergeant and a number of privates, were scattered around at various distances behind him, hugging the ground, weapons at the ready.

Bob was now close enough to speak directly to the two Japanese soldiers without using the megaphone. He kept reassuring them. They would crawl a few feet, stop and listen to Bob's appeals, and then crawl some more. The first one was by then about thirty feet away on his hands and knees, and Bob was talking to him in Japanese in a conversational tone. Just then, a shot rang out from behind Bob, and, in front of his eyes, the Japanese soldier's head snapped back, a hole blown through his forehead, and he collapsed in a motionless heap. Bob was filled with a sudden and inexpressible rage. He turned to see where the shot had come from, and the others were looking at a fellow Marine who had been lagging behind and hadn't "gotten the word," as they said in the Corps. As he caught up to the group, all he saw was a Japanese soldier crawling toward his fellow Marines, and he reacted as he'd been trained to eliminate the threat.

Bob was enraged. Using a selection of well-chosen Marine obscenities, Bob screamed at him that the Japanese soldier was surrendering, and there should have been no shooting. Neither the Marine who had fired nor any of the others in the squad seemed too upset. It had been a mistake to shoot, of course, but the Japanese soldier was the enemy, and it was their job to kill the enemy. It was an attitude Bob ran up against all the time, going back to his poorly received lectures on that topic in Hawaii prior to the Saipan operation.

Bob crawled forward and approached the second Japanese soldier as he lay huddled on the ground, not knowing what to expect. He was terrified, having just watched his friend shot and killed before his eyes. Bob got close enough to explain what happened and tell him that the Marine who did the shooting was out of line. Pausing for a moment, it struck Bob that an American Marine had followed his training to kill the enemy under any circumstance, while the presumably ruthless Japanese soldiers were the ones making the choice to overcome their training in order to save their lives by surrendering.

Bob spent the rest of the day talking groups of civilians into coming out. Some caves had people in them, others didn't, and a pattern developed. The Marines would identify a likely cave opening. Bob would broadcast repeated appeals on his handheld electric megaphone. If there was no response and no one appeared, the Marines would form a triangle, with two men on the forward corners covering another Marine holding a satchel charge. That Marine would creep up to the cave entrance, toss the charge in, and then scramble back quickly to take cover before it exploded. As smoke was billowing from the cave, the Marines would approach cautiously and peer in to make sure nothing was moving.

Bob also learned to rely on his sense of smell. An uninhabited cave was usually odorless. Caves containing people gave off the aroma of unwashed bodies and human waste. Often he could approach to within twenty or thirty feet of a cave and be fairly certain if people were inside or not.

Late in the day, the Marines returned to their defense perimeter for the night. This was something they did religiously because of the threat of Japanese infiltration if they were not buttoned down by the time it was dark. One afternoon Bob and a group of Marines were in the open along the coast road working a group of caves in the inland cliffs. The sun was low on the horizon, and the Marines were getting antsy. Bob had been broadcasting for about a half hour up toward a cave in the escarpment. Several civilians had already straggled down, and Bob was sure more were up there. The squad sergeant was impatient. He had loaded the Marines onto a truck to head back, and he informed Bob they were ready to go. Just then, a small Japanese girl who had come down told Bob in polite Japanese that her parents were still hiding in one of the caves.

Bob turned to the sergeant and said he wanted to give the girl a chance to talk her parents into coming out. He turned back to the girl, handed the battery amplified megaphone to her, and explained how to use it. He spoke slowly in Japanese, coaching her to say she was fine and her parents should come down now. The girl had been in the caves for a week without food and only a little water, and she had surrendered with a relative. She didn't seem afraid, and she started to talk into the megaphone immediately, pleading with her parents to come out, her high-pitched voice reverberating thinly among the caves in the cliff face above. She stopped, and there was silence. Nobody moved. The sergeant cleared his throat nervously, and then pointed out firmly that they really needed to be getting back. The Marines in the truck thought the same, and Bob could feel their stares behind him, but he knew it took time for the surrender appeals to work. In this situation, the Marines were typically willing to trade time for satchel charges. Bob looked down at the girl's sad face and urged her to try once more. After a few more plaintive appeals, Bob finally told her they had to stop for the day, but maybe they could come back later. She nodded silently. It was unclear if her parents were actually up among those cliffs, and Bob never found out if they were or not.

During the nights on Saipan, people were on the move. Because Marines stayed put after sunset, the Japanese became emboldened to go out and look for food and water under cover of darkness. Bob also prowled around outside the Marine perimeter after sunset. Sometimes, if he heard civilians talking as they moved through the bush, he could convince them to come with him. At other times, he could hear Japanese soldiers discussing whether they should move to a new position, and there was intelligence value in that information. Usually what he overheard in the darkness was more mundane, the prime topic being food, and where they could find large jungle snails or other edible things.

Going out by himself in the dark looking for people who could be talked into surrendering made sense to Bob. Being in the POW capture business, it was a prime time to find refugee civilians and scattered soldiers when they were roving around. The self-preservation instincts of every Marine on Saipan were exactly the opposite and dictated they stay within the protective confines of their perimeter during the most dangerous night hours. But Bob welcomed the darkness as an opportunity to get his job done.[17]

One night, Bob had ranged far past the 2nd Marine Division perimeter toward the 4th Marine Division sector. He was navigating terrain he had noted on a topographic map before he left the 2nd Marine Division lines. Suddenly he was challenged by a 4th Division Marine in the darkness. Though he rarely kept track of the passwords that were supposed to be used to pass through the lines, he was able to demonstrate his friendly intentions by asking to see the billeting officer. The Marine humor Bob used to talk his way through the front line implied he would spend the night with their unit and would need someone to show him where to stay. The fact that the Marines were dug in on a low hill in a forward position in the bush in the middle of the night made Bob's desire to see the billeting officer just that much more humorous and worked better than any password.

In another of those unlikely small-world coincidences, like running into Otis Cary on the beach in the chaos of the first morning of the invasion, it turned out that Dan Williams, Bob's childhood friend from Shanghai and a JLO in the 4th Marine Division, just happened to be with the group of Marines Bob had stumbled across. The two old friends hadn't seen each other since they'd left the Boulder campus, and they were eager to get updates on everything that had happened since they had last spoken in Colorado. Dan had been in the invasion of Kwajalein Atoll, and his first interrogation experience involved interviewing a wounded Japanese sailor plucked from the ocean near the island after an enemy ship had been sunk. Dan posed a series of carefully formed questions in Japanese, but the only words the POW spoke in Japanese were, "I hurt."[18]

Bob brought Dan up to date and recounted some of his experiences in the Tarawa invasion. He said he had been frustrated by the small number of Japanese POWs taken at Tarawa, with the major problem being they didn't know surrender was an option. He then related his subsequent successful experiences with amplified surrender appeals on Saipan. In another remarkable coincidence, while comparing notes there in the dark at 3:00 a.m. in a foxhole on Saipan, they realized that Father Cho, who landed near Bob on D-day with Otis and Decker, was in the same cabin with Dan on the ship to Saipan from Hawaii. Dan then added that as he was wading ashore on D-day a piece of shrapnel hit his pack and burrowed itself into his Japanese-English dictionary.[19]

Dan went on to tell Bob that the previous afternoon his unit had come across an affable Japanese soldier outside a large concrete bunker who cheerfully spoke to them in perfect English with the greeting, "Hi, my name is George, and I'm from Honolulu."[20] George then went on to explain that he had grown up in Hawaii and had been sent to Japan for school right before Pearl Harbor. The Japanese military had drafted him, and he ended up on Saipan. Apparently he didn't have very high status in his unit, because he had been left behind to guard about twenty Asian "comfort women," usually captive Filipino or Korean girls sent out to service the Japanese army in the field.[21] They were starving and exhausted and cowering inside the bunker. "George from Honolulu" was quite relieved to have survived his experience in the Japanese army, and the Marines left him in charge of the girls for the night, with a promise to return at dawn to transport them all to the rear area and safety.

The time flew by as Bob and Dan caught up on all their experiences. This amazing meeting finally broke up after about two hours as the first signs of dawn began to lighten the sky. Bob headed back toward the 2nd Marine Division positions, and Dan turned his thoughts to what he was going to do with George and the comfort women. It was only in later years that they appreciated how unusual their meeting was, and how, if one or both of them had been killed, it could have been their last conversation. They were both in combat and under fire, but at the time they gave it little thought. Both were preoccupied with what they had to do next and didn't give much thought to the possibility of being injured or killed. Bob returned to D-2 shortly after dawn, and another day of loudspeaker work began. Later that morning, Dan found George waiting patiently where he'd left him with the women and arranged for him and his group to be transported to Jish's camp.

As the Americans surged to the far northern coastal cliffs, the island was declared "secure" on July 9, 1944.[22] This was a relative term because the mopping-up operations continued, and the remaining combat was taking place mostly on the far north end of the island. Shortly after July 9, Pelzel gave Bob the contact information for a Marine platoon, and Bob drove north in his jeep. After a dusty trip up the coral coast road, he found the unit getting ready to move out. Subsequent events followed a then-familiar routine. When caves were encountered, using the loudspeakers, Bob broadcast appeals to give up and come out. Sometimes civilians or military would come down from the caves. Other caverns were silent and the Marines threw satchel charges into the openings just in case.

It was late morning and Bob had set up his jeep loudspeakers amid the shattered stalks of a sugarcane field a short distance away from a contorted set of uplifted limestone cliffs and ridges. Up ahead he saw a Japanese soldier come out and take cover behind some large rocks. The soldier gestured to him to come closer. Bob picked up the portable megaphone and started working his way across the sugarcane field. The Marine lieutenant in charge of the operation in that sector watched Bob carry the strange contraption forward and motioned to one of his sergeants to follow with his squad.

Bob got to within about fifty yards of where the Japanese soldier was taking cover and started to talk over the megaphone, using all the familiar appeals. The soldier shouted back in Japanese something about a group that was willing to come out, but they didn't think it was safe. They were afraid the Americans would shoot them. Bob replied that the Marines would honor their desire for a safe passage. His earlier experience with the trigger-happy Marine was still vivid in his mind, so he said he'd prove he was not lying by coming up to talk to the soldier directly.

With that, Bob took off his helmet, unslung his carbine from his shoulder, removed his sidearm and camouflage jacket, and started walking slowly toward where the Japanese soldier was hiding. This was to demonstrate that he was unarmed and not threatening, the hope being that the Japanese soldier would honor his intentions. Bob could feel the stares of the Marines behind him. They certainly must have thought he was stark-raving crazy, because they all believed the Japanese were murderous robots programmed only for violence and treachery. But Bob knew that civilians would give up, and even some Japanese soldiers had seen how senseless it was to continue resisting in a lost cause.

He had become familiar enough with Japanese traditions to know he should try to encourage the soldier to surrender with dignity and thus save face, a key element of their culture. But he also had no way of knowing whether all the Japanese in the cave felt the same way. It was just as likely that one of the soldiers farther back and out of sight would shoot anyway, just like the U.S. Marine had killed the enemy soldier crawling toward Bob as he was trying to surrender.

Bob was about twenty feet away, and he could see the Japanese soldier peering from behind a large boulder. Talking directly to him in soothing Japanese, Bob said he was an American Marine who had studied some

Japanese, but his language skills were not very good, and he hoped he could be understood. So there he stood, in the open, unarmed, about to face a group of Japanese combat soldiers. Behind him were heavily armed Marines itching to shoot the enemy. He didn't know which group worried him the most.

The Japanese soldier came forward cautiously. Behind him were about ten others, making their way in single file to where Bob waited. The first soldier who had been talking to Bob stopped and stood directly in front of him. The others formed a straight line just behind their commander. All stood at attention. Then the Japanese officer unbuckled the leather belt that held a samurai sword in its scabbard, took it in both hands, bowed, and presented it to Bob. The rest of the Japanese soldiers also bowed. Bob received the sword solemnly. He resisted the impulse to bow in return, lest the Marines behind him take it as a sign of submission. Remaining as solemn as possible in the midst of this improbable scene, he then led the group back down from the cliffs, through the remains of the sugarcane field, and past the astonished stares of the Marines.

After making arrangements for the surrendered Japanese soldiers to be transported back to the POW camp, his next assignment took him to a group of Marines who were clearing some caves nearby. As Bob approached he heard explosions and could see about twenty Marines, one with a flamethrower, working up near some cave entrances in the cliffs. He hopped out of the jeep and was told by a lieutenant in charge of the operation that he was too late, they couldn't wait, and they had already cleared out the caves in question. Bob trotted up to where the group of Marines was working. He could hear the metallic *whoosh* as a fresh jet of bright-orange flame erupted out of the end of the hand-held nozzle of the flamethrower. Strapped to the Marine's back were two brown steel tanks full of jellied gasoline, and he was leaning forward to brace himself against the force of the jet of burning liquid-gel shooting out of the nozzle toward the cave entrance in front of him.

A number of civilians had come out of the caves at some point during the Marines' sweep of the area. They were waiting to get on trucks to take them to the camp farther south. They were a bedraggled-looking group and stood silently, still unsure as to whether or not the Marines would open fire and gun them down as the Japanese military had been telling them. Bob could see that several were injured.

Lying next to the dusty road was another civilian, a woman, and she was so horribly injured that no one could bear to look at her. Bob walked over to where she lay, and he could see that she had been severely burned by the flamethrower. She also had additional injuries from shrapnel. Her clothes were blackened tatters. Her skin, what was left of it, was crusted bright red with sickening black splotches. Bob forced himself to look at her face. Most of it was burned away, and he couldn't see her eyes. Incredibly she was still breathing, her chest twitching, spasms of breath rasping in and out of an opening that had once been her mouth.

Bob had seen a lot of gruesome sights in combat, Marines and Japanese with body parts burned, blasted, or blown off, and he'd consciously become callous and hardened himself to it. But this was different. It went beyond what he'd seen before and affected him in a way he couldn't have anticipated. As he looked down at this disfigured human being in the final throes of an agonizing death, it was reminiscent of his dying mother, and of his father injecting her with morphine, the magic "sleep medicine." Bob took a morphine syrette from a pouch on his belt, dropped to his knees beside her, uncovered the needle, and stuck it into her blackened arm. Her body continued to twitch, the labored breathing even louder than before. Bob turned to a Marine standing nearby and demanded another syrette. At first the Marine didn't move, not quite understanding why this woman, who would be dead in a few moments anyway, warranted the valuable drug. Bob had to yell at him to give him the morphine. The Marine jumped forward and dug out one of the little cylinders from a pouch on his belt. Bob grabbed it, pulled the cap off to expose the needle, turned to the woman, and stuck the needle into her arm. She calmed a bit. Her breathing slowed somewhat, but she was still shuddering in agonizing spasms. Bob called to another Marine nearby, asking for a third syrette, and he injected still more morphine into her burned body. This seemed to relax her. The convulsions stopped, and the labored breathing subsided quietly until she lay perfectly still, her agony over.

Bob swallowed hard, put his helmet back on, and looked up to see a Marine truck approaching. It skidded to a halt in a cloud of white coral dust, and a 4th Marine Division Japanese language officer, or JLO, jumped out and started herding the civilians who had come out of the caves toward the open gate at the back. He was pushing those nearest to him and yelling at them to hurry up. Bob could see the JLO was tired and frustrated, but at the same time he was out of line. There was no reason to harass these pathetic people who had just been saved from what they thought was certain death. They were farmers and women and children and they didn't need to be bullied. Weak and thirsty, they hadn't eaten anything for weeks, and were having difficulty clawing their way up into the bed of the truck. Bob could feel anger welling up inside him.

The Marine JLO started kicking one of the civilians and yelled again for them to hurry up. That did it. Bob went over to the truck, pulled the sidearm from the holster on his belt, brought the pistol up level with his gaze, and shouted that if one more civilian was kicked he'd pull the trigger. The JLO turned to stare at the pistol aimed at him, a look of utter astonishment on his face. It got very quiet suddenly and no one moved. The enlisted Marines standing around had never seen an officer threaten another one with a gun. All eyes were on Bob's pistol aimed squarely at his fellow Marine.

The JLO said in a wavering voice that he could report Bob for court-martial. In a barely controlled rage, Bob snapped, "Do it!"[23] There was a pause. No one said anything. Bob then announced that he was taking charge of the civilians. With that, he went over to where the frightened refugees were huddled at the back of the truck and started helping them get in. The other Marines stood in stunned silence. They couldn't believe what they had just seen. When the last civilian was loaded, Bob told the driver to head south. The truck accelerated in a cloud of white dust. The JLO never reported Bob, and nothing more came of it.

The next morning, Bob forced himself to put the traumatic incidents of the day before out of his mind. The best thing was to get back to work. Reed Irvine, a boyish-faced graduate of the Boulder Japanese language school, joined Bob and they went back to the area in the north part of the island where mopping-up operations were still taking place. They took with them a Japanese civilian, a former sugarcane farmer on Saipan. He had been released into Bob's custody by Jack Williams, an Army civil affairs officer who, after the war, ended up serving as the senior U.S. foreign service officer in Korea. On Saipan he was in charge of the farm project that put captured Japanese civilians to work raising vegetables and other food to help feed the ever-growing population in the camp. Jack had issued the man a khaki long-sleeve shirt and pants, a Marine pith helmet, and an armband stating in English and Japanese that he was helping the Americans.

They all loaded into the loudspeaker jeep and bumped along the rutted and dusty track until they finally got to the Japanese airstrip at the northern end of the island. It was sited spectacularly on a plateau perched between windswept Marpi Point on the ocean side and a set of high limestone cliffs looming menacingly above it on the inland side. As usual, the coral limestone formations were riddled with natural caves. The remains of the Japanese army, as well as many civilians, were pinned into those caves.

They stopped to watch a Marine artillery piece blasting away at some cave entrances they could see in the cliff face above them. With each startlingly loud bang of the howitzer the big gun would recoil, bouncing back on its rubber tires. Then up on the escarpment there would be an explosion marking the impact of the shell, and a shower of limestone fragments would cascade down the cliff to disappear into the vegetation below. A grayish-white splotch was left where each shell had hit. They were sharpshooting at the cave as if they were aiming a rifle at a bull's-eye, much like the destroyer Bob had seen firing away at the Japanese truck on the shoreline at Tarawa.

After watching for a while, Bob and the others got back into the jeep and continued along the rough track. Here the road paralleled the coral runway. The small airstrip had been built as a fighter base by the Japanese, and it was now being put to good use by the tiny Marine artillery spotter aircraft. These were the same airplanes Bob had employed to drop the surrender leaflets he had printed back in Honolulu. Suddenly one of the men walking along the road yelled out. He thought he'd seen Japanese soldiers. Bob stopped the jeep and, followed by Reed and the Japanese civilian in his pith helmet, trotted over to where several Marines had gathered to peer down into a hole in the ground. It was actually the entrance to a cave. It looked like it had been enlarged for use as an air raid shelter. Bob looked down into the cavern cautiously and at first could see nothing. He asked the Marine whether he was sure there were Japanese soldiers down there. The Marine looked to be only about eighteen years old, but he said calmly that he was sure he'd seen movement. He then reached for a grenade to drop into the hole, but Bob stopped him and said he'd try to talk to anyone who may be inside.

Crouching next to the hole, he spoke Japanese into the darkness below: please come out; many of your people are now in a safe camp; we don't want to shoot you, but we can't allow you to stay in there; we don't want to drop a hand grenade in there; and so on. He saw movement and could hear voices conversing in low tones, but he still couldn't see them clearly. They were only about ten feet below the surface. Bob offered to lift them out, and one shouted back in defiant Japanese that it was impossible. The Marines around the hole looked at each other. It was the first time they had heard the enemy speak. Bob continued the soothing conversation, pointing out the futility of resistance. The battle was over, and they could come out honorably and peacefully. One of the Japanese had shifted over to a spot where he could look up at Bob, and he again said emphatically that they weren't coming out.

Bob was about to speak again when he sensed a sudden movement below. By reflex, he yelled to the Marines to get back and simultaneously shoved Reed as he leapt back from the hole. Just then, there was a loud *wham!* The earth shook beneath them, and a jet of gray smoke and coral gravel shot into the air from the explosives the Japanese soldiers had detonated. The Marines looked at Bob as he picked himself up off the ground. He crept back cautiously to look into the hole and, in the dim, smoky light, saw the gory carnage of blasted bodies.

Before anyone could say anything, they heard shouting. Off to their left, a dozen Marines were crouched at the edge of the cliffs overlooking the ocean. Bob, Reed, and the Japanese civilian joined them at the edge of a sheer vertical drop, a three-hundred-foot free fall into the heaving dark-blue swells that were slamming into the dripping-wet rock face. Each wave hit with a dull *whump*, followed by an explosion of sun-lit, sparkling, white spray. The view was spectacular. In later years this site would become a scenic overlook for tourists, one of the most awesome and frequently visited spots on the island. It became known as "Suicide

Cliffs." Bob and the other Marines in the group were about to witness why the name was chosen.

Everyone at the edge of the precipice was straining to peer down the cliff line toward Marpi Point to their right. Just then one of the Marines yelled, "There goes another one!" Bob looked over just in time to see a person in midair, plummeting downward and then soundlessly impacting the coral shore far below. Immediately the body was swallowed up by a massive wave and tons of water. Bob followed the trajectory of the jumper back up to the cliff edge about two hundred yards to their right, and he could see a woman and several children standing there. Just as quickly, she threw the children over the edge one by one, and then she jumped. It was a horrific yet transfixing sight. A Marine photographer with a small, handheld movie camera arrived and began filming. Several more civilians appeared at the edge of the precipice in the distance and threw themselves into space, plummeting to their deaths hundreds of feet below. The Marines were helpless to stop them. Blocked by a hodgepodge of jagged limestone formations along the hazardous edge of the cliff, they couldn't easily get to where the civilians were jumping.

Bob went back and got the jeep, drove cautiously forward, and attempted to edge up to the drop-off. The terrain was rough, and he couldn't maneuver close enough. Several more civilians were making their way to the cliff edge. Bob pulled out the portable megaphone, leaned over the edge as far as he could, and started broadcasting. He wondered if the amplified sound could be heard above the roar of the ocean as the massive waves thundered into the cliff face. Occasionally, amidst the spray and froth, floating bodies could be seen. Wave after wave picked up the limp forms and slammed them on the rocks. Bob handed the megaphone to the Japanese civilian helper to see if he could have any better luck. The civilians didn't seem to hear, or if they did, they ignored the appeals. There was a strange sense of urgency to the jumpers. None of them paused at the edge for very long. They were determined to end their lives. It was uncomfortably hypnotic to watch people hurling themselves willfully to their deaths, one after another.

A war correspondent Bob knew who had just arrived on the scene asked him excitedly if he'd ever seen anything like this, and whether they were all going to kill themselves. Bob had to admit that the sight of Japanese civilians jumping off a cliff into the ocean left a compelling impression. On the other hand, he knew that many hundreds of civilians had already surrendered, and he felt strongly that many more would give up rather than commit suicide.

By now a larger crowd of Marines had gathered, and a couple more combat photographers with cameras had joined the group. The prevailing view among the Marines was that the Japanese were solving their problem for them—they didn't have to dig or blast them out of their hiding places in bunkers or caves. The Marines could just watch as they ended their lives. When the lineup of jumpers finally came to an end, the Marines moved on and the correspondents returned to their jeeps to drive back to their quarters. They had a good story and they knew it.

The noted war correspondent Robert Sherrod was on Saipan and heard about the civilians jumping to their deaths that day. He wrote an article for *Time* magazine in which he wondered if the whole Japanese race would commit suicide if the United States invaded.[24] Bob wanted to set the record straight with an article of his own, stressing that thousands of civilians surrendered on Saipan rather than commit suicide. But Sherrod was a good friend of the Marines, and Bob's article wasn't released for publication in *Far Eastern Survey* until nearly ten months later in May of 1945.[25]

Aside from the suicides, the subject of stragglers and holdouts was not a central one for D-2. Their main concern, first and foremost, was winning the military battle for Saipan and supplying urgently needed intelligence information required by Division headquarters to make that effort successful. After the island had been secured, who cared about a few stragglers? It was an uphill fight for Bob to get the top brass interested in the subject. Whenever he could, he would bring this up with Col. Jack Colley and his assistant, Tom Dutton.

One day he was doing just that with Colonel Colley. The head of D-2 was dressed as usual in Marine dungarees and a khaki T-shirt darkened with perspiration. Bob stressed again that there were probably still hundreds of civilian and military roaming in the hills. Colley wanted Dave Shoup, the head of D-3, Division operations, to hear it, so they went to see him. Shoup was one of the heroes of the Tarawa invasion. In the confusion of the landing, he had proved himself to be a supremely capable combat commander who kept the attack going while hopelessly pinned down near the sea wall, and he had been awarded the Medal of Honor for it.[26] Bob had seen him in action under fire at Tarawa, and he knew his reputation was justified.

On arrival at Shoup's command post, one of his staff officers accompanied the D-2 group into the tent. Shoup greeted them and, with his bull neck, rock-solid jaw, and buzz haircut, he looked every inch the Marine warrior. Colonel Colley started the meeting by first summarizing D-2's assessment of remaining civilians and military on Saipan. Shoup wanted to know the basis for that assessment. Colley pointed to Bob, who stated that there were at least several hundred more civilians and probably additional Japanese soldiers hiding in the bush. Shoup then wanted to know how many Bob had actually seen. His honest answer was about fifteen or twenty. Shoup laughed and said maybe there were just fifteen or twenty out there.[27] But Bob persisted in his argument, and Shoup authorized mop-up patrols designed to provide the opportunity for Bob to first find and then convince more of the enemy to surrender. Shoup passed this information along to General Watson, the 2nd Marine Division commander, and he came to appreciate Bob's efforts to bring in stragglers and holdouts.

It turned out that continued patrols and mopping-up operations uncovered not several hundred but several thousand more civilians roaming around in the bush or hiding in caves. The combination of Bob's work with the jeep-mounted loudspeakers, handheld amplified megaphones, and surrender leaflets; the contributions from U.S. Army interpreters, many of whom were Japanese American Nisei; the efforts of Bob's Japanese language officer colleagues in the 2nd and 4th Marine divisions; and the roles played by some individual Marines and Navy civil affairs personnel resulted in at least 15,000 Japanese civilians, local Chamorro natives, and Carolinian islanders coming out of hiding and being placed in the internment camp by the end of the war.[28]

As the mopping-up operations continued to grind along, Bob accompanied patrols frequently to areas where there were suspected military or civilian holdouts. On one such excursion, things went wrong. Bob was with a squad of Marines, and the sergeant in charge was leading them along a sloping limestone ledge where there were caves. Below them was a sheer drop-off and a vegetation-covered cliff. They came across a small encampment, indicating there were Japanese civilians nearby. Hearing the Marines approaching, they had abandoned their pathetic little camp hastily. A couple of sheets of corrugated tin from a wrecked roof had been rigged as a crude rain catchment system, with the water draining into a few bottles. Scattered around were the remains of their food supply, mostly the shells of giant African snails that had been brought to Saipan by earlier settlers and were now ubiquitous on the island. Some were as big as fists. The Marines tore the camp apart and began throwing things over the edge of the cliff.

Suddenly there was a loud *pop!* in the distance, and Bob felt a bullet zip by inches in front of his face. Then another *pop*, a second shot, and another bullet whizzed by. A Marine standing just above him on the sloping ledge screamed in pain and fell down, writhing in agony. Immediately the rest of the members of the patrol dropped flat on the ground. The Marine who had been shot continued yelling and was thrashing around wildly. The shot that had passed just in front of Bob's face had struck the Marine who had been standing a little higher up on the sloping ledge. The wound was serious. The bullet had torn into his hip and lodged in his groin. An ugly splotch of dark-red blood was spreading across the hip and crotch areas of his trousers.

Marines nearby crawled over and saw immediately what had happened. They all had ashen looks on their faces. One muttered that it was the worst thing that could happen to a guy. By this time the injured Marine had stopped screaming and had recovered a bit from the initial shock of being shot. But when he realized exactly where he had been wounded, he started yelling again, this time pleading loudly for one of his friends in the squad to shoot him. This had an unnerving effect on the entire group. More than ever they wanted to kill the Japanese sniper who had taken the shot. A couple of Marines rigged up a corrugated tin sheet for a stretcher to haul their wounded buddy up to an access road on the bluff above to catch a ride on a truck. With great effort they tried to wrestle him onto the metal sheet. He resisted and continued to plead with them to shoot him. Of course none of them would consider killing a fellow Marine, no matter what his injuries.

Bob peered over the ledge through the vegetation to the coastal track more than one hundred feet below. He saw several Marines patrolling along the road, so he turned on his portable megaphone and asked if they had seen any Japanese snipers. The amplified sound echoed down toward them, and the Marines looked up and yelled back that they'd seen brush moving above them and thought there were Japanese up there.

With a sickening realization, Bob knew then that the injured member of his patrol was a victim of friendly fire—he had been shot by one of his fellow Marines on the road below. The others in the squad heard the exchange, and they looked at each other angrily. The sergeant spat in disgust and said that everyone had been briefed just hours before as to where the patrols were going that day. The briefing was designed specifically to keep Marines from inadvertently firing at each other. An accidental shooting was inexcusable.

Bob was furious and shouted through the megaphone that they had just hit a Marine. War was bad enough without your own people shooting at you. The Marines below now realized what had happened and looked shaken. By yelling back and forth, Bob got the identification of the unit that had done the shooting. He intended to report the incident.

A fine drizzle had started to make an already miserable day even worse. The ground was slippery as they struggled to move the injured Marine uphill onto flatter terrain. He was still writhing on the corrugated tin sheet that was dripping with a combination of blood and rain water. Someone gave him a shot of morphine. They finally made their way up to the plateau and a truck was waiting. Bob told the sergeant in charge of the squad he'd ride in the truck and make sure the wounded man was delivered to the hospital safely, and he climbed into the back with the then-unconscious Marine. As the truck lurched off down the track, it left behind a distraught group of men. Friendly fire was bad enough, but getting shot in the groin was almost the worst wound they could imagine.

After a bumpy drive, they approached the hospital that consisted of a group of large olive-drab tents, their roofs marked with bright-red crosses painted on white backgrounds. Wounded Marines were still being brought in from the mopping-up operations at the north end of the island. The term "mopping up" sounded innocuous enough, but clearly it was still a dangerous and sometimes lethal activity. As the truck ground to a stop, Bob jumped out and motioned for a couple of orderlies, dressed in blood-stained white gowns, to come over and unload the injured Marine. They lifted him gently off of the corrugated tin sheet, laid him out on a stretcher, and carried him into one of the tents. Bob followed and entered to find a scene reminiscent of a bustling restaurant, except the diners were young Marines laid out on stretchers, and the waiters and waitresses were haggard-looking doctors and nurses. They were moving around in a choreographed swirl of activity as they attended to their bloodied customers.

Rapid decisions had to be made regarding which Marines should receive treatment first. A doctor, with a nurse at his side, approached Bob and crouched over the Marine to make a preliminary examination. Bob pointed out that it was a friendly-fire injury, the shot apparently going through the hip and into the crotch. The nurse looked quickly at Bob, and then cut the Marine's trousers off with a scissors as the doctor helped her. Bob looked away from the bloody mess, still furious that this had happened. The doctor motioned for a couple of orderlies and told them to take the Marine into surgery. He turned to Bob and said it was a miracle the bullet missed the femoral artery, or he'd have bled to death already.

Then the doctor moved on to the next stretcher. Bob touched the shoulder of the nurse as she stood up to follow, and he asked where the Marine would end up after surgery. He wanted to look back in on him to check his recovery. She turned toward him with a pleasant but tired look, clearly showing the strain of dealing with the inevitable burden of her job. Like all the hospital staff in triage, she had bright-red bloodstains on her white uniform. Her thick black hair was neatly tucked up and under her white nurse's cap. The dark circles under her watery blue eyes indicated she hadn't slept in a while, but otherwise she was strikingly attractive. Bob didn't contemplate for long the fact that his judgment may have been compromised by not having seen an American woman in quite a while. She told him he'd be in the ward in another hospital tent, and that if she saw Bob return she would point him in the right direction. She had a competent air of pleasant friendliness. Then she turned and caught up with the doctor, who was kneeling beside an unconscious Marine on the next stretcher in line.

Bob reported the incident when he got back to D-2 and turned in the names of the Marines who had fired on them and their unit. Pelzel told him nothing would happen, and Bob knew it, too. There were friendly fire incidents all the time on Saipan. It was part and parcel of the violent chaos that surrounded them. Bob was told the wounded man would still get the Purple Heart, even though he was shot by another Marine. That seemed like faint compensation given the grim nature of his wounds.

Later that week, Bob headed back to the hospital. After inquiring at the desk just inside the main hospital tent, he was directed to the far end. He walked past the rows of beds where young men lay in various forms of repose with bandages, slings, casts, and drip bottles over and around them in all kinds of improbable configurations. A few of them were talking to each other, but most lay quietly, staring upward at nothing in particular, undoubtedly contemplating whether their wounds were serious enough to get them shipped off the island and out of harm's way. If asked, most would respond that they were eager to rejoin their buddies, even if it meant more combat. Bob spotted the nurse who had attended to the friendly-fire Marine. She looked revitalized, wearing a clean, white uniform, and she recognized Bob as he approached. Before he could say anything, she said the Marine was going to survive, but it was doubtful that he would ever be able to have children because there was just too much damage to the organs. The situation had been explained to him, and they had tried to point out how lucky he was to be alive at all.

She then motioned Bob to follow as she headed toward the last bed at the end of the tent. The Marine looked up expectantly as Bob approached. His first question was about his squad and how they were doing. Bob said they were okay and he'd pass along the good news of the successful surgery. He mentioned the Purple Heart, but that didn't seem to make much of an impression. The boy asked again eagerly about his squad-mates, and Bob assured him they were all fine. After more small talk for a few minutes, Bob bade him farewell and said he'd be back to check on him from time to time. The nurse was standing nearby, and she walked with

Bob outside the hospital tent. The sun was edging toward the horizon to the west of the island, and the huge orange ball shimmered above the glistening ocean. Several small, delicate cumulus clouds overhead were lit in pastel shades of orange and purple. Bob and the nurse stood there staring at this incongruous burst of breathtaking tropical beauty amidst the ragged, bullet-shredded palm trees silhouetted against the sunset. In an offhand kind of way, Bob mentioned some scenic spots nearby that weren't bombed or shot up. This seemed to perk her up, and she said her name was Denise.[29] She figured Bob was the wounded Marine's commanding officer, but he set her straight and said he was a Japanese language officer, a Marine combat interpreter, and had been assigned to the squad only temporarily. His job was to look for Japanese civilians and soldiers hiding in the bush and try to convince them to give up. Denise wondered if Bob had been wasting his time, because she heard all the Japanese on the island were killing themselves. He bristled a bit because this was a common misconception on Saipan. He pointed out that he was spending most of his time finding living refugees. There were already several thousand civilians in a place called Camp Susupe near the ruined village of Charan Kanoa, with about one hundred military POWs in a separate camp nearby. Not all of them were committing suicide. In fact, more and more were being brought in very much alive every day.

Denise hadn't heard anything about the large number of enemy survivors, but that came as no surprise because the nurses were isolated from the rest of the military men on Saipan for their own protection. Like all Marines on the island, Bob had heard about the nurses who had arrived a month after the landing. They were the only American women within hundreds of miles, dropped into the middle of thousands of heavily armed and hormone-driven young men.[30] This was clearly a potentially volatile situation. The nurses were all officers, so according to military regulations, social contact was allowed only with other male officers. But Saipan was a combat zone, and inevitable tensions would arise if enlisted men saw officers socializing with nurses in that environment. As a consequence, the nurses were off-limits and ensconced in a guarded compound surrounded by a high fence topped with barbed wire. In effect, they were prisoners on the island, locked up like crown jewels in a vault.

As they stood there looking at the sunset, Bob wondered if he could arrange to meet her outside the confines of the hospital. He tentatively volunteered to accompany her to one of the secluded beaches he knew about, but only if she dared to. Her eager response surprised him. She definitely wanted to escape, if only briefly, the stress of working at the hospital and the confinement of the nurses' compound. Without a doubt she wanted to see another part of the island, a place that didn't involve blood, bandages, or hospital beds.

Bob sensed the desperation in her voice, but he also recognized it would be a nearly impossible operation. They thought about it for a few minutes, and then plotted a strategy. Bob would pose as her driver and pick her up in a jeep. They would make it look like he was accompanying her to one of the forward field hospitals. The guards wouldn't know one way or the other. Bob said his jeep had loudspeakers mounted on the hood, but they could give it a try. They were like two kids plotting to play hooky from school right under the principal's nose. Denise told him to come by the nurses' compound at about 5:00 p.m. the next day when she got off her shift. She would bring along a swimsuit she hadn't even unpacked yet.

The next day at the appointed time, Bob hopped into the jeep and drove over to the nurses' compound. Armed guards were standing at the opening in the barbed wire–topped fence that surrounded a cluster of tents. Bob was wearing a clean set of combat fatigues with his lieutenant's bars clearly visible, looking for all the world like an officer who was there to take a nurse somewhere on official business. As the jeep pulled to a stop, the two guards, both privates, looked at Bob but otherwise didn't move. Denise approached the gate from inside the compound, looking very prim in a clean, olive-drab nurse's uniform. She had a handbag that looked to be carrying official documents. As she passed through the gate, both Marine guards saluted crisply. Their reward for this otherwise boring guard duty was seeing American women at close range, which was more than most of the men on Saipan could do.

Denise returned the guards' salutes and hopped into the jeep. Bob looked straight ahead and drove the jeep away from the compound before turning south on the coast road, in the opposite direction from where the fighting was still sputtering away farther north. Soon there was only tropical vegetation lining the road, and not a trace of military activity. Bob glanced at Denise and she had a broad smile on her face. It was like they had successfully pulled off a jail break.

As they bounced along the road, she thanked Bob for springing her from the nurses' compound and letting her see parts of the island that hadn't been ruined. Soon he turned the jeep onto a side road heading for the coast. It was no more than a rough track, but he'd found it on one of his forays into the bush in the earlier stages of the island campaign when he was ranging farther afield looking for civilians hiding in the area. He parked the jeep out of sight, and they walked the last thirty yards before emerging on a deserted white-sand beach. The reef offshore was absorbing the force of the ocean swells, and they broke with a nearly uninterrupted dull roar in the distance. Small wavelets lapped softly on the gleaming sand. The low sun was shimmering off the ocean, and palm trees arched lazily overhead. It was as if they had entered a tropical paradise, a dumbfounding incongruity on an island that had seen so much death and destruction.

Denise stopped in her tracks, overwhelmed with the scene. Then she asked where she could change. Bob pointed to a clump of vegetation behind the beach. She scampered behind the bushes and emerged a few minutes later wearing a stunning white one-piece swimsuit. Bob then changed into his swim trunks behind the same clump of bushes and rejoined Denise on the beach. She sat on the sand with a nonchalant grace, her legs drawn up so that her forearms rested on her knees. Her dark hair, now hanging loose and tumbling around her shoulders, was backlit and glowing from the low sun above the ocean horizon.

After a few moments, she jumped up and ran into the welcoming warm, clear water, and Bob followed. They splashed and floundered around like two kids in a neighborhood swimming hole. They had left behind the carnage and shocking violence of combat, the civilian suicides, the ragged refugees and Japanese military, and the groaning of wounded Marines fighting pain and shock. All of it seemed very far away on that tropical late afternoon.

They got out of the water reluctantly and sat on the beach to dry off, both taking in the idyllic scene in this beautiful deserted spot. She lounged back on the sand and felt something through the back of her swimsuit. Sitting up quickly, she cried out and turned to see what was underneath her. There were ashes from a cooking fire on the beach, and among the remains were blackened sticks of wood. She twisted her head around to look at the charcoal marks on the sheer white material and yelled something angrily about how stupid someone was to leave burnt wood on the beach. Immediately she realized she had overreacted. Her outburst was a clear indication of the tension that had built up over the previous weeks of unrelenting work in the hospital to patch up the shattered bodies of young Marines. She finally calmed down, and they turned their attention to the sunset, mindful they couldn't be out after dark. As soon as the sun disappeared over the ocean horizon, they changed back into their uniforms quickly, and Bob reassumed his role of chauffeur for a nurse returning from an official meeting.

During the mopping-up operation on Saipan, Japanese civilians were being brought into Camp Susupe by a number of Americans, in addition to Bob and the other Marine language officers. Some of this work was being done by nisei interpreters from the Army, and occasionally other Marines would turn over civilians they had rounded up. One was a diminutive enlisted Marine, a private named Guy Gabaldon. His helmet appeared oversized and his fatigues draped on him so that he looked like a kid who was trying to dress up in his father's suit. With his short stature and his aviator-style sunglasses, he appeared to be anything but a typical Marine. Guy was not bashful about talking up his exploits on Saipan, and by his own account he had brought in many hundreds of Japanese all by himself. Several months later he would be shot in the wrist when he and his fellow Marines were ambushed by Japanese holdouts.[31]

Somehow Gabaldon could get away from his unit and go out on his own, looking to round up Japanese civilians in the bush. He was raised in an ethnic Japanese community in Los Angeles, and he came to learn a brand of Japanese that included a lot of street slang. Given his background growing up with Japanese-Americans, it was unclear to everyone why he treated the civilian refugees on Saipan so roughly. He called himself "Lone Wolf" and was determined to set a record for the number of Japanese he brought in.[32] Bob had several encounters with "Gabby," as he was known to the JLOs. The most disturbing was when he witnessed

Gabaldon break the jaw of an elderly Japanese civilian for not answering a question quickly enough.[33] Other Marines who saw Gabby in action also witnessed his abuse of Japanese civilians.[34]

His exploits on Saipan earned him a Silver Star. After the war, Gabby related his wartime experiences to a friend with Hollywood connections, and in 1960 they made a movie true to Guy's version of events.[35] Shortly thereafter, his Silver Star was upgraded to a Navy Cross.[36] A later documentary film further extolled Guy's side of the story.[37]

It was the view of the JLOs at the time that most of the "enemy" Gabaldon rounded up were civilian refugees, not Japanese military.[38] A number of Marines claimed that Gabby probably brought in only about half of the 1,500 prisoners he boasted about.[39] Guy was more or less helping in what the other Japanese language specialists were trying to accomplish on Saipan. All of them were determined to search out as many civilians and military as possible and save them from being killed. The eventual 15,000 or so civilians who surrendered on Saipan were a credit not only to the Marine JLOs like Bob in the 2nd and 4th Marine divisions, but also to U.S. Army nisei interpreters and their Caucasian commanding officers, and rank-and-file Marines like Gabaldon. What distinguished Gabaldon was his attitude, and the fact that he later made it seem as if he alone was bringing in surrendered Japanese on Saipan. While the JLOs treated the civilians as hapless refugees, in Gabaldon's mind they were all enemy combatants, and he promoted his exploits relentlessly.[40] His death in 2006 finally ended his personal quest to have his Navy Cross upgraded to the Congressional Medal of Honor. After the war, he married an ethnic Japanese woman he met in Mexico and had the distinction of being the only Marine Corps veteran of the Saipan campaign who ended up living out his life on Saipan, the scene of his World War II experiences.[41]

But Gabby was only a passing acquaintance, and during the Saipan campaign Bob was more concerned about the welfare of his childhood friend from Shanghai, Dan Williams, a JLO in the 4th Marine Division. The only time Bob saw Dan on Saipan was their chance encounter in the middle of the night during the battle. It turned out they barely missed making contact once more, when Dan came through Saipan again with the 4th Marine Division on his way to the Iwo Jima invasion in early 1945. Bob was still on the island and went out to the ship when he heard the 4th Marine Division JLOs were there. Right before Bob arrived, Dan had gone ashore, and they missed connecting. But some of the other JLOs were still on the ship, and Bob talked to a couple of his old buddies from Boulder. One was Ray Luthy. Shortly thereafter the convoy sailed for Iwo, and about a week later Bob saw Ray back in a Saipan hospital. Just after he hit the beach during the first morning of the Iwo Jima landing, an artillery shell exploded next to him. Ray was evacuated to one of the transports offshore. After amputating what was left of his leg, they shipped him back to Saipan.

For the next year Bob was stationed on Saipan, his longest assignment during the entire war, though there were a couple of interruptions. First, in late July 1944, there was the matter of the invasion of nearby Tinian Island for him to deal with, and another opportunity to convince more Japanese to surrender. It was there that he would encounter a remarkable Japanese soldier whom he would not soon forget.

EIGHT

A Human Connection with the Enemy: Tinian, 1944

As July 1944 wore on and mopping up continued on Saipan, Bob knew the invasion of the neighboring island called Tinian could not be far away. Sure enough, one morning all of the language officers were called into a meeting with Pelzel, Colley, and Dutton at D-2 headquarters, and they were briefed on the upcoming landing. Colley, thin, pale, and sweating as usual, was businesslike and direct. Though they had all been in the tropics for more than a month, it looked like Colley was even more pallid than when they first landed.

He spread out a map on the table and said they would load up in LSTs, just like the Saipan landing. The big difference was they were right next door to Tinian, only five miles distant, so their time at sea would be minimal. The plan was for the 2nd Marine Division to make a feint down toward the south end of the island where the main town was located adjacent to some long white-sand beaches, seemingly perfect for an amphibious landing. Aerial photo analysis by D-2 had shown that most of the enemy defenses were built in and around those areas, and the Japanese fully expected the landing to take place there. Instead, after offloading Marines into the amphibious landing craft and milling around off the south shore, they would abruptly go back to the ships and reboard. Meanwhile, the 4th Marine Division would be landing at the north end of the island on a couple of very narrow beaches.[1] The gaps in the limestone rocks behind those strips of sand totaled only a couple of hundred yards, making for a tricky landing indeed. The element of surprise was critical, otherwise the Americans would be clobbered trying to come ashore in such a small area. The feint to the south would be essential to keep the main Japanese force anchored there while the Marines were inserted in the lightly defended north. It would be like a boxer missing with a left jab that distracted his opponent, followed by an unseen body blow with his right.

The businesslike atmosphere in D-2 had the air of a corporate board meeting to plan the takeover of a rival company. They had all come a long way since the chaotic mess of the Tarawa operation. This would be Bob's third island invasion, and he realized the Marines now knew what it took to do one of these landings right. Because the feint to the south did not require intelligence officers, it had been decided that D-2 for the 2nd Marine Division, Bob's group, would land with the 4th Marine Division in the north.

A couple of days later, on July 24, the Marines and their amphibious vehicles loaded onto the LSTs. They made their way the short distance over to nearby Tinian, the closed double doors in the blunt-nosed bows bashing against the waves. The battleships of the fleet were already in position and were pounding the southern part of the island. The now-familiar dull booms of their guns reverberated inside the steel LSTs like the rumble from a distant thunderstorm. Precisely according to plan, the LSTs arrived off the south coast and launched the amtracs filled with Marines. They started circling as the battleships leveled the town.[2] Fountains of black smoke and orange flame shot into the air with the impact of each huge shell, and it was difficult to see how they could figure out what they were shooting at. By now the Marines knew this was more for effect than to disable the deeply dug-in Japanese. But the Marines figured it must have made the enemy think about why the Americans would expend that much firepower if they didn't intend to land there.

While all of this was occupying the attention of the Japanese forces in southern Tinian, the main invasion force was approaching the north end of the island. Because the beaches in front of the narrow gaps in the limestone ledges along the shore limited the number of amtracs that could land at any one time, the amphibious vehicles were queued up in lines at prearranged intervals. This allowed time for one group of vehicles to land, unload, turn around, and head back to the ships, while the next group of amtracs came in.³ Later groups of amtracs would land their troops a short distance inland following the Marine advance.

Bob was loaded in one of these amphibious vehicles, identical to the one he had been wedged in for the Saipan landing. By the time their turn came to go in to the beach, it was afternoon. But there was something very different from his previous experiences on Tarawa and Saipan. As they neared the beach there was almost total silence: no sound of nearby shelling—the battleships were still quite a distance away, busily blasting the southern part of the island—and no alarming pinging sounds of enemy bullets ricocheting off the sides of the amtrac. Bob and the other Marines looked at each other and wondered aloud if the elaborate feint had actually worked.

There was another difference. The young Marines crammed into the amtrac with Bob were now battle-tested veterans from the Saipan operation, and there was hardly any small talk. They were focused on the task at hand, like a winning football team about to take the field, knowing what it would take to crush the opposition. The treads of the amtrac ground hard on the edge of the reef, lurching upward into the shallower water that covered the coral. The driver gunned the engine and the vehicle bumped along until it was entirely out of the water and driving over the narrow sand beach. Because they were part of a later wave, they kept right on going and headed a short distance inland to unload.

Bob peered out over the side as they crossed the beach and could see that the opening in the limestone rocks was only wide enough to allow about three amtracs at a time to pass through. There were several more of those narrow openings to the left and right, and the amphibious vehicles were streaming through all of them and heading inland. It was like a precision airdrop of paratroopers behind enemy lines. Bob's amtrac was following the one in front of it, and another was right behind. They wove through a scattering of coral boulders and scrub vegetation behind the immediate shoreline, and then they were churning over broad expanses of sugarcane fields.

Almost the entire island of Tinian was relatively flat, perfect for agriculture, but also ideal for the coral airfield the Japanese had built amidst the sugar cane near where the Marines landed. In only a couple of weeks, the partially built Japanese runway would begin to be unimaginably expanded to become the Americans' largest complex of runways and air bases in the Pacific. A few months later, Bob would be back on Saipan watching armadas of gleaming silver B-29s, launched from airfields on Tinian, joining those taking off from Saipan and Guam, all flying north to blanket nearly every major Japanese city with incendiary bombs whose fires would burn most structures in those urban centers to the ground. In just over a year, the planes carrying the two atomic bombs bound for Hiroshima and Nagasaki would take off yards from where Bob's amtrac was now driving. But what was on the minds of the Marines on July 24, 1944, was survival, and they were concentrating on their assigned task of clearing the Japanese from the island using whatever means they had at their disposal.

There was only an occasional gunshot, and Bob couldn't tell if it was trigger happy Marines or a few Japanese defenders on this nearly deserted north end of the island. There was more firing coming from the direction of the nearby Japanese airstrip, as Marine units began to encounter Japanese troops. Bob's amtrac ground to a halt, and the driver yelled for the Marines to get out. They jumped over the sides and Bob went out last, landing amidst the broken sugarcane stalks that had been crushed by the advancing amtracs that had gone before. The Marines immediately spread out and moved forward at a brisk trot. They had been prepared to land under fire as they had on Saipan, but the deception of the fake landing in the south had worked. There was little resistance.

Bob looked to the right and noticed a narrow-gauge railroad track used for the miniature trains the Japanese had built to haul harvested sugar cane to the now-leveled town at the south end of the island. There was a low rise and the steel rails followed a cut in the small hill. He recognized Boulder JLS classmate Frank Turner and a couple of other officers who were trying to rig a tarp across the cut to provide a shelter for D-2 operations. Bob hustled over to help them. Frank and John Pelzel greeted Bob and noted with considerable satisfaction that the plan had worked—the landing had been no problem whatsoever. American commanders later classified the Tinian operation as one of the best-executed island amphibious invasions of the Pacific war.[4]

Because the Japanese were thrown off by the feint to the south end of the island, followed by the surprise landing in the north, they never really recovered. Mostly combat veterans brought in from China, the Japanese were faced with having to attempt to turn their southern defenses around to face the Marines rushing down from the north.[5] In the end, it was too late for that to be effective, and they ended up retreating to caves in the far south end of the island in escarpments and cliffs only slightly less imposing than those on the north end of Saipan.

The rapidity of the Marine advance didn't allow time for Bob to attempt many surrender appeals. He was assigned to a frontline unit, and their imperative was to move forward as quickly as possible. Before his jeep with the loudspeakers was offloaded on the island a couple of days after the initial landing, Bob used the portable megaphones on a few occasions. He didn't have much luck with surrenders initially, as the Japanese army units in the caves were more determined to resist than to give up.

If the Marines did happen to give him a chance to try for surrenders, and his appeals to the Japanese to come out didn't work, the now-familiar triangulation technique came into play. As on Saipan, Marines on two points of the triangle would shoot at the cave entrance, and a third Marine with a satchel charge, the point of the triangle, would creep forward. On signal, the two who were shooting would stop, and the other Marine would leap up and toss the bag with the explosive charge into the cave, and then jump back as the firing resumed. A couple of seconds later, the pops from their rifles were drowned out by the dull *whoomph* as the charge went off inside the cave and smoke and debris flew out from the entrance. This scene was repeated over and over as the Marines advanced relentlessly. They could see the Japanese were on the run, and they wanted to exploit the situation as expeditiously as possible.

Occasionally, as the Marines moved across the island, a single Japanese soldier would pop up and start firing from a concealed position. Then the Marines would form a moving arc as they closed in. This enabled them to focus their fire on the Japanese defender's position, while staying out of each other's way. It took a little while to organize, like positioning cowboys for a cattle drive, but it was quite effective as the arc would move and converge on the hidden enemy. On one occasion, Bob watched as about twelve Marines carefully formed an arc that closed in and eliminated a single Japanese machine gunner.

At one point, Bob's unit encountered a cave in another of a series of low, limestone ridges. The Marines were on a roll on their way toward the south end of the island, and in spite of Bob's requests, they insisted they didn't have time to give him a chance to use his megaphone. He was back about fifty yards from the cavern entrance as the Marines concentrated on setting up the triangle formation to cover the satchel charge. Suddenly a shot rang out from behind Bob, and he felt a bullet whiz past his right ear. Expecting that the shooter was a Marine who hadn't gotten the word, he turned and was ready to raise hell when he saw the head and shoulders of a Japanese soldier above a large rock, rifle aimed directly at him. Bob ducked down instinctively and yelled a warning to the Marines up ahead. They all turned and crouched down. Bob's ears were ringing from the sound of the shot, it was that close. The Marines motioned silently to each other and, like a finely tuned drill team, started to arrange themselves in the deadly arc. In their well-practiced way, they closed in on the Japanese soldier. He popped up to shoot again, and the Marines immediately opened up with automatic weapons fire. One of the Marines had a BAR, the unwieldy but deadly effective Browning automatic rifle. Because the BAR was heavy, it was usually carried pointing straight up in the air. The Marine's left arm was wounded and bandaged, so he was balancing the BAR with only his right arm. When the Japanese soldier suddenly emerged, the wounded Marine started firing the BAR while it was still pointed in the air. As he dropped it onto his wounded left arm, it was firing all the way down. The line of bullets from the weapon ripped into the Japanese soldier from head to waist, almost cutting him in two. It was all part of the routine for the Marines, and they immediately turned their attention back to the cave entrance.

As the Americans continued their rapid and relentless drive to the south, Bob had located his loudspeaker jeep and was working as part of a larger force under the command of Maj. Bill Chamberlin, a Marine commander who, like Dave Shoup, had emerged from the combat on Tarawa with a reputation as a can-do warrior.[6] The Marines had driven the remaining Japanese military and civilians into the limestone escarpments and ridges at the southeastern end of Tinian. As on Saipan, there were coastal cliffs and some of the cornered civilians had been jumping into the ocean to their deaths. Because the Marines had overrun nearly the entire island, the language effort by now was being given a little more time to be effective. A patrol boat was hovering offshore to assist in broadcasting surrender appeals and otherwise to shoot into the caves in the cliffs that towered above the ocean.

When the squad Bob was accompanying arrived, an operation to clear a complex of caves had already begun. An officer standing nearby said a large group of Japanese civilians and military had holed up in a monstrous cave in the face of the cliff below them. Bob noticed a radio operator who was in contact with the patrol boat offshore. He went over and heard a voice on the radio say the boat's guns had bracketed the cave entrance. Bob asked the radio operator to inquire if any civilians had tried to climb out of the cave and up the cliff face in an attempt to surrender. Just then, another voice came over the radio, saying people had been seen standing in the mouth of the cave, but they hadn't given any indication of a willingness to surrender, and, by the way, there were loudspeakers on the patrol boat and they were standing by ready to assist. After a couple of questions, Bob determined there was an interpreter on the ship, a Japanese-American sergeant attached to the U.S. Army. Exactly how a nisei Army interpreter ended up on a Navy patrol boat with loudspeakers at his disposal was unclear, but he could prove to be useful in helping convince the Japanese to give up peaceably.

Chamberlin was the officer in command, and he was on high ground some distance away. Bob asked the communications man if he could speak to him over the radio. Chamberlin came on, and Bob pointed out that there was an interpreter and loudspeakers on the patrol boat. The combination of appeals from where Bob was at the top of the cliffs and the amplified broadcasts from offshore could produce surrenders. Chamberlin replied curtly that there was no time for that. Bob persisted and Chamberlin finally gave him a half hour to try. Bob then argued that he needed a few hours to first make the appeals and then give the civilians a while to work their way out of the cave and up the cliff face without being shot from others inside who may not like the idea of surrender. Chamberlin was adamant—he could only wait one half hour. Not willing to give up, Bob continued his pleas for more time, and finally Chamberlin relented. He would delay his assault for one hour, but not a minute more. Then he would order the patrol boat to commence firing into the cave.

With this time constraint weighing heavily on his mind, Bob quickly unloaded his portable megaphone from the jeep. He instructed the radio operator to relay a request for the nisei sergeant on the ship to start broadcasting appeals toward the cave from his position offshore, stressing that they only had an hour until the firing started. Meanwhile, Bob tried using the amplified megaphone by pointing it over the edge of the cliff, though he doubted he could be heard by the Japanese below. He couldn't even see the cave beneath him in the vertical rock face.

In the meantime, the clear, fluent Japanese from the nisei interpreter began echoing from the loudspeakers on the ship. He was using similar types of appeals to the ones Bob had relied on throughout the Saipan campaign. This went on for about one half hour. Nothing was happening. After nearly forty-five minutes, Bob asked the radio operator to query the ship to find out if they could see any Japanese trying to make their way out of the cave and up to the top of the cliffs. The nisei interpreter on the ship reported he couldn't see any movement at all. This presented them with an extremely frustrating situation. Given enough time, Bob was sure he could get at least some of the Japanese in the cave to come out. A few minutes later, Chamberlin was on the radio and said the hour was up. Bob pleaded for a little more time, but Chamberlain declined, saying his operation had been delayed long enough, and he ordered the patrol boat to open fire into the cave with white phosphorous. It was nasty stuff, arguably one of the worst weapons the Marines possessed. Those who weren't killed by the initial concussion of the phosphorous shell were burned to death in a searing blaze of blinding, white-hot combustion. It was brutal, but Chamberlain knew it was the quickest way to take out the cave. The ship started firing, and Bob turned away as he heard the thudding sounds of the shells impacting the cliff face below.

He looked around for his squad and spotted them in full combat mode, clearing the area of snipers. As they came across Japanese corpses, they would quickly search the bodies for souvenirs, mindful that they were under fire and could not spend too much time in one spot. Bob was very familiar with this behavior, having seen it throughout the Saipan campaign, and even at Tarawa. The souvenirs could include officers' samurai swords, the most sought-after items, but also popular were enemy pistols that could be sent home easily. Many Japanese soldiers carried rising sun flags, signed by their friends for good luck, often folded inside their helmets. These made for great souvenirs because they were portable and easily pocketed by the Marines. Another item the Marines always looked for on an enemy body was the "belt of a thousand stitches." Before leaving home, friends and relatives of a Japanese soldier would stitch outlines of dragons or other figures on a silk sash that was then tied around the soldier's waist. Each stitch was supposed to bring good luck and protection in battle. Given the number of these souvenirs that Marines took from dead Japanese, the sashes didn't seem to work very well for their intended purpose. After finding such items, the combat Marines would keep the choicest prizes for themselves and trade or sell the rest to rear area troops, Seabees working on the airfields, or sailors on the ships.

Bob also was obligated to search Japanese corpses, but he was less interested in souvenirs and more concerned with maps, diaries, or other items of intelligence value. He noticed a dead Japanese soldier nearby and was about to check the pockets, when he noticed a small pistol lying next to the body. The corpse looked like it had been torn apart violently by wild animals, but it had in fact had been disemboweled by an exploding mortar shell, and the pistol was covered with gore and maggots. Bob was shoving the pistol gingerly with the toe of his boot, contemplating whether it was worth trying to clean it off and save it as a souvenir, when a young Marine private standing nearby pleaded to let him have the enemy weapon. Coming to the quick conclusion that it wasn't worth the hassle of cleaning it up, he told the Marine to take it. The private grabbed the pistol eagerly and held it in his hands as carefully as if it were a rare archaeological artifact, and then he wiped it off on his dungarees. The boy was smiling like someone who had just opened a prized Christmas present.

The squad worked their way through rough terrain until they finally approached a series of cave entrances in a jumble of limestone formations. Bob had climbed up quite close to one and was talking to someone inside at close range, civilian or military, he couldn't tell. Soon, a uniformed Japanese soldier appeared cautiously at the entrance of the cave, apparently prepared to surrender. Bob asked him his name and rank, knowing that if he could address the soldier on a more personal basis it established a better sense of trust. The soldier stated he was Warrant Officer Nakazawa.[7] A warrant officer in the Japanese army was a top enlisted rank, similar to a gunnery sergeant in the Marines.

After about fifteen minutes of conversation, Warrant Officer Nakazawa finally agreed to come out. He cautiously emerged from the darkness of the cave, squinting in the bright afternoon sunshine. He saw the other Marines positioned below the cave entrance, but none had their weapons pointed at him. As usual, Bob had emphasized the importance of shouldering weapons so the warrant officer could see he wouldn't be shot.

When asked if there were any more soldiers in the cave, and if Bob should go in to talk to them about coming out, Warrant Officer Nakazawa answered with a resounding, "No!" He knew his comrades would not take kindly to an American officer entering their cave, and they would likely shoot first and ask questions later. Bob then asked Nakazawa if he would agree to enter the cave and try to talk them into coming out. Somewhat to Bob's surprise, he said he would. Though Japanese civilians and some Koreans had assisted Bob with his surrender appeals on Saipan and Tinian, this was the first time a member of the Japanese Imperial Army had agreed to lend a hand.

This was encouraging news, but first Bob wanted to get Nakazawa back to the POW camp, give him water, feed him, and let him regain some strength. He had endured weeks of combat, and then surrender, and now he seemed near the point of collapse. The Marines in the squad covering them also looked beat. There was unrelenting tension because they never knew if the Japanese holed up in caves would surrender or shoot at them. They had to be ready at all times for either eventuality. Bob decided to call it a day.

As they climbed down from the mouth of the cavern, Bob thanked Nakazawa for coming out. The warrant officer seemed resigned and only nodded. They walked together to the truck waiting below, and Bob asked him a few questions about the situation on Tinian. Nakazawa seemed to relax a little and said it had become clear to him the battle was lost, he could see there was no use fighting any more, and it was pointless to die.

Though Bob was still no fan of the Japanese military, he was surprised to hear such a thoughtful appraisal of the situation on Tinian, especially because Nakazawa was a warrant officer and a combat veteran.

The next day, he and Bob returned to the cave with a squad of Marines. They set up their triangle formation, but instead of a Marine with a satchel charge, they were covering Nakazawa as he worked to get closer to the entrance. This was a dangerous moment. His comrades were well armed. Many were inclined to shoot anyone who wanted to give up, even their superiors. He was taking a serious personal risk. Reaching the opening, he shouted something in Japanese. From deep in the cave a voice told him to go away. Nakazawa looked at Bob, turned back to the cave and yelled that he was coming in, and he cautiously edged through the jagged coral limestone outcrops and disappeared into the dark opening. Then the period of anxious inaction began.

The Marines in the squad were nervous, scanning the rock formations around them. Fifteen minutes had passed when they heard yelling and then a shot from inside the cavern. The Marines ducked and tightened their grips on their weapons. Suddenly, Nakazawa ran from the cave holding his bleeding arm. From behind him were muffled shots, an explosion, and smoke billowed out of the cave. He came to rest next to Bob, his face twisted in a painful grimace. He had been shot in the forearm and blood was soaking his shirt and dripping from his fingers. Bob asked anxiously what had happened. Nakazawa, with a half-smile through the pained expression on his face, replied that the Japanese soldiers in the cave had disagreed with his request to come out.

Bob took Nakazawa back to the temporary POW stockade. There his arm was patched and set in a cast and arm sling. But now what to do with him? Putting Nakazawa in with other POWs had its own set of risks because some of the Japanese had not surrendered willingly. A number of them had been captured after being knocked unconscious from shelling, or they were wounded so badly they couldn't avoid being taken prisoner. If they found out Nakazawa had been wounded trying to help the Marines, his life could be in danger. Bob explained the situation to him and he nodded silently, resigned to whatever fate awaited him in the POW compound.

The next day, Bob met with John Pelzel at the new D-2 command post. They had moved to the southern part of the island from their tarp-covered railroad cut. John said that Colonel Shoup had heard about Nakazawa and wanted to talk to him. Bob remembered his brief encounter with Shoup on Tarawa, and his previous experience with him on Saipan. In the face of the colonel's skepticism, Bob had tried to convince him that there were many more hundreds of civilians left in the island's jungles. Bob was somewhat leery of Shoup's reputation for being a determined bulldog of a man, a fierce warrior in all the greatest traditions of the Marine Corps, and not particularly sympathetic to efforts aimed at convincing Japanese to surrender. But Bob's impression from his conversation on Saipan was that Shoup was actually mentally inquisitive and alert. Perhaps he would recognize the value of what Nakazawa had tried to do.

Bob checked out one of the D-2 jeeps and picked up Shoup at his command post. It was a short drive to the POW compound. Shoup was chomping silently on a cigar and gave no indication he remembered Bob from their previous meeting. They went inside the stockade and found Nakazawa in a tent, sitting on a cot. When he saw them enter, the warrant officer rose to his feet with some difficulty as he cradled the cast on his arm, and then bowed stiffly. Shoup only waved his cigar dismissively in Nakazawa's direction and sat down heavily on the neighboring cot.

Bob motioned for Nakazawa to take a seat, and then settled next to him. Shoup faced Bob and without hesitation started right off by saying he'd heard about Nakazawa, how he had surrendered and then tried to help the Americans by getting some of his fellow Japanese soldiers to come out. He'd also heard Nakazawa had been shot by one of his own countrymen in the process. Without pausing, Shoup then asked Bob, "What I want to know, and what I want you to ask him, is why is he a traitor?"[8]

The blunt question shocked Bob. First of all, he didn't know the exact Japanese word for "traitor," and even if he did, he wouldn't put the question that way. For effective interrogation, conversations needed to coax out information without intimidating the person. He turned to Nakazawa and said in Japanese that his commanding officer wanted to know why he was willing to assist in persuading Japanese to give up. Nakazawa nodded and, addressing Bob as "lieutenant," said that the war on Tinian was over for the Japanese and he didn't want to see people die needlessly. It was an insightful answer, thoughtfully worded. Shoup was impatient and demanded to know what was being said, even before the warrant officer had finished. Bob turned to Shoup and said that Nakazawa wanted to help save lives, and that he didn't want to see his countrymen die for no reason.

For the next several minutes, he went back and forth between Shoup and Nakazawa, struggling with Shoup's direct confrontational questions, and then trying to translate Nakazawa's thoughtful and reasoned responses. Finally, like a kindly uncle, Nakazawa said he understood Bob's dilemma. He could sense Shoup's confrontational style and the difficulties involved in tactful translation. Because he knew that Bob understood the situation, he suggested a better alternative was to just explain it to Shoup in his own words and not worry about the details of the translation.

Bob nodded, turned to Colonel Shoup, who was losing patience, and tried again to make clear how an enemy combatant could see the battle was lost and agree to help the Marines convince other Japanese to come out. It was a humanitarian issue of not wanting to expend lives needlessly. Shoup didn't buy it and repeatedly tried to get Bob to probe the mind of the warrant officer to determine why such a fanatical foe would suddenly turn into an ally and attempt to facilitate the defeat of the Japanese Imperial Army, seemingly betraying his own country. Finally Shoup stood up, announced he'd heard enough, and stalked out of the tent. Nakazawa rose to his feet at the same time. Bob thanked him quickly before following Shoup out to the jeep. As they drove back to the command post, Shoup sat for a few moments silently mulling over the conversation he'd just had with his enemy. He finally shook his head and said, "We'll never know what makes these Nips tick."[9]

Bob came to the surprising realization that, in this situation, he knew what made the Japanese warrant officer tick, but he actually knew less about what made Shoup tick. It was disconcerting for him to contemplate that he identified more with his former hated enemy than his own commanding officer. Colonel Shoup was thorough and super-competent in his role, which was to secure the island as rapidly and efficiently as possible by military means. He viewed himself as an extension of his country, and by winning the battle on Tinian he was achieving the aims of the government of the United States. He just couldn't imagine a situation where he, as a Marine commander, would not only surrender, but also assist the Japanese enemy to convince other Marines to do so. On one level, Bob could see Shoup's point of view, but he could also identify with Warrant Officer Nakazawa as an intelligent, humanistic person, keeping his dignity in a situation of utter and devastating defeat. It was a mismatch of minds, perceptions, and beliefs, with no real communication. Language was not the barrier.

Over the next few days the fighting on Tinian wound down. There was the usual mopping up and the ongoing task of calling many more civilians and military out of hiding using the jeep-mounted loudspeakers and handheld amplifier megaphones. Sometimes he was joined by Reed Irvine, the JLO who had assisted him on several occasions on Saipan.

At one stop in front of a large cave, Bob and Reed spent about an hour making amplified broadcasts. Finally, a group of what looked like civilians emerged cautiously and approached their jeep. After drinking a lot of water and sitting down on the ground, one of the men, a Japanese from Okinawa who was clutching an infant, pointed to another member of the group and, in Japanese, angrily accused him of being a soldier who had tried to convince them all to kill themselves, and had even threatened to murder them all if they surrendered to the Americans.

The accused man plaintively pleaded innocence, and Bob was put in the position of making a call—send him to the civilian camp or the military POW camp. Soon a group of Marines had gathered to hear the argument, though none of them could understand a word of the Japanese being spoken. Bob and Reed were at a loss, but they were finally convinced when several more civilians, who also had been in the cave, agreed the man in question was definitely a Japanese soldier. So off he went to the POW camp.

A short distance away, several Marines were clearing some caves using explosive charges. Outside one of the cave entrances was a semiconscious Japanese soldier sprawled on the rocks. His head was turning from side to side and he was muttering inaudibly, but otherwise he seemed unhurt. He appeared to have been blasted into a stupor from the concussion of one of the satchel charges. Bob leaned over the soldier and began speaking Japanese, asking him his unit, where he had been assigned, and all the usual questions to determine if he had information of strategic value. The man spoke back in Japanese, still in a semiconscious state. This went on for a couple of minutes, with Bob and the soldier talking back and forth. Suddenly he looked up as if he were seeing things clearly for the first time and, in an astonished tone, blurted out that he didn't speak

English. He failed to realize that he had, in fact, been speaking in his native tongue to an American Marine who was conversing with him in his own language. Bob said he had indeed been speaking Japanese, and that he would be well taken care of and given food and water and medical attention. The soldier was still too stunned to walk without assistance, and Bob asked a couple of nearby Marines to make sure he got to a truck for transport to the POW camp.

His duties finally finished on Tinian, Bob returned to Saipan and promptly came down with dengue fever. He was laid up in the hospital there for a couple of agonizing weeks. Sometimes called "break-bone fever," dengue fever is transmitted by a mosquito bite, just like malaria, and it is only slightly less serious. All the Americans on Saipan and Tinian were popping atabrine pills to stave off malaria, but there was nothing to take for dengue. The high fever, delirium, and overwhelming achiness that sets into the joints made the Marines say about dengue that first you're afraid you're going to die, and then you're afraid you're not. To make matters worse, if anything could be worse than the agony of dengue fever, the nurse Bob had earlier smuggled out of the compound for a trip to the beach was no longer working at the hospital. She had been rotated back to the States. He finally recovered just in time to be sent on a brief diversion for another possible island invasion.

The 2nd Marine Division shipped out to Okinawa in late March 1945. The 1st and 6th Divisions were assigned to be the main invasion force, with the 2nd to provide a feint off the southeastern Okinawan coast, just as they had done at Tinian. Then the 2nd was to be held in reserve and brought ashore if the landing stalled.[10] When the huge armada arrived at Okinawa, it wasn't like Tarawa, where the Japanese were shelling the American ships before the landing even started. Instead, there was little initial opposition from the Japanese defenders as the invading American troops went ashore and proceeded inland. But during the diversionary maneuver on the first day, the ships with the 2nd Marine Division troops were attacked by kamikazes.[11] Bob's ship escaped unscathed, but he watched as the ship next to his was hit and burst into flames, followed by another nearby. There was a lot of firing, and at first he couldn't see what the gunners on his ship were shooting at. There was no formation of Japanese planes, just individuals coming in from all directions. He saw a few shot down, some in fireballs, but some got through, and he was up on deck watching the show.

Bob had never heard the Japanese word "kamikaze" used to describe a suicide pilot. He was familiar with the term in reference to the "divine wind," which was a typhoon that hit while the Mongol fleet was attempting to invade Japan from China in the thirteenth century. It saved the day for the Japanese when the storm sunk the Mongol invasion boats. Seven centuries later, the military rulers of Japan envisioned the suicide pilots to be a 1940s version of the "divine wind" that could rescue their country from the Americans.[12]

After waiting around for a while, the 2nd Marine Division was sent back to Saipan.[13] The initial minimal enemy resistance meant they were not needed and there was nothing more for them to do. The landing was on April 1 and Bob's twenty-third birthday was April 8. He thought it was a perfect birthday present—he didn't need a cake; survival was a great gift. After the departure of the 2nd Marine Division, the Marines and U.S. Army troops wheeled to the south on Okinawa, and thousands of Japanese started fighting back from cemeteries and caves and tunnels. It was then that the real struggle began, and it turned into one of the most savage battles of World War II.[14]

After his return to Saipan and until mid-1945, Bob was mostly working with civil affairs to restore agriculture and fisheries. One of his projects was to help put the skipjack bonito fishing boats back into operation.[15] His main task was to make sure the boats were captained and crewed by Japanese and Okinawan civilians who could be trusted not to escape to other islands.

Before the invasion, there had been a sizable fishing industry based on Saipan aimed at producing katsuobushi, or dried bonito tuna fillets, mainly for export to Japan. After the battle, the Americans restored the fishery to catch skipjack, a small tuna fish, to feed the thousands of Japanese civilians, the native Chamorros and Carolinians, and the Japanese POWs on Saipan. Because the operation ended up working out so well, they also were able to supply fresh fish to the large number of U.S. military forces on the island. There was so much excess production that the U.S. Navy brought in a freezing plant, and skipjack was supplied to naval vessels and even sent back to Hawaii.

While Bob was helping restore the skipjack industry on Saipan, the 2nd Marine Division was preparing for the assault on Japan proper. By this time, Bob had participated in three island invasions, had tallied a great many service points in the process, and was long overdue for leave. Only the shortage of JLOs had kept him on Saipan. Finally, with the accumulated points for his duration of service overseas, his combat activities, and the Bronze Star he had been awarded for his efforts in convincing so many civilians and military to surrender, he was sent back to the United States for a brief home leave prior to the upcoming invasion of Japan.

To begin his month-long break in the States, he first traveled on a Navy seaplane, called a PBY, from Saipan to Hawaii. All the way back to Honolulu, Bob was obsessing about the hula dancer's husband who had vowed to kill him. This was to be his climactic return to face the outcome of the ill-fated affair that had been on his mind since he had left for the Saipan invasion the year before. His stress level rose with every mile the seaplane drew closer to Hawaii.

He decided the best thing to do when he arrived was to contact his friends Richard and Iris to ask their advice on how to avoid the vengeful husband. Immediately after he got off the plane at Pearl Harbor, he made the call, but before he could ask the question he really wanted answered (namely, was the jilted husband lurking nearby?), Richard invited Bob to dinner at their home. After a tense taxi ride and a warm welcome, it didn't seem appropriate to blurt out his question immediately. During dinner there was the usual small talk, centered mainly on what Bob had been doing and what had been going on in Honolulu. Finally, unprompted by Bob, Richard asked if he remembered the hula dancer and her husband. Bob tried to appear nonchalant and replied that he indeed remembered the couple. Richard and his wife went on to relate an extraordinary story.

It turned out that before Bob met her at their wedding, the dancer and her husband had been having a bad time, not getting along, and their marriage had been on the rocks. Then Bob made his unexpected entrance, and they were forced to confront their troubled relationship. After Bob left Hawaii for Saipan, they talked a lot about what they should do, ultimately deciding to stick with their marriage and work out their problems. Unbeknownst to him, Bob had helped them get back together. Amazingly, they referred to him as the dancer's "second honeymoon."

They had left word with Richard and Iris to let them know the minute Bob showed up in Hawaii, so they could take him out to dinner to thank him. Extremely relieved, Bob argued convincingly that he would just as soon let the matter rest and not see them again. He had successfully survived combat on three islands, and he didn't want to press his luck by confronting the couple, even if he had been her "second honeymoon."

NINE

Japanese Language and World War II in Retrospect: Boulder, 2002

As 2002 rolled around, the chief archivist at the University of Colorado and unofficial keeper of all things from the World War II Japanese Language School, David Hays, realized that the sixtieth anniversary of the establishment of the JLS in Boulder had arrived. It seemed like the time was right to organize the first-ever reunion of JLS graduates.

Bob was eager to attend, and he flew in from San Francisco. He was a spry eighty years old, but he was limping slightly. He complained in his usual good-natured way that his hips had worn out. He later got a titanium hip replacement, and he didn't let it slow him down as he kept up his trips back and forth to Taiwan. It was there that he had based a successful career in business consulting all over Asia. The Taiwan business was the culmination of quite an eventful postwar life.

Shortly after finding out he wasn't going to be killed by the husband with murderous intent in Honolulu, he arranged transportation back to the United States for his leave. He was on a small aircraft carrier, the USS *Makassar Strait*, headed down the ship channel leading from Pearl Harbor to the open ocean when guns started going off. Just then, it was announced over the public address system that the war was over. The sailing plans of the ship didn't change, though, and out across the Pacific they went. The next stop was San Pedro, California.

Abandoning plans for his leave, Bob made his way to Washington, D.C., where he met with General Watson, the same General Watson who had awarded Bob his Bronze Star citation on Saipan. Though he was now commandant of the Marine Corps, he made time to talk to Bob because he remembered the citation and his unusual service on Saipan. Bob told the general he wanted to stay in the Marines and go back to China. When the general found out Bob had been attending Harvard when the war broke out, he recommended that he finish his degree before deciding whether to return to active duty with the Marines. So back to Harvard Bob went, changing his major from biology to Far Eastern studies. He never did return to active duty, but he stayed in the Marine Corps Reserve for the next twenty years, eventually ending up with the rank of major.

One of the classes he took was an advanced course on Chinese language. There was only one other person in the class, a strikingly attractive student from Radcliff named Jane Packard Pratt. They hit it off right away, partly because she had an upbringing in China similar to his. As the granddaughter of a medical missionary in Beijing, she and two of her sisters, as well as their mother, had been imprisoned in China by the Japanese for a while at the beginning of the war.[1] After spending some time in an internment camp, they got out of China on the Swedish ship *Gripsholm*, made famous for peaceful civilian exchanges early in the war as the United States and Japan clashed on Pacific island battlefields.[2]

Bob graduated from Harvard in June 1946, magna cum laude. It was the first commencement to take place since the end of the war. He spoke as the combined valedictorian for the classes of 1942, 1943, 1944, 1945, and 1946. Receiving honorary degrees that morning were some of the wartime leaders, including General Eisenhower from the Army, Admiral Nimitz from the Navy, and General Vandegrift from the Marines.

Bob and Jane were married that year, and he subsequently completed his master's degree at Harvard in China regional studies in 1948, securing a job shortly thereafter at the Pentagon as a China affairs analyst for the U.S. Army. He was to have worked as a civilian analyst in Nanjing (Nanking) in the late 1940s, but the Communists were in the process of taking over China and closing U.S. attaché offices. Bob shifted from the Attaché Service to the U.S. Information Service and accepted a similar position in Nanjing. He was on his way to his assigned post with his family, but just before they got there, Nanjing fell to the Communists.

It was then decided that his job would be based in Shanghai instead. Bob greeted this news enthusiastically because this would give him a chance to return to the city of his birth. He left his wife and two small sons at the U.S. Consulate Residence in Taipei and went on ahead to make arrangements for them to follow. He was in Shanghai for the month of April, but the Chinese Communist forces, having taken the Nationalist capital city of Nanjing, were advancing rapidly toward Shanghai from the north. He witnessed the pathetic retreat through Shanghai of Nationalist army troops. The refugee government fled to Canton and relocated to Taiwan at the end of the year.[3]

The onrushing Chinese Communists spread panic among the foreign expatriates. The United States ramped up efforts to evacuate Americans who faced being trapped in the city. Even though he had official status, Bob was barely able to secure a seat on what was to have been the last American plane out of Shanghai to Taiwan. He made his way to the airport and was ready to board, when he received a frantic message from a friend in Taipei, Louis de Groot, requesting help to get a flight to Taiwan for his wife, Emma. Louis and Emma were Canadian missionaries of Dutch origin serving in Taipei with the Mackay Presbyterian Mission, which ran a major hospital and a nurse training school. Emma had required special surgery, for which there were no specialist surgeons available in Taiwan, so she had been sent to Shanghai for the operation. Though she had not yet fully recovered, it was imperative to get her back to Taiwan before the Chinese Communists closed down Shanghai.

She arrived at the airport as Bob made hurried inquiries, only to find out to his dismay that there was a catch. Emma de Groot did not qualify for American emergency evacuation, and there were no more available flights. There was only one alternative. With official permission, Bob gave his assigned seat to her. As he watched her board the plane, he wondered how he was going to get out of Shanghai. Perhaps he could improvise an escape by catching a train to Canton, and then travel by boat to Taiwan. To his immense relief, several days later an additional American evacuation flight from Shanghai to Taiwan became available. Bob was then able to rejoin his family who were anxiously waiting in Taipei for his return.

Bob served the next three years in Taiwan as director of the U.S. Information Service (USIS). After the Chinese Nationalist government was reestablished in Taiwan, what had been the American Consulate General was elevated to be the American Embassy, headed by Ambassador Karl Rankin. Bob became the embassy's public affairs officer, while concurrently directing the USIS. Bob's USIS colleagues in Taipei included two fellow JLS classmates from Boulder and wartime JLOs, Dave Osborn and Chuck Cross. In Taiwan, Dave served concurrently in the USIS and as a political officer for the embassy. Chuck was Bob's junior assistant in the USIS. Many years later, Dave became political adviser to the U.S. representative in Beijing, and Chuck Cross became the American ambassador to Singapore.

Although work in Taiwan was interesting, Bob did not enjoy the governmental bureaucratic framework of his job. He accepted an offer from the San Francisco–based Committee for a Free Asia (CFA) to serve as its field representative for Malaya/Singapore. He was to be based in Kuala Lumpur. The aim of the CFA was to counter Communist political influence. At first a clandestine operation, the CFA was later reconstituted as The Asia Foundation, with much broader functions, and private as well as some U.S. congressional funding.[4] Malaya, together with Sarawak and Sabah on the island of Borneo, later combined to become present-day Malaysia, and Singapore became a separate country.

As the field representative of CFA, in 1952 Bob moved to Kuala Lumpur. With official British concurrence, he initiated projects to counter Communist influence and terrorism. He arrived to find "The Emergency," as the British called it, in full swing in Malaya. It was a mainly Chinese Communist–led campaign of lethal terrorism against the British and Malay officialdoms and their supporters. The Communist terrorist guerillas (dubbed "CTs") were well armed with military weaponry left over from the war of resistance against the Japanese forces that had invaded and occupied Malaya and Singapore in 1942, almost immediately after Japan's attack on Pearl Harbor.[5]

Inevitably, Bob's work became well known to the CTs and grew increasingly hazardous. He was tracked and followed, and on one occasion he narrowly escaped ambush and assassination, only because he happened to be absent from a local group of civilians with whom he regularly went hunting for feral pigs in the nearby jungle on weekends.

During Bob's time in Malaya, Vice President Richard Nixon and his wife, Pat, were touring Asian countries on behalf of newly elected President

Eisenhower. The Nixons visited Kuala Lumpur in October 1953 on a fact-finding tour to learn whether there was a chance the Communist guerillas might win their war against the British Commonwealth forces. Bob participated in welcoming the Nixons on arrival, arranged for them to meet various Malayans during their stay, and helped with security measures.

After his three years in Malaya, Bob returned to work for The Asia Foundation in San Francisco for the next ten years. He built a home in Marin County on the shore of the Belvedere Lagoon, where he and Jane and their four children lived until they moved temporarily to Washington, D.C., in 1963. Bob was invited by the National Academy of Sciences (NAS) to serve as associate director of the Pacific Science Board to promote scientific projects and cooperation among nations of the Asia Pacific region. His senior colleague was Harold Jefferson Coolidge, Harvard-educated biologist and world-renowned wildlife conservationist.

During the next six years, Bob traveled frequently to Asian countries for the NAS to promote a wide range of science development projects in diverse Asian countries, ranging from Indonesia and the Philippines in Southeast Asia, to Taiwan and Korea in northeast Asia. During this time, he helped establish and conduct a major program of science and technology cooperation between the United States and Taiwan, administered jointly by the NAS and its Chinese counterpart in Taiwan, the Academia Sinica.

Following his years in Washington with the NAS, Bob decided to enter the world of business enterprise. He was recruited in 1969 by a Detroit company called COMAC. The owners aimed to get into the field petroleum drilling equipment supply business as part of the booming offshore oilfield development activity taking place in Southeast Asia. Based in Singapore for COMAC, Bob worked for three years until its parent firm in Detroit was paralyzed by antitrust action. At that point, Bob started his own consulting business in Singapore. He named it Development Management Ltd. (DML), and it was incorporated in Hong Kong. Besides promotion and sales of oilfield supplies, among the diverse projects Bob helped to develop and manage was one in aquaculture for the Malaysian Borneo state of Sabah. The idea was to establish a new industry, the commercial farming of marine algae, which provided the raw materials for production of carrageenans by the Maine-based firm Marine Colloids. The enterprise progressed well and took up much of Bob's time for several years.

In 1984 Bob moved to Taiwan and continued his consulting practice from Taipei. For about two years he served as agriculture and special reports officer for the American Institute in Taiwan (AIT), which had become America's unofficial embassy there when President Carter set up the official American Embassy in Beijing. Bob was recruited by the Seattle-based engineering consulting firm Kramer, Chin & Mayo to start and help manage an emerging seawater aquaculture project in north China. Located along the Bohai Gulf coast, not far from Tianjin (Tientsin), the project consisted of converting extensive salt flat drying areas into shrimp cultivation ponds, as well as producing shrimp food, shrimp culture, and processing, freezing, and packing shrimp products for export. Owned by a Chinese regional state farm (Nandagang), the project was profitable, netting $2 million the first year. This was because there was a good crop, strong world demand, and high prices for the product, the large "China White Shrimp."

Bob lived at the shrimp project site in China for a year, and then returned to Taiwan, where he became the representative and sales agent for two firms in the field of tunnel construction. One was a Canadian company that manufactured tunnel boring equipment, Lovat Tunnel Boring Machines. The other, CONDAT Lubrifiants, was a French company that manufactured special chemicals and lubricants used in tunnel boring. Bob played a key role in providing the products and related services used for a giant tunnel projects in northern Taiwan. It provided a link for vehicle traffic from the capital city of Taipei with the island's east coast. In connection with that project, Bob went to Russia seven times to recruit excellent, but unemployed, Russian engineers and operators for the tunneling machines.

After their early years in Taiwan, Jane was with him in Southeast Asia, first in Malaya, then in Singapore. Later on, she mostly resided in their Belvedere home in California while Bob traveled. Having worked at the Library of Congress in Washington, D.C., and later earning a professional degree in librarianship, Jane served as a librarian for Marin County. Although Bob and Jane had divorced, Bob moved back to California from Taiwan in 1995. Medical diagnoses indicated that Jane had an incurable cancer, from which she died in October 1996 in Marin County. Five years later, in 2001, in Santa Rosa, California, Bob married Bao-Mei Liu, former Taiwan corporate executive secretary and Taipei office manager of DML, Bob's Hong Kong–incorporated consulting firm. The eldest daughter of a Taiwanese middle-class family and fluent in three languages, Bao-Mei graduated with honors from two universities in California to become a financial analyst for the Kaiser Permanente medical organization in Santa Rosa, California.

Bob's childhood chums from Shanghai who became JLOs all turned into overachievers. Bucky Freeman's father, Mansfield, the man Bob remembered as a judge in the foreign court in Shanghai, teamed up with C. V. Starr to start a company called American Asiatic Underwriters before the war. It was a large Asian insurance company that ended up with the more familiar name AIG. Bucky, known more formally by his full name, Houghton Freeman, ended up working for AIG and founded the Freeman Foundation to fund academic grants for the teaching of Asian studies to academic institutions.[6] Bucky's lifelong pal, another of the Shanghai kids and fellow JLS classmate, Bill Allman, worked with Bucky for a time and did very well in the business world, as well.

Bob's older brother, George, graduated from the JLS in Boulder a few months after Bob and became a JLO in the Navy. During the war he served at the Allied Translator and Interpreter Service (ATIS) in Brisbane, Australia. ATIS was a joint American and Australian military intelligence operation under the command of General MacArthur. George joined a number of Boulder JLOs who also served there. At war's end, George was sent to Japan to take part in the decommissioning and sinking of Japan's submarine fleet.

For some years, George worked for the University of California administration in Berkeley. At the outbreak of the Korean War, George, still a Naval Reserve officer, was called back to intelligence duty in Tokyo. He subsequently served in the American Embassy in Vietnam, and he was in Saigon during the years of turmoil before and after the November 1963 coup d'état assassination of President Ngo Dinh Diem. Long since retired, George resides in Southern California. His eldest daughter, Diana, and her family live nearby.

Dan Williams' life paralleled Bob's in many ways. They grew up together in Shanghai, went to the JLS in Boulder together, were both Marine combat interpreters, served together on Saipan, and lived near each other for years in the Bay Area. Dan ended up pursuing a successful career in finance and living with his wife, Jan, north of San Francisco. After Bob's move back to California from Taiwan, they once again live near each other and visit frequently.

John Pelzel, the wartime 2nd Marine Division Headquarters intelligence section (D-2) senior officer, was Bob's best man at his wedding in 1946 in Cambridge at the on-campus Harvard Chapel in Harvard Yard. After the war, Pelzel, who had a doctorate in cultural anthropology, returned to Harvard and served as director of Harvard's Peabody Museum and director of the Harvard Yenching Institute and Library of East Asian Studies. He became one of America's leading professors of Asian studies.

Otis Cary, Bob's JLS roommate first at Berkeley and then in Boulder, never became a missionary in Japan like he had so hoped to do, but he did end up spending most of the rest of his life in the country of his birth. He was an academic who lived in Japan and helped bring democratic practices and reform to Doshisha University after the war. During that time he met the emperor's younger brother, Prince Takamatsu, and suggested that the prince urge the emperor to travel out among his subjects so he could get to know them better. Following Otis' advice, the prince mentioned this idea to his brother, and the emperor did just that, to great acclaim. Otis lived in Kyoto for many years, authored numerous books on Japan and Asia, and cofounded the Center for American Studies at Doshisha.[7] Bob stayed in touch with Otis off and on over the years, but as he aged, Alzheimer's claimed the brilliant mind and agile intellect that had made him one of the most influential of the Japanese-speaking former JLOs in postwar Japan.

Through the course of his life, Bob stopped hating Japan, but another Boulder classmate of Bob's, Donald Keene, fell in love with that country. Late in life he gave up his U.S. citizenship and moved to Japan, where he intends to live his final years. While Bob was trying to bring in live POWs, Don was translating captured diaries. He was a sensitive, poetic, esthetic, student type, and it is easy to imagine the strong impact of the admirable human and cultural qualities revealed in those Japanese documents. The diaries were written mostly by young Japanese soldiers his age, who were soon to die. Subsequent academic devotion to Japanese literature and history must have completed his conversion.

All of Bob's old classmates were on his mind when he showed up for the JLS reunion in 2002. It was the first time he had been back to Boulder since his graduation in early 1943. He recognized the faculty club on campus where he had eaten all his meals. It still looked pretty much the same as it did in 1942. But the Boulder campus of the early 1940s was only a fraction of the size of the early 2000s version. Trees had grown and matured and partially obscured the older buildings. There also had been much infilling with postwar construction that changed the look of the place. But there were a few landmarks that were still unmistakable. One was the stately, fortress-like Macky Auditorium where Florence Walne administered the JLS from an office on the ground floor. It had been the first stop Bob made when he arrived in Boulder initially, and it was where the graduation ceremony for his class was held. Another building he remembered was the old Memorial Center, now the economics building. The library also was recognizable as a place where JLS classes were regularly convened.

Dan Williams was at the reunion, as well. Still known for his amazing memory, he could clearly recall the dorm where they had lived, including exactly where his own room was, where Bob's room was, and where Bob's brother, George's, room was. He could describe in detail the path he took after entering the west door to go downstairs and around a corner to his room.

Part of the JLS reunion was a luncheon held at the Alumni Center, a stately, old, redbrick mansion tucked into one corner of the CU campus. Bob was very familiar with this particular landmark. It was the former residence of the university president, the place where the blonde from his JLS days in Boulder had lived upstairs. Many were the evenings he said goodnight to her on the steps of the front porch.

A buffet was set up under an expansive, open-sided canopy tent on the lawn behind the sprawling, old, Victorian house. It was a warm June day, and the reunion participants were chatting amiably. The JLS reunion of 2002 was unique. Many other veterans' groups from World War II had been getting together regularly for years after the war, their allegiances formed around their combat units, bomb groups, or the ships on which sailors spent months or even years together at sea. What made the JLS graduates different was that once they left Boulder, they were scattered to the four winds and assigned to different Navy and Marine units all over the Pacific. Few were able to form deep bonds to these units because they were often attached for short periods of time before moving on. Most of the JLS graduates had not been back to Boulder since completing their wartime Japanese language training and departing for the far reaches of the Pacific. It also marked the first time many had seen each other since the war.

There were about forty veterans and a few of their nisei teachers in attendance, in addition to their wives or adult offspring. Ari and Ida Inouye were there, as well. Ari had been one of the JLS instructors, and he was reputed to have been one of their best teachers. Another attendee was a tall, white-haired veteran with an elegant handlebar mustache and beard, none other than Jish Martin, the Navy JLO who had helped run the civilian camp on Saipan.

Bob and Jish hadn't seen each other since their days on Saipan, and they discussed their experiences during the war eagerly. They brought up the topic of Guy Gabaldon, and how "Gabby" would bring in straggling lines of Japanese civilians, cursing at them in Japanese and shoving them. Then Gabby would turn around and tell Jish how much he identified with the Japanese because he was raised by Japanese-American nisei in Los Angeles.[8] Bob had gone back to Saipan for the fiftieth anniversary in 1994 and had run into Gabby, who'd been living on Saipan for years. Gabaldon was proud of the fact that he was the only Marine veteran of the Saipan campaign who actually returned to take up residence on the island. Bob and Gabaldon actually got along pretty well. Gabby toured Bob around Saipan and flew him to nearby Tinian in his small plane to have a look at the old airfields, war relics, the site where the atom bombs had been loaded into the B-29s *Enola Gay* and *Bocks Car*, and, of course, the beach where Bob landed during the Tinian campaign.[9]

Bob and Jish recalled the Hollywood movie about Gabaldon's alleged Saipan exploits, with Tab Hunter, more than six feet tall, and a smooth operator, incongruously playing Gabby, who was barely five feet tall, rough, and feisty. Neither Bob nor Jish seemed resentful that Gabby had portrayed himself to the media and the public as the only Marine on Saipan who captured any Japanese, when in fact there were a number of Marine JLOs, U.S. Army nisei, Caucasian interpreters, and naval civil affairs personnel, like Otis Cary and John Decker, who were either actively bringing in Japanese military and civilians who had surrendered or were contributing to that effort.

Later the JLS veterans gathered at the University Memorial Center, the student union building on one edge of the CU campus. David Hays had organized the dedication of a marker commemorating the JLS. The text on the bronze plaque summarized the history of the school and the unique contributions of the graduates to the war effort. The veterans crammed into a relatively small space with too few chairs for the dedication, reminding Bob of his early JLS days in the cramped classrooms at Berkeley.

Later that afternoon was a reception in the old Faculty Club on the Boulder campus where the JLS students had taken their meals while learning Japanese. The room was filled with congenial octogenarians, and in that way it was a typical gathering of World War II veterans. Their conversations, however, were not the usual war stories, and they revolved around breaking Japanese codes, translating captured documents, inducing surrenders, and interrogating Japanese POWs.

One of the veterans was seated on an electric scooter. It was Ray Luthy, and it was the first time Bob had seen Ray since discussing the Iwo Jima invasion with him after Ray reappeared on Saipan minus a leg. It was amputated on a ship offshore after a Japanese shell exploded near him on the beach at Iwo. He was fitted with an artificial limb after the war and had been wearing it ever since. Dan Williams also landed on Iwo Jima, along with some other JLOs, but Ray was the only one seriously wounded.

Near the end of the reunion, there was a panel discussion in the ornately restored theater in Old Main, the first structure built on the CU campus in the 1870s. There were a number of talks about the history and impact of the JLS-trained language officers in the Pacific war. During the discussion session, a JLO named Larry Vincent stood and brought up what turned out to be a hot-button issue with the veterans. He said his fellow Marines were all racist and shot the Japanese POWs he had captured. This drew a number of sharp comments from the former JLOs, either agreeing or disagreeing. But several said they wanted to hear what Bob had to say about the role racism played in the Pacific war, given that he seemed to have had the most combat experience of any of them.

All eyes turned to Bob as he stood up slowly. He then gave a carefully worded account of how he initially hated the Japanese but later learned tolerance, first from the sensei at the JLS in Berkeley and Boulder, and then from some of the Japanese civilians and military he encountered on Saipan and Tinian. He agreed that a major challenge was to convince his fellow Marines to take prisoners rather than kill them. But he figured their attitude had less to do with racism and more to do with their training—they were taught many methods and techniques to kill the Japanese, and they viewed that as their primary mission. Once they got into combat, they heard stories about Japanese treachery, feigning first to surrender, and then suddenly producing weapons or explosives to kill Marines who approached them. That, and the Japanese propensity to fight to the death in the face of hopeless situations that cost more Marine lives, formed a determination on the part of the Americans not to risk taking prisoners and killing them instead.

For the Marines in the Pacific, their upbringing taught them that taking a human life was not acceptable, yet they were trained and desensitized to overcome that upbringing and kill the Japanese enemy. The Americans would routinely talk tough before a battle and fight the Japanese with a ruthless intensity, but when civilian refugees would surrender, the Marines would often show empathy in ways directly opposite to their actions in fighting the Japanese military. Bob had come to realize that some circumstances bring out the very worst in people, and some bring out the very best, and most humans are fully capable of both. He was an eyewitness to that great range of human behavior and had, in the end, found life-affirming humanity in the midst of the brutality of war.

NOTES

Prologue: A Remarkable Incident on Saipan, Western Tropical Pacific, 1944

1. Haruko Taya Cook and Theodore F. Cook, *Japan at War* (New York: The New Press, 1992), 291–92.
2. Major Carl W. Hoffman, *Saipan: The Beginning of the End* (Historical Branch, G-3 Division, Headquarters, U.S. Marine Corps, 1950), 45.
3. Uchizono Yozo, letter to Glenn Slaughter, *The Interpreter* (Archives, University of Colorado at Boulder Libraries, 2002), Number 45.
4. Cook and Cook, *Japan at War*, 288–89.
5. Cook and Cook, *Japan at War*, 291.
6. Robert Sheeks' experiences and observations throughout this book are taken from voice tape interviews conducted by the author in 1995, 2000, and 2002. Where quotations are given, the voice tape interviews will be specifically cited.
7. Rex Alan Smith and Gerald A. Meehl, *Pacific War Stories: In the Words of Those Who Survived* (New York: Abbeville Press, 2004), 453–54.
8. Benis M. Frank, *Marine Corps Gazette*, obituary for William K. Jones, 1998. Jones was awarded the Silver Star for his actions during the Tarawa invasion in November 1943. During that battle he received a field promotion to lieutenant colonel before he was twenty-seven years old, and he was reputed to be the youngest Marine of that rank. He went on to win the Navy Cross for his leadership under fire on Saipan and Tinian at age twenty-eight.
9. Col. Joseph H. Alexander, *Utmost Savagery* (Annapolis: Naval Institute Press, 1995), 231; Capt. James R. Stockman, *The Battle for Tarawa* (Marines in World War II Historical Monograph, Historical Section, Division of Public Information Headquarters, U.S. Marine Corps, 1947), 73.
10. Hoffman, *Saipan: The Beginning of the End*, 8.
11. Rex Alan Smith and Gerald A. Meehl, *Pacific Legacy: Image and Memory from World War II in the Pacific* (New York: Abbeville Press, 2002), 149; Interview with Scott Russell, Historical Preservation Officer, Saipan, December 30, 1987.

12. 2nd Marine Division, FMF, In the Field, P/A Directives, D-2. Robert Sheeks collection.
13. Cook and Cook, *Japan at War*, 287.

Chapter 1. An Unusual Childhood: Shanghai, 1932

1. Saburo Ienaga, *The Pacific War 1931–1945* (New York: Pantheon Books, 1968; English Translation 1978 by Random House), 65; Donald Jordan, *Chinese Boycotts Versus Japanese Bombs: The Failure of China's "Revolutionary Diplomacy" 1931–32* (Ann Arbor: University of Michigan Press, 1991), 259, 277.
2. Donald A. Jordan, *China's Trial by Fire: The Shanghai War of 1932* (Ann Arbor: The University of Michigan Press, 2001), 16.
3. Robert Sheeks' recollections of his childhood experiences growing up in Shanghai taken from voice tape interviews conducted by the author in 1995, 2000, and 2002.
4. Jordan, *China's Trial by Fire*, 1.
5. Eric Niderost, *The Lost Leathernecks* (*World War II Magazine*, November, 2005), 35.
6. Dan Williams' recollections of his childhood experiences growing up in Shanghai taken from voice tape interviews conducted by the author in 2003.
7. Dan Williams' recollections of his childhood experiences growing up in Shanghai taken from voice tape interviews conducted by the author in 2003.
8. Niderost, *The Lost Leathernecks*, 35. The Shanghai Volunteer Corps was designated to protect the International and French Concessions, supplemented by troops from the respective home governments. Thus, the French Concession had troops sent by France for security to supplement the Shanghai Volunteer Corps and the U.S. 4th Marine Regiment.
9. Jordan, *China's Trial by Fire*, 42. Combat in Chapei between Japanese marines and the Chinese 19th Route Army broke out the night of January 28, 1932.
10. Niderost, *The Lost Leathernecks*, 40.
11. Greg Leck, *Captives of Empire: The Japanese Internment of Allied Civilians in China 1941–1945* (Bangor, PA: Shandy Press, 2007), 675.
12. Jordan, *China's Trial by Fire*, 47.
13. Dan Williams' recollection, voice tape interview conducted by the author and follow-up email messages in 2003.
14. Jordan, *China's Trial by Fire*, 192.
15. Ibid, 27.
16. Dan Williams' recollection, voice tape interview conducted by the author and follow-up email messages in 2003.
17. The name of the British family, the friends of the Sheeks who evacuated Shanghai, has been lost to history. For the purposes of this story, they are referred to as the Mitchell family.
18. This particular atrocity could have been perpetrated by members of any one of several groups of the Japanese military engaged in the invasion of Shanghai. Japanese marine naval forces were the first to enter into combat with the Chinese army in Shanghai. They were joined subsequently by units of the Japanese army as the

fighting intensified. There were also Japanese civilian militia, or vigilante units, who called themselves ronin after the samurai from the shogun era. All were involved in combat and committed various atrocities against the Chinese, some reported, some not. Thousands of Chinese civilians in Shanghai simply disappeared and could not be accounted for. They were either the victims of combat or atrocities. Ienaga, *The Pacific War 1931–1945*, 65; Jordan, *China's Trial by Fire*, 42, 80, 111, 192.

19. Ienaga, *The Pacific War 1931–1945*, 66. Jordan, *China's Trial by Fire*, 231.

Chapter 2. Japanese Language Immersion: Berkeley, California, and Boulder, Colorado, 1942–43

1. Ienaga, *The Pacific War 1931–1945*, 171–80; John Keegan, *The Second World War* (New York: Penguin Books, 1989), 256–67.
2. Roger Dingman, *Deciphering the Rising Sun* (Annapolis: Naval Institute Press, 2009), 5–6.
3. Irwin Leonard Slesnick and Carole Evelyn Slesnick, *Kanji and Codes: Learning Japanese for World War II* (Bellingham, WA: Self-published, 2006), 76.
4. Slesnick and Slesnick, *Kanji and Codes*, 77.
5. Ibid., 78.
6. Ibid., 87–88.
7. Ibid., 79.
8. Account of the Japanese language class from Robert Sheeks' recollections (voice tape interviews in 2000 and 2002), Dan Williams' recollections (voice tape interviews in 2003), and from Dingman, *Deciphering the Rising Sun*, 14, 29–51; Slesnick and Slesnick, *Kanji and Codes*, 74–76.
9. Slesnick and Slesnick, *Kanji and Codes*, 13.
10. Bob Sheeks' description of Japanese language from voice tapes and follow-up emails; Dingman, *Deciphering the Rising Sun*, 29–30.
11. Dingman, *Deciphering the Rising Sun*, 18; Slesnick and Slesnick, *Kanji and Codes*, 94.
12. This exchange was recounted by Bob Sheeks in voice tape interviews conducted by the author in 2000 and 2002.
13. Dingman, *Deciphering the Rising Sun*, 19–21.
14. Ibid., 22.
15. Dan Williams' recollections from voice tape interview conducted by the author in 2003.
16. Leck, *Captives of Empire*, 675.
17. Dingman, *Deciphering the Rising Sun*, 33.
18. Ari Inouye recollections, unpublished manuscript.
19. *The Interpreter*, The U.S. Navy Japanese/Oriental Language School Archival Project, Archives, University of Coloardo at Boulder Libraries, Number 65, July 1, 2003.
20. Slesnick and Slesnick, *Kanji and Codes*, 85.
21. Bob Sheeks, voice tape interview conducted by the author in 2002.
22. Bob Sheeks voice tape interview conducted by the author in 2002, and follow-up email correspondence.

23. Bob Sheeks voice tape interview conducted by the author in 2002, and follow-up email correspondence.
24. Dan Williams voice tape interview conducted by the author in 2003.
25. Bob Sheeks voice tape interview conducted by the author in 2002
26. John Keegan, *The Second World War* (New York: Penguin Books, 1989), 292–93.

Chapter 3. Combat Training: Camp Elliott, and on to the Pacific, 1943
1. Dingman, *Deciphering the Rising Sun*, 67.
2. Filmography for Sid Salkow: http://www.imdb.com/name/nm0758508/filmotype
3. Dingman, *Deciphering the Rising Sun*, 66.
4. Robert Sheeks letter to Paul Dull, February 17, 1943, twenty handwritten pages, Robert Sheeks collection.
5. Filmography for Doris Dowling: http://www.imdb.com/name/nm0235835/
6. Filmography for Virginia Mayo: http://www.imdb.com/name/nm0562920/
7. Deanna Swaney, *Samoa* (Berkeley: Lonely Planet Publications, 1994), 154.
8. Margaret Mead, *Coming of Age in Samoa* (New York: Morrow Quill, 1928), 42.

Chapter 4. Adventures in Japanese Language: New Zealand and Noumea, New Caledonia, 1943
1. William Manchester, *American Caesar* (New York: Dell Publishing, 1978), 324. MacArthur established his office in an old insurance building at 401 Collins Street in Melbourne.
2. Robert Leckie, *Delivered from Evil* (New York: Harper and Row, 1987), 214; Keegan, *The Second World War*, 330.
3. For more details on the Marine camp at Paekakariki, see: http://home.clear.net.nz /pages/42mbjeep/US%20Marines%20Page.htm
4. Col. Joseph H. Alexander, *Utmost Savagery* (Annapolis: Naval Institute Press, 1995), 44.
5. Peter Turner, Jeff Williams, Nancy Keller, and Tony Wheeler, *New Zealand* (Hawthorn, Australia: Lonely Planet Publications, 1998), 15–16.
6. Filmography for Ida Lupino: http://www.imdb.com/name/nm0526946/; filmography for Louis Hayward: http://www.imdb.com/name/nm0371775/
7. *American Men and Women of Science* (AmMWSc 73S), New York: R. R. Bowker Co., 1973, eds. 38, 40.
8. Col. Joseph H. Alexander, *Utmost Savagery*, 76.
9. For a description of the World War II experiences of New Zealand women, see Deborah Montgomerie, *The Women's War: New Zealand Women 1939–45* (Auckland, N.Z.: Auckland University Press, 2001). For a more complete account of the role of New Zealand women during the war, see Eve Ebbett, *When the Boys Were Away: New Zealand Women in World War II* (Wellington, N.Z.: Reed, 1984). War brides in New Zealand: http://histclo.com/essay/war/ww2/cou/us/live/w2usl-bride.html
10. Dingman, *Deciphering the Rising Sun*, 69. A combat interpreter, Lt. Ralph Cory, was one of the twenty-three Marines killed on the patrol led by Division intelligence chief Lt. Col. Frank Goettge.

11. The name of the ethnic Japanese army interpreter who assisted Bob in Noumea is lost to history. For the purposes of the story here, he is called Sergeant Watanabe.
12. Bob Sheeks voice tape interviews conducted by the author in 2000 and 2002.
13. Carl Boyd and Akihiko Yoshida, *The Japanese Submarine Force and World War II* (Annapolis: Naval Institute Press, 1995), 43.
14. Edwin P. Hoyt, *Japan's War* (New York: Cooper Square Press, 1986), 113.
15. Bob Hackett and Sander Kingsepp, *HIJMS Submarine I-17: Tabular Record of Movement* (Contributions from Dr. Higuchi Tatsuhiro of Japan, Steve Eckardt of Australia, and Andrew Obluski of Poland, 2001): http://www.combinedfleet.com/I-17.htm
16. Bert Webber, *Retaliation: Japanese Attacks and Allied Countermeasures on the Pacific Coast in World War II*, (Corvallis: Oregon State University Press, 1975), 30–31.
17. Carl Boyd and Akihiko Yoshida, *The Japanese Submarine Force and World War II*, 24–26.
18. Jess W. Carr, "Vs-57 and the Sinking of Japanese Submarine I-17," *Naval Aviation News*, September–October, 2001, 14–15.
19. Bert Webber, *Retaliation*, 14–16.
20. Ibid., 158.
21. Patrick Barta, "Tricky Digs," *The Wall Street Journal*, July 12, 2006. http://www.eca-watch.org/problems/asia_pacific/kanaky/WSJ_Inco_Kanaky_12july06.htm.

Chapter 5. First Combat: Japanese Surrender Not an Option on Tarawa, 1943

1. Stockman, *The Battle for Tarawa*, 25.
2. Alexander, *Utmost Savagery*, 3.
3. Stockman, *The Battle for Tarawa*, 9. The island group then known as the New Hebrides is now called Vanuatu.
4. The term "amtrac" refers to an amphibious tractor. It was designed to be self-propelled when floating in water, as well as on land. In deeper water the cleated treads spun and moved the vehicles forward slowly. In shallow water, the tracks pulled the vehicles up on the reef, and they could then be driven to shore. Technically called "LVTs" ("landing vehicle tracked"), sometimes referred to as "alligators," they were made of steel that afforded some protection to the men inside. Several models of LVTs were built during the course of the war. A "Higgins boat," or "LCVP" ("landing craft vehicle personnel"), was made mostly of wood with a flat steel door at the front that could be lowered to allow men to land on a beach. Unlike amtracs that could move forward while either in deep water or driving on land, Higgins boats needed about four feet of water to remain floating, and they proved problematic in Pacific island invasions over island-fringing coral reefs, where the depth of the water, even at high tide, was rarely more than about three feet. Col. Joseph H. Alexander, *Utmost Savagery*, 58–59, 73.
5. Stockman, *The Battle for Tarawa* 1; Eric M. Hammel and John E. Lane, *76 Hours: The Invasion of Tarawa* (New York: Belmont Tower Books, 1980), 37.
6. Alexander, *Utmost Savagery*, 82.
7. Ibid., 69–71.

8. Stockman, *The Battle for Tarawa*, 5.
9. Alexander, *Utmost Savagery*, 73–78.
10. Ibid., 76.
11. Stockman, *The Battle for Tarawa*, 4.
12. Alexander, *Utmost Savagery*, 59–60.
13. Stockman, *The Battle for Tarawa*, 4.
14. Ibid., 12.
15. Ibid., 12.
16. Ibid., 13.
17. Ibid., 15.
18. Alexander, *Utmost Savagery*, 111.
19. Stockman, *The Battle for Tarawa*, 16; Alexander, *Utmost Savagery*, 135.
20. Robert Sherrod, *Tarawa: The Story of a Battle* (New York: Duell, Sloan and Pearce, 1944), 68.
21. Alexander, *Utmost Savagery*, 135.
22. Stockman, *The Battle for Tarawa*, 25.
23. Ibid., 17.
24. Alexander, *Utmost Savagery*, 141.
25. Stockman, *The Battle for Tarawa*, 25.
26. The destroyer was either the USS *Ringgold* or USS *Dashiell*. Both were in close to shore performing various fire missions the first day of the invasion. Alexander, *Utmost Savagery*, 148.
27. Bob Sheeks' recollection of the exact words spoken by Hermle, voice tape interview conducted by the author in 2000.
28. Assistant Division surgeon, Capt. French Moore, supervised the evacuation of numerous casualties, and he later returned to the *Monrovia* with a group of Marines with serious wounds. Stockman, *The Battle for Tarawa*, 26.
29. Stockman, *The Battle for Tarawa*, 26.
30. Alexander, *Utmost Savagery*, 146.
31. Ibid., 249.
32. Ibid., 161.
33. As a consequence of the miscommunication between Dave Shoup, General Hermle, and the command ship, Bob witnessed at close hand the disastrous landing of the 1st Battalion, 8th Marines on the second morning of the battle. Alexander, *Utmost Savagery*, 146.
34. United States Marine Corps History Division, Who's Who in Marine Corps History, Major General Merritt Austin Edson: http://www.tecom.usmc.mil/HD/Whos_Who/Edson_M.htm
35. Alexander, *Utmost Savagery*, 170–71.
36. BBC News, *Sinking Feeling in Tuvalu*: http://news.bbc.co.uk/2/hi/asia-pacific/2219001.stm
37. The issue of why the depth of the water over the reef was insufficient for the Higgins boats was only resolved in 1987 when Donald Olson, a professor at Southwest

Texas State University, performed an analysis that showed it was a rare combination of factors that combined to keep the depth at high tide lower than normal. Alexander, *Utmost Savagery*, 76–77.

38. Stockman, *The Battle for Tarawa*, 26.
39. Ibid., 26.
40. Ibid., 41.
41. Ibid., 43.
42. Voice tape interview with Bob Sheeks performed by the author in 2000.
43. Hammel and Lane, *76 Hours*, 269.
44. A few years after the war ended, John Pelzel was in Japan, staying at a local residence in Tokyo. The landlady introduced John to a Japanese university student living in the same house. They got to talking and John asked the student where he had served during the war. It turned out he had been a pilot and was initially based at Tarawa. Just before the Marines invaded the island, his unit flew their planes to the Marshall Islands, a couple of hundred miles to the northwest. John asked whether he had ever flown back to Tarawa, and the student told him he had flown from the Marshalls back to Tarawa once during the battle and had strafed and bombed the runway on Betio. It turned out that it was his guns that had pounded not a yard away from Bob and Pelzel. John and the Japanese ex-pilot became quite good friends and stayed in touch over the years. If that pilot's aim had been a yard closer, Bob and Pelzel likely would not have lived to tell the story. In this case, the margin between life and death was about three feet.
45. Stockman, *The Battle for Tarawa*, 56.

Chapter 6. Between Campaigns: Hawaii, 1943–44

1. Cdr. Edward C. Raymer, *Descent into Darkness* (Novato, CA: Presidio Press, 1996), 66; *Diary of a Corsair Pilot in the Solomons, New Caledonia*: http://www.scuttlebuttsmallchow.com/wdiary4.html
2. Hoyt, *Japan's War*, 265.
3. Surrender leaflet text taken from copies saved by Bob Sheeks, Robert Sheeks collection.
4. Ibid.
5. Ibid.
6. Ibid.
7. Ibid.
8. Field order, D-2 2nd Marine Division, May 7, 1944. Robert Sheeks collection.
9. Surrender texts to be used in the field, Bob Sheeks collection.
10. Voice tape interview with Bob Sheeks conducted by the author in 2002.
11. Intelligence Section, Marine Division and Joint Intelligence Center, Pacific Ocean Areas, *Study of Japanese Defenses of Betio Island (Tarawa Atoll), Part I: Fortifications and Weapons*, 20 December, 1943. National Archives: WWII Geographic File "Gilberts," Record Group 127, Boxes 35-36, 370/D/1/5. Bob also helped prepare the other two volumes of this three-part series, *Part II: Communications and Power*

Plants, 1 January, 1944, and *Part III: Base Installations*, 20 January, 1944. All are filed in the National Archives Record Group 127, Boxes 35-36, as noted above.

Chapter 7. They All Didn't Commit Suicide: Saipan, 1944

1. Maj. Carl W. Hoffman, *Saipan: The Beginning of the End* (Historical Section, Division of Public Information, Headquarters, U.S. Marine Corps, 1950), 27–29; Harold J. Goldberg, *D-Day in the Pacific: The Battle of Saipan* (Bloomington: Indiana University Press, 2007), 40–47.
2. The temporary retreat by this small group of Marines was likely a response to a counterattack by Japanese defenders who charged down the beach from the north, straight into a crowded area where the regimental command post had just been established and wounded Marines were being collected. After some initial confusion, the Marines reformed a firing line and killed all the Japanese who had counterattacked. Hoffman, *Saipan*, 53.
3. Ibid., 71–72.
4. Ibid., 79.
5. Ibid., 5.
6. Goldberg, *D-Day in the Pacific*, 104–5.
7. Hoffman, *Saipan*, 88–89.
8. Goldberg, *D-Day in the Pacific*, 109.
9. Voice tape interview with Bob Sheeks and Jish Martin conducted by the author in 2002.
10. Second Marine Division, FMF, In the Field, P/A Directive Text. Robert Sheeks collection.
11. United States Marine Corps, Logistics Operations School, Marine Corps Combat Service Support Schools, Camp LeJeune, North Carolina. *Student Outline: Introduction to Amphibious Embarkation Planning*. 17 pp.
12. Bob Sheeks voice tape interview conducted by the author in 2000.
13. For an overall description of the Tanapag banzai charge, see Goldberg, *D-Day in the Pacific*, 175–85; and Hoffman, *Saipan*, 223–26.
14. Goldberg, *D-Day in the Pacific*, 190.
15. Ibid., 189.
16. Smith and Meehl, *Pacific Legacy*, 149. Interview with Scott Russell, Historical Preservation Officer, Saipan, December 30, 1987.
17. Voice tape interview with Bob Sheeks performed by the author in 1995.
18. Voice tape interview with Dan Williams performed by the author in 2003.
19. Ibid.
20. Ibid.
21. Ienaga, *The Pacific War 1931–1945*, 184.
22. Hoffman, *Saipan*, 243.
23. Bob Sheeks voice tape interview conducted by the author in 2000.
24. Robert Sherrod, "The Nature of the Enemy," *Time*, August 7, 1944, archived at: http://www.time.com/time/magazine/article/0,9171,886174,00.html.

25. Robert B. Sheeks, "Civilians on Saipan," *Far Eastern Survey*, May 9, 1945, 112.

26. Alexander, *Utmost Savagery*, 249.

27. Bob Sheeks voice tape interview conducted by the author in 1995.

28. Though impossible to know for certain because of the evacuation efforts that had begun earlier in 1944, it has been estimated that between 16,000 and 20,000 civilians were living on Saipan at the time of the American landings. Of these, roughly 3,000 died during combat operations, about 1,000 killed themselves or were killed in and around the areas of last resistance in the Marpi Point region, and at least 15,000 survived to be interned in the camps on Saipan. Haruko Taya Cook, "The myth of the Saipan suicides," *Quarterly Journal of Military History*, 1995, 18–19; Dingman, *Deciphering the Rising Sun*, 150.

29. The nurse's name has been lost to history. For the purposes of the story, she is called Denise.

30. *The Army Nurse Corps: A Commemoration of World War II Service*, 27: http://www.history.army.mil/books/wwii/72-14/72-14.HTM

31. An account of Guy Gabaldon's exploits appear in Guy Gabaldon, *Saipan: Suicide Island* (Saipan: Self-published, 1990).

32. Interview with Guy Gabaldon performed by the author, Saipan, December 1987. Goldberg, *D-Day in the Pacific*, 197.

33. Bob Sheeks voice tape interview conducted by the author in 2002.

34. Sgt. David Dowdakin, quoted in Goldberg, *D-Day in the Pacific*, 198.

35. "Hell to Eternity," 1960 feature-length movie summary: http://www.imdb.com/title/tt0053901/

36. Goldberg, *D-Day in the Pacific*, 197.

37. "East LA Marine: The Untold True Story of Guy Gabaldon," 2008 documentary film: http://www.imdb.com/title/tt1265593/

38. Bob Sheeks voice tape interview conducted by the author in 2002.

39. Goldberg, *D-Day in the Pacific*, 198.

40. Gabaldon, *Saipan: Suicide Island*, 5–6. Interview with Guy Gabaldon conducted by the author, Saipan, December 1987. "East LA Marine: The Untold True Story of Guy Gabaldon," 2008 documentary film: http://www.imdb.com/title/tt1265593/

41. Interview with Guy Gabaldon conducted by the author, Saipan, December 1987.

Chapter 8. A Human Connection with the Enemy: Tinian, 1944

1. Maj. Carl W. Hoffman, *The Seizure of Tinian* (Historical Branch, G-3 Division, Headquarters, U.S. Marine Corps, 1951), 24, 31, 39.

2. Ibid., 43.

3. Ibid., 48.

4. Goldberg, *D-Day in the Pacific*, 208.

5. Hoffman, *The Seizure of Tinian*, 8,

6. Stockman, *The Battle for Tarawa*, 46–47. Hoffman, *The Seizure of Tinian*, 109–10.

7. The Japanese warrant officer's name is lost to history, but for the purposes of this narrative he will be referred to as Nakazawa.

8. Voice tape interview with Bob Sheeks conducted by the author in 2002.

9. Ibid.

10. Joseph H. Alexander, *Storm Landings: Epic Amphibious Battles in the Central Pacific* (Annapolis: Naval Institute Press, 1997), 151, 153.

11. Ibid., 155.

12. Hoyt, *Japan's War*, 336.

13. Alexander, *Storm Landings*, 165.

14. Ibid., 166.

15. Voice tape interview with Bob Sheeks conducted by the author in 2000.

Chapter 9. Japanese Language and World War II in Retrospect: Boulder, 2002

1. Leck, *Captives of Empire*, 675.

2. Ibid., 675.

3. For a full account of the history of modern China, see R. Keith Schoppa, *The Columbia Guide to Modern Chinese History* (New York: Columbia University Press, 2000). See also http://www.history.com/this-day-in-history/chinese-nationalists-move-capital-to-taiwan.

4. Online Archive of California, Overview of the Committee for a Free Asia collection: http://www.oac.cdlib.org/findaid/ark:/13030/kt129030s1/

5. "Malayan Emergency, 1948–1960": http://www.britannica.com/EBchecked/topic/895044/Malayan-Emergency

6. Freeman Foundation: http://www.macalester.edu/freemangrant/about_Free-man.html

7. Doshida University Cary Collection: http://www.doshisha.ac.jp/english/libraries/about/collection.php

8. Voice tape interview with Bob Sheeks and Jish Martin conducted by the author in 2002.

9. Voice tape interview with Bob Sheeks conducted by the author in 2000.

BIBLIOGRAPHY

Alexander, Joseph H. *Utmost Savagery*. Annapolis: Naval
   Institute Press, 1995.
———. *Storm Landings: Epic Amphibious Battles in the Central Pacific.*
Annapolis: Naval Institute Press, 1997.
American Men and Women of Science. (AmMWSc 73S) 38th and 40th editions, New
   York: R. R. Bowker Co., 1973.
Barta, Patrick. "Tricky Digs." *The Wall Street Journal,* July 12, 2006.
Boyd, Carl, and Akihiko Yoshida. *The Japanese Submarine Force and World War II.*
   Annapolis: Naval Institute Press, 1995.
Carr, Jess W. "Vs-57 and the Sinking of Japanese Submarine I-17." *Naval Aviation
   News,* September–October, 2001.
Dingman, Roger. *Deciphering the Rising Sun.* Annapolis: Naval Institute Press, 2009.
Cook, Haruko Taya, "The Myth of the Saipan Suicides." *Quarterly Journal of Military
   History,* 1995.
Cook, Haruko Taya, and Theodore F. Cook. *Japan at War.* New York: The New Press,
   1992.
Ebbett, Eve. *When the Boys Were Away: New Zealand Women in World War II.*
   Wellington, N.Z.: Reed, 1984.
Frank, Benis M. *Marine Corps Gazette.* Obituary for William K. Jones, 1998.
Gabaldon, Guy. *Saipan: Suicide Island.* Saipan: Self-published, 1990.
Goldberg, Harold J. *D-Day in the Pacific: The Battle of Saipan.* Bloomington: Indiana
   University Press, 2007.
Hammel, Eric M., and John E. Lane. *76 Hours: The Invasion of Tarawa.* New York:
   Belmont Tower Books, 1980.
Hoffman, Carl W. *Saipan: The Beginning of the End.* Historical Branch, G-3 Division,
   Headquarters, U.S. Marine Corps, 1950.
———. *The Seizure of Tinian.* Historical Branch, G-3 Division, Headquarters, U.S.
   Marine Corps, 1951.
Hoyt, Edwin P. *Japan's War.* New York: Cooper Square Press, 1986.
Inouye, Ari. World War II recollections, unpublished manuscript.

Intelligence Section, Marine Division and Joint Intelligence Center, Pacific Ocean Areas. *Study of Japanese Defenses of Betio Island (Tarawa Atoll), Part I: Fortifications and Weapons*, 20 December 1943. National Archives: WWII Geographic File "Gilberts," Record Group 127, Boxes 35-36, 370/D/1/5.

———. *Study of Japanese Defenses of Betio Island (Tarawa Atoll), Part II: Communications and Power Plants*, 1 January 1944. National Archives: WWII Geographic File "Gilberts," Record Group 127, Boxes 35-36, 370/D/1/5.

———. *Study of Japanese Defenses of Betio Island (Tarawa Atoll), Part III: Base Installations*, 20 January, 1944. National Archives: WWII Geographic File "Gilberts," Record Group 127, Boxes 35-36, 370/D/1/5.

Ienaga, Saburo. *The Pacific War 1931–1945*. New York: Pantheon Books, 1968. Random House English Translation, 1978.

Jordan, Donald A. *Chinese Boycotts Versus Japanese Bombs: The Failure of China's "Revolutionary Diplomacy" 1931–32*. Ann Arbor: University of Michigan Press, 1991.

———. *China's Trial by Fire: The Shanghai War of 1932*. Ann Arbor: University of Michigan Press, 2001.

Keegan, John. *The Second World War*. New York: Penguin Books, 1989.

Leck, Greg. *Captives of Empire: The Japanese Internment of Allied Civilians in China 1941–1945*. Bangor, PA: Shandy Press, 2007.

Leckie, Robert. *Delivered From Evil*. New York: Harper and Row, 1987.

Manchester, William. *American Caesar*. New York: Dell Publishing, 1978.

Mead, Margaret. *Coming of Age in Samoa*. New York: Morrow Quill, 1928.

Montgomerie, Deborah. *The Women's War: New Zealand Women 1939–45*. Auckland, N.Z.: Auckland University Press, 2001.

Niderost, Eric. "The Lost Leathernecks." *World War II Magazine*, November, 2005.

Raymer, Edward C. *Descent into Darkness*. Novato, CA: Presidio Press, 1996.

Schoppa, R. Keith. *The Columbia Guide to Modern Chinese History*. New York: Columbia University Press, 2000.

Sheeks, Robert B. "Civilians on Saipan." *Far Eastern Survey*, May 9, 1945.

Sherrod, Robert. *Tarawa: The Story of a Battle*. New York: Duell, Sloan and Pearce, 1944.

———. "The Nature of the Enemy." *Time*, August 7, 1944.

Slesnick, Irwin Leonard, and Carole Evelyn Slesnick. *Kanji and Codes: Learning Japanese for World War II*. Bellingham, WA: Self-published, 2006.

Smith, Rex Alan, and Gerald A. Meehl. *Pacific Legacy: Image and Memory from World War II in the Pacific*. New York: Abbeville Press, 2002.

———. *Pacific War Stories: In the Words of Those Who Survived*. New York: Abbeville Press, 2004.

Stockman, James R. *The Battle for Tarawa*. Marines in World War II Historical Monograph, Historical Section, Division of Public Information, Headquarters, U.S. Marine Corps, 1947.

Swaney, Deanna. *Samoa*. Berkeley: Lonely Planet Publications, 1994.

Turner, Peter, Jeff Williams, Nancy Keller, and Tony Wheeler. *New Zealand.* Hawthorn, Australia: Lonely Planet Publications, 1998.
Uchizono Yozo, letter to Glenn Slaughter. *The Interpreter.* Archives, University of Colorado at Boulder Libraries, 2002. Number 45.
Webber, Bert. *Retaliation: Japanese Attacks and Allied Countermeasures on the Pacific Coast in World War II.* Corvallis: Oregon State University Press, 1975.

Web sites
BBC News. *Sinking Feeling in Tuvalu:* http://news.bbc.co.uk/2/hi/asia-pacific/2219001.stm
Committee for a Free Asia collection, Online Archive of California: http://www.oac. cdlib.org/findaid/ark:/13030/kt129030s1/
Diary of a Corsair Pilot in the Solomons, New Caledonia: http://www.scuttlebuttsmallchow. com/wdiary4.html
Doshida University Cary Collection: http://www.doshisha.ac.jp/english/libraries /about/collection.php
East LA Marine. 2008 documentary film: http://www.imdb.com/title/tt1265593/
Edson, "Red Mike." United States Marine Corps History Division, Who's Who in Marine Corps History, Major General Merritt Austin Edson: http://www.tecom. usmc.mil/HD/Whos_Who/Edson_M.htm
Filmography for Doris Dowling: http://www.imdb.com/name/nm0235835/
Filmography for Ida Lupino: http://www.imdb.com/name/nm0526946/
Filmography for Louis Hayward: http://www.imdb.com/name/nm0371775/
Filmography for Sid Salkow: http://www.imdb.com/name/nm0758508/filmotype
Filmography for Virginia Mayo: http://www.imdb.com/name/nm0562920/
Hell to Eternity. 1960 feature-length movie summary: http://www.imdb.com/title /tt0053901/
I-17 Japanese submarine: Hackett, Bob, and Sander Kingsepp, HIJMS Submarine I-17: Tabular Record of Movement (Contributions from Dr. Higuchi Tatsuhiro of Japan, Steve Eckardt of Australia, and Andrew Obluski of Poland, 2001): http://www.combinedfleet.com/I-17.htm
Malayan Emergency, 1948–1960: http://www.britannica.com/EBchecked/topic / 895044/Malayan-Emergency
Modern China history: http://www.history.com/this-day-in-history/chinese-nationalists-move-capital-to-taiwan
Noumea nickel smelter: http://www.eca-watch.org/problems/asia_pacific/kanaky/WSJ _Inco_Kanaky_12july06.htm
Nurses on Saipan: *The Army Nurse Corps: A Commemoration of World War II Service:* http://www.history.army.mil/books/wwii/72-14/72-14.HTM
Paekakariki, New Zealand, Marine camp: http://home.clear.net.nz/pages/ 42mbjeep /US%20Marines%20Page.htm
Saipan suicides: http://www.time.com/time/magazine/article/0,9171,886174,00.html
War brides: http://histclo.com/essay/war/ww2/cou/us/live/w2usl-bride.html

INDEX

Gerald Meehl is the co-author (with Rex Alan Smith) of *Pacific Legacy: Image and Memory from World War II in the Pacific* (Abbeville Press, 2002); *Pacific War Stories: In the Words of Those Who Survived* (Abbeville Press, 2004); and (with Dave Levy) *Fast Boats and Fast Times: Memories of a PT Boat Skipper in the South Pacific* (Authorhouse, 2008). He has traveled extensively in the South Pacific and has visited and photographed every major Pacific island battlefield of World War II. He is a senior scientist at the National Center for Atmospheric Research in Boulder, Colorado.

The **Naval Institute Press** is the book-publishing arm of the U.S. Naval Institute, a private, nonprofit, membership society for sea service professionals and others who share an interest in naval and maritime affairs. Established in 1873 at the U.S. Naval Academy in Annapolis, Maryland, where its offices remain today, the Naval Institute has members worldwide.

Members of the Naval Institute support the education programs of the society and receive the influential monthly magazine *Proceedings* or the colorful bimonthly magazine *Naval History* and discounts on fine nautical prints and on ship and aircraft photos. They also have access to the transcripts of the Institute's Oral History Program and get discounted admission to any of the Institute-sponsored seminars offered around the country.

The Naval Institute's book-publishing program, begun in 1898 with basic guides to naval practices, has broadened its scope to include books of more general interest. Now the Naval Institute Press publishes about seventy titles each year, ranging from how-to books on boating and navigation to battle histories, biographies, ship and aircraft guides, and novels. Institute members receive significant discounts on the Press's more than eight hundred books in print.

Full-time students are eligible for special half-price membership rates. Life memberships are also available.

For a free catalog describing Naval Institute Press books currently available, and for further information about joining the U.S. Naval Institute, please write to:

Member Services
U.S. Naval Institute
291 Wood Road
Annapolis, MD 21402-5034
Telephone: (800) 233-8764
Fax: (410) 571-1703
Web address: www.usni.org